THE GOSPEL
AND THE CHURCH

Lives of Jesus Series

LEANDER E. KECK, *General Editor*

THE GOSPEL
AND THE CHURCH

by ALFRED LOISY

With an Introduction by
BERNARD B. SCOTT

FORTRESS PRESS
PHILADELPHIA

The text of *The Gospel and the Church* herein reprinted is the translation by Christopher Home which was published in 1903 by Isbister & Company Limited in London and reprinted in 1912 by Charles Scribner's Sons in New York.

Introduction and Selected Bibliography COPYRIGHT © 1976 BY FORTRESS PRESS.

Library of Congress Catalog Card Number 75–13050

ISBN 0–8006–1274–4

4587J75   Printed in U.S.A.   1–1274

FOREWORD
TO THE SERIES

In a time when a premium is placed on experimentation for the future and when theological work itself values "new theology," the reasons for reissuing theological works from the past are not self-evident. Above all, there is broad consensus that the "Lives of Jesus" produced by our forebears failed both as sound history and as viable theology. Why, then, make these works available once more?

First of all, this series does not represent an effort to turn the clock back, to declare these books to be the norm to which we should conform, either in method or in content. Neither critical research nor constructive theology can be repristinated. Nevertheless, root problems in the historical-critical study of Jesus and of theological reflection are perennial. Moreover, advances are generally made by a critical dialogue with the inherited tradition, whether in the historical reconstruction of the life of Jesus or in theology as a whole. Such a dialogue cannot occur, however, if the tradition is allowed to fade into the mists or is available to students only in handbooks which perpetuate the judgments and clichés of the intervening generation. But a major obstacle is the fact that certain pivotal works have never been available to the present generation, for they were either long out of print or not translated at all. A central aim, then, in republishing certain "Lives of

Jesus'' is to encourage a fresh discovery of and a lively debate with this tradition so that our own work may be richer and more precise.

Titles were selected which have proven to be significant for ongoing issues in Gospel study and in the theological enterprise as a whole. H. S. Reimarus inaugurated the truly critical investigation of Jesus and so was an obvious choice. His *On the Intention of Jesus* was reissued by the American Theological Library Association in 1962, but has not really entered the discussion despite the fact that questions he raised have been opened again, especially by S. G. F. Brandon's *Jesus and the Zealots*. Our edition, moreover, includes also his previously untranslated discussion of the resurrection and part of D. F. Strauss's evaluation of Reimarus. That Strauss's *Life of Jesus* must be included was clear from the start. Our edition, using George Eliot's translation, also takes account of Strauss's shifting views as well. Schleiermacher's *Life of Jesus* is being translated, partly because it is significant for the study of Schleiermacher himself and partly because he is the wellspring of repeated concern for the inner life of Jesus. One of the most influential expressions of this motif came from Wilhelm Herrmann's *The Communion of the Christian with God,* which, while technically not a life of Jesus, emphasizes more than any other work the religious significance of Jesus' inner life. In fresh form, this emphasis has been rejuvenated in the recent work of Ernst Fuchs and Gerhard Ebeling who concentrate on Jesus' own faith. Herrmann, then, is a bridge between Schleiermacher and the present. In such a series, it was also deemed important to translate Strauss's critique of Schleiermacher, *The Christ of Faith and the Jesus of History,* for here important critical issues were exposed. Probably no book was more significant for twentieth-century study of Jesus than Johannes Weiss's *Jesus'*

Proclamation of the Kingdom of God, for together with Albert Schweitzer, Weiss turned the entire course of Jesus-research and undermined the foundations of the prevailing Protestant theology. From the American scene, Shailer Mathews's *Jesus on Social Institutions* was included. There can be no substantive dialogue with our own theological tradition which ignores his work, together with that of Shirley Jackson Case. Case's *Jesus: A New Biography* was originally planned for inclusion, but its availability in two other editions has made that unnecessary. Finally, Alfred Loisy's *The Gospel and the Church* has been added to the series, partly for its intrinsic merit and partly because this was the most important contribution from the Roman Catholic tradition. Both Catholics and Protestants will profit from this trenchant reply to Harnack's *What is Christianity?* Doubtless other works could have been included with justification; however, these will suffice to enliven the theological scene if read perceptively.

In each case, an editor was invited to provide an introductory essay and annotations to the text in order to assist the reader in seeing the book in perspective. The bibliography will aid further research, though in no case was there an attempt to be comprehensive. The aim is not to produce critical editions in the technical sense (which would require a massive apparatus), but a useable series of texts with guidance at essential points. Within these aims the several editors enjoyed considerable latitude in developing their contributions. The series will achieve its aim if it facilitates a rediscovery of an exciting and controversial history and so makes our own work more fruitful.

The present volume is edited by Bernard Brandon Scott, a lay Catholic New Testament scholar. Upon receiving his B.A. from St. Meinrad College in St. Meinrad, Indiana in 1963 he earned an M.A. at Miami University in Oxford, Ohio in 1968. In 1971 he received his Ph.D. from Vanderbilt University, having been awarded both a Kendrick Grobel Fellowship and a Woodrow Wilson Doctoral Dissertation Fellowship. His dissertation, which analyzed the debate between Harnack and Loisy, laid the foundation for his Introduction to the present volume. Since 1971 he has taught New Testament at the St. Meinrad School of Theology, and in 1975 became its Academic Dean as well. He is currently a member of the Parable Seminar of the Society of Biblical Literature, and is preparing a commentary on the Gospel of Mark.

LEANDER E. KECK

CONTENTS

ix

INTRODUCTION

Bernard B. Scott

The struggle of Christianity to accept a critical examination of its Sacred Scriptures has been, and continues to be, an extremely arduous task. The situation has been no different in Roman Catholicism than elsewhere.[1] Raymond E. Brown has recently pointed out what he considers to be the three stages of this process.[2] From 1900 to 1943 Roman Catholicism was pre-critical, in fact anticritical.[3] The second stage was begun by the encyclical *Divino Afflante Spiritu* (1943) of Pius XII. This encyclical marks a cautious acceptance of critical scholarship. The results of this critical method can be seen in the decrees and actions of Vatican II. In 1955 the Secretary of the Pontifical Biblical Commission affirmed the freedom of the critic in regard to prior decrees of the Commission, and in 1964 the Commission's "Instruction on the Historical Truth of the Gospels" encouraged the acceptance of a

1. Keith D. Stephenson, "Roman Catholic Biblical Scholarship: Its Ecclesiastical Context in the Past Hundred Years," *Encounter* 33 (1972): 303-28.
2. Raymond E. Brown, *The Virginal Conception and Bodily Resurrection of Jesus* (New York: Paulist Press, 1973), pp. 3ff.
3. Brown has observed: "The first period (1900-1940) was dominated by the rejection of modern biblical criticism, an attitude forced on the Church by the Modernist heresy" (ibid). Cf. also idem "Church Pronouncements," *The Jerome Biblical Commentary* (Englewood Cliffs, N. J.: Prentice-Hall, 1968), p. 625.

fully critical methodology in gospel research.[4] Brown
maintains that this freedom of the critic will lead to a
third stage, which he sees as now in progress, in which
the implications of modern criticism will work their way
through the fabric of Roman Catholic theology and life.

Alfred Loisy's *The Gospel and the Church* comes from
a period that antedates Brown's first stage and moreover
is in many ways a cause of that first stage. It represents
the first flowering of critical scholarship within Roman
Catholicism. Loisy believed that a historical examination
of the origins of Christianity would demonstrate that it
had developed, and that an awareness of this development would force the Roman Catholic Church to change
once again in order to meet the needs of modern society.
Loisy's aim was twofold: establishing critical scholarship
within Roman Catholicism and working out the implications of that scholarship for the stance of the church
within modern society. The first part of that aim is now
assured; the second is the task which Brown sees emerging.

The occasion for the publication of *The Gospel and the
Church* was the publication of Adolf von Harnack's *Das
Wesen des Christentums* (1900), whose English title, *What
is Christianity?*, obscures the theme expressed in the German, *The Essence of Christianity*. Loisy's response was
intended to be not only a critique of Harnack but also
an apologetic for his own vision of Catholicism. The second part of his project was a failure. Soon after its publication the book was condemned by the archbishop of
Paris, Cardinal Richard, and placed on the Index of Forbidden Books. Loisy was excommunicated in 1908 and his
position, identified as Modernism, was condemned by the
encyclical *Pascendi* of Pius X. Loisy was *vitandus* ("to be

---

4. Brown, "Church Pronouncements," pp. 625–26, 631; Joseph Fitz-
myer, "The Biblical Commission's Instruction on the Historical
Truth of the Gospels," *Theological Studies* 25 (1964): 386–408.

avoided") not only in everyday contact but, more importantly, in Roman Catholic scholarship. This *vitandus* involved critical scholarship itself and thus marked the beginning of what Brown calls the pre-critical stage of modern Roman Catholicism.

In the first place, then, Loisy's *The Gospel and the Church* offers the opportunity to examine the beginnings of Catholic critical scholarship with a view toward seeing the implications of that scholarship for the task of contemporary theology. Because the book marks a beginning, we can observe in it the shift from one intellectual horizon (traditional Catholicism) to another (historical consciousness). Second, although in an ecumenical age Loisy's apologetic concerns may be somewhat out of place, his critique of Protestant liberalism raises the question whether there is a distinctive Protestant and/or Catholic critical position. Finally, Loisy stood at a pivotal point in the history of New Testament scholarship. The impact of the eschatological interpretation (J. Weiss, A. Schweitzer) and the History of Religions School (W. Wrede, W. Bousset) produced a profound shift in interpretation. Loisy was not only cognizant of these movements, but made substantial contributions to them.

This Introduction is divided into two parts, the first dealing with Loisy and Modernism and the second more specifically with *The Gospel and the Church*. The first part will examine the career of Loisy up to his excommunication, the question of Modernism, Loisy's use of the hypothesis of historical development, and his principal theme of the kingdom and the church. The second part will summarize Harnack's *What is Christianity?* and examine two of the most significant issues which divide Harnack and Loisy. Finally, there will be an attempt to assess the significance of Loisy.

I.

LOISY AND MODERNISM

THE CAREER OF ALFRED LOISY

The career of Loisy did not run in a straight line. It was filled with twists and turns, punctuated by violent controversy and condemnation. Loisy's work raised so great a storm of protest that Pius X, in his condemnation of Modernism, called this system "the synthesis of all heresies." [5]

Loisy's early life offered no indication of his future as a heresiarch.[6] He was born in 1857 at Ambrières, a small village in the upper valley of the Marne River. His family had been farmers for several generations. His education was unexceptional and completely within the Catholic system. While at the Collège de St. Dizier (high school) he decided to study for the priesthood, and shortly before his eighteenth birthday entered the diocesan seminary at Châlons-sur-Marne. The theological education there was mediocre, but Loisy was a model student and scrupulous in his religious attitudes. He remarks that only his study

---

5. *Pascendi*, as quoted in Paul Sabatier, *Modernism*, trans. C. A. Miles (New York: Charles Scribner's Sons, 1909), p. 309.
6. Loisy reviewed his life twice, in *Choses passées* (1913) and in *Mémoires pour servir à l'Histoire religieuse de notre Temps*, 3 vols. (Paris: Nourry, 1930). *Choses passées* was translated into English by Richard Wilson Boynton as *My Duel with the Vatican* (New York: E. P. Dutton, 1924).

of Greek and Hebrew relieved the boredom. He was marked out by his teachers as a student of intellectual promise and was recommended for further studies to the newly founded Institut Catholique at Paris in 1878; there he became a student of the famous church historian Abbé Duchesne. Loisy's health broke before the end of the year, and he returned home to recuperate. He was ordained to the priesthood on June 29, 1879, and was assigned to rural parishes for two years.

During this period of recovery Loisy maintained contact with Abbé Duchesne and continued his studies privately. He was allowed to return to the Institut in 1881 after his recovery. With his return to his studies the course was set for the first stage of his career, which would be closed by his expulsion from his teaching position at the Institut in 1893.

The state of biblical studies in France during this period contrasted sharply with that in Germany. Protestant theology and scholarship were established in the leading German universities with prestigious chairs. Catholic education in France, however, had been outlawed after the Revolution and was not allowed again until 1875, when the Instituts Catholiques were established at various universities.[7] The right and duty of the historian to investigate the Bible with the modern critical tools was secure in Germany at this time. This situation did not exist in France, where criticism in Roman Catholic circles was either unknown or rejected.

The most influential French Catholic exegete of the period was Abbé Vigouroux, then teaching at the Seminary of Saint Sulpice. Loisy attended his lectures on Biblical

---

7. A. Latreille and R. Remond, *Histoire du Catholicisme en France* (Paris: Éditions Spes, 1962), 3:430. The history of the struggle between the state and the church over the control of education in France is an extremely complicated story.

Rationalism in 1882 and gives an illuminating example of his procedure:

> One found it easy, for example, to abandon all belief in the flood of Genesis after hearing the professor explain gravely that the passages attributed to the Yahwist writer are a description of what was going on in the Eternal mind, while the passages called Elohist . . . have regard to the revelation of these thoughts to Noah, and their practical execution; that, the flood covering only the then inhabited portion of the earth, the ark was plenty large enough to contain all the animal species known to Noah; that a calculation had been made, and the ark shown to be capable of enclosing six thousand, six hundred and sixty-six species, allowing so much cubic space to each couple—and much more of the same sort![8]

Loisy concluded that one could believe such reasoning only if he had made up his mind in advance to accept any reasons that led to a foregone conclusion.

At the same time, Loisy was also attending the lectures of Ernest Renan at the Collège de France. There can be little doubt that Renan was the foremost biblical scholar in the French world outside the Catholic sphere.[9] Loisy says that he attended the lectures in order to learn the method of the master with a view to confounding him with his own evidence.[10] Although Loisy attended Renan's lectures for three years, he never met him; Renan's influence was considerable, however, not in specifics, but in offering Loisy an alternative to the orthodoxy of Vigouroux,

---

8. *My Duel,* p. 89. M.-J. Lagrange likewise acknowledges that Vigouroux's refutation of the German rationalists was too defensive to accomplish its purpose. See Francis M. Braun, *The Work of Père Lagrange,* trans. Richard T. A. Murphy (Milwaukee: Bruce Publishing Company, 1963), pp. 5–6.
9. H. W. Wardman, *Ernest Renan* (London: Athlone Press, 1964). Renan's *Vie de Jésus* had been published in 1863 and had caused a considerable reaction among French Catholics (cf. Wardman, chap. 4). His monumental *Origines du Christianisme* had been published only a few years before Loisy attended his lectures.
10. *My Duel,* p. 94; *Mémoires,* 1:121.

an alternative that Loisy had already begun to discover on his own. "What Renan had to say about the composition of the Biblical books contained few surprises for myself." [11] Under the influence of Renan and Duchesne, Loisy had turned to Germany for his decisive influence.

While pursuing his studies, Loisy was also appointed professor of Hebrew at the Institut. He finished his doctoral dissertation "on the doctrine of inspiration according to the Bible, and to the ancient ecclesiastical writers from the Apostolic Fathers down to Tertullian." [12] When the thesis was presented to the rector of the Institut, Monsignor d'Hulst, it was returned with the remark that although the position taken was the only tenable one, "its publication was impossible to contemplate." [13] Loisy summarized his rejected thesis as follows:

> In a few clear-cut phrases of the preface and the conclusion I said that the inspiration of the Scriptures, having to do with existing writings, capable of analysis, was a belief to be controlled by the study of the books in question; that the psychology of the inspired authors was visibly the same as that of all men who write; that the element of the divine which might be added by inspiration changed not at all the nature of the writings to which it pertained . . . that, if revelation was contained in the Bible and without error, as was declared by the Vatican Council, it must be under a relative form, proportioned to the time and the environment in which these books emerged, and to the general knowledge of that time and environment.[14]

11. *My Duel*, p. 93.
12. Ibid. p. 97; *Mémoires*, 1:130–33.
13. Loisy eventually received his doctorate in theology from the Institut in 1890 when a new thesis entitled *History of the Old Testament Canon* was accepted. His doctorate in Assyriology was never officially granted by the École Pratique des Hautes Études because of the considerable expense that would have been involved in the publication of his thesis, which was a reconstruction of the Annals of Sargon. See *My Duel*, p. 117, and *Mémories*, 1:133.
14. *My Duel*, p. 98.

Loisy's activities began to draw attention. In 1892, he began the publication of a journal, *L'Enseignement Biblique,* and for some time his teaching had been under suspicion, especially by the · fathers of Saint Sulpice. Following the publication of his analysis and comparison of the Babylonian myths of creation and flood with those of Genesis, Abbé Icard, Saint Sulpice superior, took his students from Loisy's class. Loisy wrote: "It will some day be cause for astonishment, even in the Church of Rome—at least so I should hope—that a Catholic University professor should have been judged highly reprehensible for having said, in the year of grace 1892, that the narratives of the first chapter of Genesis are not to be taken as literal history." [15]

From this point, Loisy's position began to deteriorate rapidly. In a sincere effort to defend his brilliant professor, Monsignor d'Hulst launched a series of articles on "The Biblical Question." Unfortunately, they were ill-conceived and did not represent the position of Loisy. In the final lecture of the 1893 school year, Loisy responded in an attempt to clarify his own position.[16] He had developed his position in five theses: the Pentateuch is not the work of Moses; the first chapters of Genesis are not a literal account of the beginnings of mankind; all the books of the Old Testament and New Testament do not possess equal historical value, and some were written "in a looser manner than modern historical writing"; "we have to concede a real development in the religious doctrine contained in Scripture"; the sacred writings, in regard to the laws of nature, share the same limitations as the rest of the authors of the ancient world.[17] These conclu-

15. Ibid., p. 162.
16. A full discussion of this episode is contained in *Mémoires,* 1:chap. 8.
17. *My Duel,* p. 149.

sions so scandalized Cardinal Richard that he convened the prelates who sat on the board of governors for the Institut; on November 15, 1893, they voted to expel Loisy.

With this decision Loisy began the second phase of his career, which would culminate in 1908 with his excommunication from the Church of Rome. Loisy's personal attachment to the Church had received a severe shock. He realized that he was no longer in favor with the authorities and that his desires for the modernization of the Church had been rejected. However, he refused to concede; he firmly believed in the task and the importance of the Church for the future of mankind.[18]

Following his removal from the Institut, Loisy was made chaplain at a convent of Dominican nuns in the Paris suburb of Neuilly. This experience, especially the teaching of the young girls under the charge of the nuns, revived his interests and sent him off in a completely new direction with renewed energy. He had always resisted the advice of his friends to confine himself to the strictly scholarly pursuit of Assyriology. He felt compelled to develop a twofold agenda: an apology for Catholicism and a study of its history that would lay the basis for a reform of Catholic theology. For Loisy, if the Church were to survive as an important element in mankind's development, it must adjust to the exigencies of modern life.

---

18. The sincerity of Loisy's Catholicism from this period until his excommunication has been the subject of considerable debate. Albert Houtin and Félix Sartiaux, *Alfred Loisy*, ed. Émile Poulat (Paris: Éditions du Centre national de la Recherche scientique, 1960), p. 1, charged that Loisy was an atheistic priest. This charge has been generally accepted by such recent commentators as John Ratté, *Three Modernists: Alfred Loisy, George Tyrrell, William L. Sullivan* (New York: Sheed and Ward, 1967), pp. 45 ff., and M. Roger Aubert, "Recent Literature on the Modernist Movement," *Concilium* (Sept. 1966): 47 ff. Loisy has been more than adequately exonerated from any duplicity by P. Guerin, "La Vie et l'Ouvre de Loisy à propos d'un Ouvrage récent," *Revue d'Histoire et de Philosophie religieuses* 42 (1961): 334–43, and Alex R. Vidler, *A Variety of Catholic Modernists* (Cambridge: University Press, 1970). Chapters two and three of Vidler contain a thorough discussion of this problem.

To further this program Loisy began work on a grandly conceived project. This work was never published in its entirety, although large parts did appear in separate articles and a major section was incorporated into *The Gospel and the Church*.[19] This unpublished work contained three major parts, introductory essays and discussions of historical considerations and the present situation. The first section dealt with current theories of religion. Loisy was critical of the popular Catholic theory as well as of the liberal Protestant position represented by A. Sabatier.[20] He strongly favored an extension of Newman's theory of development.[21] In a chapter entitled "Religion and Revelation."[22] Loisy elaborated his own theory of the constituent element of religion as its social and institutional dimensions. This first section was followed by five chapters dealing with historical considerations: "The Religion of Israel,"[23] "Jesus Christ," "The Gospel and the Church," "The Gospel and Christian Dogma," and "The Gospel and Catholic Worship." These chapters led one to "confront directly the problems and the difficulties of the present."[24] A transitional chapter from the historical problems to the modern situation was

19. A summary of the contents and arguments of this unpublished volume can be found in *My Duel*, pp. 173–96, and *Mémoires*, 1:chap. 16.

20. Published under one of Loisy's pseudonyms, A. Firmin, "La Théorie individualiste de la Religion," *Revue de Clergé français*, 1 January 1899, pp. 202–15. *Revue de Clergé français* hereafter referred to as RCF. Firmin was Loisy's middle name. For a full discussion of the use of pseudonyms by the Modernists see Émile Poulat, *Histoire, Dogme et Critique dans la Crise Moderniste* (Paris: Casterman, 1962), pp. 621–78.

21. A. Firmin, "Le Développment chrétien d'après la Cardinal Newman," RCF, 1 December 1898, pp. 5–20.

22. Published in three essays: A. Firmin, "La Définition de la Religion," RCF, 1 April 1899, pp. 193–209; "L'Idée de la Révélation," RCF, 1 January 1900, pp. 250–71; "Les Preuves et l'Économie de la Révélation," RCF, 15 March 1900, pp. 126–53.

23. A. Firmin, "La Religion d'Israel," RCF, 15 October 1900, pp. 337–73.

24. *My Duel*, p. 178.

entitled "The Intellectual Regime of the Catholic Church."
The final three chapters were Loisy's attempt at synthesis:
"Dogma and Science," "Reason and Faith," and "Religion and Life." These final four chapters were never published, although Loisy later regretted that he did not
publish the chapter "The Intellectual Regime" before
he left the church; he felt that its publication might have
contributed to the clarification of the situation in which
Modernism arose.

Loisy resigned his chaplaincy at Neuilly following a
severe illness in 1899, and in December of that same year
he was appointed to a lectureship at the École Pratique
des Hautes Études. For the first time in his life, Loisy
enjoyed a teaching position that was not subject to inter-
ference by the ecclesiastical authorities.[25] But this new
freedom did not alter his concerns; he refused the temptation to withdraw into purely scholarly concerns and continued to feel that his work had vital implications for
the Church.

When Harnack's *Das Wesen des Christentums* was first
published, Loisy paid little attention to it. But by 1902
the situation had changed. Harnack's lectures had been
translated into French [26] and were being received favorably
by some Catholics.[27] Using the materials from his unpublished manuscript, Loisy published *The Gospel and the
Church*, which he conceived as a refutation of Harnack;

25. Loisy felt that he would have been better received at the École
had he left the church. See *My Duel*, p. 212.
26. The translation, which was very poor, was done by Blanche
Calmard du Genestoux under the pseudonym Jacques de Coussange
and was published by the Protestant house of Fischbacher in May,
1902. A second, much improved edition was published in 1907 by
an anonymous translator. Loisy did not use the French translation
as the basis of his criticism but the German original. Cf. Poulat,
Histoire, Dogme, p. 46.
27. *Mémoires*, 2:167; Loisy, *Autour d'un petit Livre* (Paris: Alphonse Picard et Fils, 1903), p. 4.

he hoped it would not only serve as an argument for the Catholic position but also convince the Church that his position was a viable alternative. The book was written between May and August, 1902, and was published in October of the same year.[28]

The reaction was swift and quite other than Loisy had hoped. In January, 1903, Cardinal Richard of Paris condemned the book and other French bishops followed suit. The obscurantist journals *L'Univers* and *La Verité français* engaged in violent, often personal polemic against both the work and its author.[29] The attention of the debate was not upon what Loisy had said or upon his controversy with Harnack, but upon the implications of his position for traditional theology. "Let us remain firm on the ground of tradition. The Christ-God constituted the Church, and thereby all Christianity, or this is only an idol of the Hellenistic spirit and Catholicism is an idolatry." [30] The accusation is not that Loisy adduced false evidence, but that his evidence was false since it did not agree with traditional theology.

Loisy responded to his critics with *Autour d'un petit Livre* (1903) and initiated a second round of debate.[31] Cardinal Richard went to Rome to request the condemnation of Loisy. On December 16, 1903, the Holy Office

28. A second edition was prepared to be published in January, 1903. This edition differed from the first with the addition of a chapter entitled "The Sources of the Gospels" (chap. 1) and the third section in chapter three on "The Son of God." The second edition was not released because of the condemnation of Cardinal Richard, but was brought out as a third edition at the end of 1903. The fourth edition was published in 1908 and the fifth in 1929; both are reprints of the third. The English translation of Christopher Home is of the third edition. I have followed Home's edition inasmuch as Loisy himself recognized this edition as definitive.
29. Poulat, *Histoire, Dogme*, Part I, chap. 6.
30. Abbé Gayraud in *L'Univers*, as quoted in Poulat, ibid., p. 127.
31. Ibid., Part II, chap. 2.

placed five of Loisy's works on the Index: *La Religion d'Israel,*[32] *Études bibliques, L'Évangile et l'Église, Autour d'un petit Livre,* and *La Quatrième Évangile.*[33]

By the end of 1903, it was clear to Loisy that the Church had rejected his approach.[34] He expected his excommunication to be forthcoming, but events actually delayed the inevitable. Loisy determined not to leave the Church but rather to be forced out.[35] He responded to the placing of five of his works on the Index with a letter to Cardinal Merry del Val, secretary of state for Pius X.

> I receive with respect the judgment of the Sacred Congregations, and I myself condemn whatever may be found in my writings that is reprehensible. . . . My adherence to the sentence of the Sacred Congregations is purely disciplinary in character. I reserve the right of my own conscience, and I do not intend, in inclining myself before the judgment rendered by the Sacred Congregations of the Holy Office, either to abandon or to retreat from the opinions which I have uttered in my capacity of historian and of critical exegete.[36]

His letter went on to comment on the relative character of historical judgments and their need for refinement and correction. Thus, all his opinions should be understood within the light of the limitations of historical criticism. Loisy himself did not really expect this letter of submission to be sufficient, but he felt that it was as far as he could go. ''My letter could not serve to dissipate the fundamental misunderstanding which exists between the

32. This pamphlet was nonexistent at the time it was placed on the Index. See *My Duel,* p. 247.
33. *Études bibliques* (1901) was a collection of Loisy's early essays; *Autour d'un petit Livre* (1903) was a response to criticism of *The Gospel and the Church; La Quatrième Évangile* (1903, second edition 1921) argued against the historical character of the Fourth Gospel.
34. *My Duel,* p. 273.
35. Ibid., p. 256.
36. Ibid., p. 250.

Church, founded on the unreal principle of its absolute authority, and the modern mind, with its untrammeled quest of truth."[37]

Cardinal Merry del Val responded through the intermediary of the archbishop of Paris. He demanded Loisy's "instantaneous retraction, without reserve, of the five condemned volumes and their contents."[38] Loisy found it impossible to disavow errors that had not been clearly defined and wondered whether the contents of all his books were equally fallacious.[39] On February 28, 1904, he wrote directly to Pius X.

> Most Holy Father:
> I well know your Holiness' goodness of heart, and it is to your heart that I now address myself.
> I wish to live and die in the communion of the Catholic Church. I do not wish to contribute to the ruin of the Faith in France.
> It is beyond my power to destroy in myself the result of my work.
> So far as in me lies, I submit myself to the judgment brought against my writings by the Congregation of the Holy Office.
> To give evidence of my good faith, and for the pacification of spirits, I am prepared to abandon the teaching chair which I occupy in Paris, and at the same time to suspend my scientific publications now under way.[40]

On March 12, again through the auspices of the archbishop of Paris, Loisy received the reply of Pius X. The Pope responded that Loisy's letter, "addressed to his heart, was not written from the heart since it failed to contain the act of obedience which has been required."[41]

37. Ibid., p. 253.
38. Ibid.
39. Ibid., p. 258.
40. Ibid., p. 262.
41. Ibid., p. 264.

On reading these words, Loisy remarked that "something gave way within me." [42]

Loisy expected the decree of excommunication shortly, but for some reason it did not come. In March of the same year he resigned his chair at the École and retired to a small cottage in Garnay. There he remained in retirement, working on his commentary on the Synoptic Gospels, until after the decree of excommunication. Finally, in 1907, the expected condemnation came down from Rome. The encyclical *Pascendi Dominici gregis* and the syllabus *Lamentabili sane exitu* were published condemning the errors of Modernism. Loisy's own excommunication was not far behind. On March 7, 1908, he was formally excommunicated; he first learned of it the next day from the news reports.

Loisy's career within the Church was finished; he then entered the final stage of his career as a professional historian of religions. Shortly after his excommunication he was appointed to the chair of history of religions of the Collège de France, a chair that had been occupied by his former teacher, Ernest Renan. Loisy remained at the Collège de France from 1909 to 1931. He died on June 1, 1940. [43]

---

42. Ibid., p. 265.
43. The inscription on his tombstone, which he directed, provides an enigmatic summary of his life.

Alfred Loisy
Prêtre
Retiré du ministère et de l'enseignement
Professor au Collège de France
Tuam in votis tenuit voluntatem

Cf. Vidler, *A Variety of Catholic Modernists*, p. 44. This third period of Loisy's career has not received the examination that it deserves. Raymond de Boyer de Sainte Suzanne, *Alfred Loisy* (Paris: Éditions du Centurion, 1968), provides an interesting summary of the final period. De Boyer, a friend of Loisy during this period, maintains that there was a consistent thrust to Loisy's thought throughout all the stages of his career.

MODERNISM

Although Loisy's scholarly work during this last period merits analysis and assessment, reissuing *The Gospel and the Church* calls for a discussion of the movement with which he was closely identified and for which he was condemned—Modernism. It should be noted that although it is Roman Catholic Modernism which is in view here, there was a parallel contemporary movement within Protestantism which was also called Modernism. In Protestant circles it evoked its opposite movement—fundamentalism. Within Catholicism, however, a discrete movement called "fundamentalism" did not emerge inasmuch as *Pascendi* had asserted the precritical tradition. Today, Loisy's career and the Modernism for which he was condemned remind both Catholics and Protestants of a common heritage in the struggle over biblical criticism.

In writing about the Modernist controversy it is very difficult to avoid a Manichaean view of history; the players tended to view each other in black and white terms. The reactions of Church authorities were harsh and extreme. Modernism was rooted out of the Roman Church, and its principal spokesmen were either excommunicated or silenced.[4]

Furthermore, it is difficult to determine what Modernism was. The Modernists themselves rejected its characterization by the encyclical *Pascendi*. The English Modernist George Tyrrell complained, "with all due respect to the Encyclical *Pascendi*, Modernists wear no uniform nor are they sworn to the defence of any system; still less to that

---

44. For an example of the extreme reaction within the Roman Church see Émile Poulat, *Intégrisme et Catholicisme Intégral: Un réseau secret international antimoderniste, La "Sapinière" 1909–1921* (Paris: Casterman, 1969). J. F. Broderick, "New Light on Modernism," *Catholic Historical Review* 57 (1971): 442–46, contains a good review of the material in Poulat.

which His Holiness has fabricated for them." [45] Loisy
expressed much the same thought. "The so-called Modernists are not a homogenous and united group, as one would
suppose if one consulted the papal encyclical, but a quite
limited number of persons, who share the desire to adapt
the Catholic religion to the intellectual, moral, and social
needs of the present time." [46] But the encyclical *Pascendi*
has an answer to this diversity among the Modernists.
"It is one of the cleverest devices of the Modernists (as
they are commonly and rightly called) to present their
doctrines without order and systematic manner, so as to
make it appear as if their minds were in doubt or hesitation, whereas in reality, they are quite fixed and steadfast." [47] When the definitive history of Modernism is
written, this Manichaean aspect will have to be explained.
Our purpose here is only to account for it in some tenta-
tive fashion.

The clash of the Modernists with Rome represents a
classic example of the confrontation of conflicting world
views. Conversation was doomed from the beginning, not
because of any intrinsic dogmatic differences, but because
the basis of conversation was missing, i.e., a shared horizon
of common meaning. The mind-set of the Roman authorities was that of traditional Catholicism. This mind-set had
flourished for almost two millenia and had been reinforced
by the intellectual and political upheaval that followed
the French Revolution. The Modernists, on the other hand,
represented the emerging mind-set of historical consciousness.

For a variety of reasons, Roman Catholicism at the

45. George Tyrrell, *Medievalism* (London: Longmans, 1908), p. 106,
as quoted in Alex R. Vidler, *The Modernist Movement in the Roman
Church* (Cambridge: University Press, 1934), p. 4.
46. Loisy, *Simples réflexions* (Paris: Nourry, 1908), p. 14, as quoted
in Vidler, ibid.
47. *Pascendi*, as quoted in Sabatier, *Modernism*, p. 236.

beginning of this century lived in a ghetto, like a queen who had been stripped of her court. Both the political and intellectual arenas had contributed to this situation. The papacy as a political institution had been humiliated by the loss of the Papal States (1860–70). The Church no longer dictated to political states, nor could it act even as an equal. Within the walls of the Vatican, the republican cries for liberty sounded like a cry for the destruction of the Church. In the intellectual sphere, the rationalism that followed upon the French Revolution was openly anti-religious. When Pius IX's encyclical *Quanta Cura* (1864) and its *Syllabus of Errors* condemned the proposition that the Pope should reconcile himself with progress, liberalism, and modern civilization, the Pope was acknowledging a fact: progress, liberalism, and modern civilization had rejected the papacy and vice versa.

While isolating itself from the outside, the Church by the end of the 19th century had centralized its internal organization in Rome under the Pope and the Curia. This movement of centralization around the Pope, which has gone under the name of Ultramontanism, resulted from a variety of forces and events.[48] Following the Revolution and the Restoration in France, the hierarchy wanted a return to Gallicanism, which maintained the interdependence of state and church. The French bishops, for example, recognized the right of the state to nominate bishops. Liberal elements within the French church, such as Félicité de Lamennais (1782–1854), resisted this Gallicanism, which they saw as a restoration of the ancien regime. The only way for the church to be free was to be separated from the state, and these Ultramon-

---

48. For a full treatment of this subject see M. Roger Aubert, *Le Pontificat de Pie IX, Histoire de l'Église*, (Paris: Bloud et Gay, 1952), 21:chap. 9, and Alex R. Vidler, *The Church in an Age of Revolution* (Baltimore: Penguin Books, 1974), chaps. 6, 13.

tanes looked to the Pope as the rallying point for this separation. Likewise, following the excesses and chaos of the Revolution, Joseph de Maistre (1753–1821) in his influential book *Du Pape* (1817) concluded that liberty was subversive and that a new order must be created to restore order. He saw the papacy as standing at the heart of that order, and in fact maintained that it was divinely constituted to serve that purpose. De Maistre combined both absolutist claims for papacy with the concept of regal absolutism. In the theological sphere, Ultramontanism reached an official high standing with the definition of papal infallibility at the First Vatican Council.

This political and ecclesiastical position reinforced, as indicated above, the inherited mind-set of traditional Catholicism. Bernard Lonergan has described this intellectual horizon as "classicist."

> It stressed not facts but values. It could not but claim to be universalist. Its classics were immortal works of art, its philosophy was the perennial philosophy, its laws and structures were the deposit of the wisdom and prudence of mankind. Classicist education was a matter of models to be imitated, of ideal characters to be emulated, of eternal verities and universally valid laws.[49]

Loisy described the Modernists as a "quite limited number of persons, who share the desire to adapt the Catholic religion to the intellectual, moral, and social needs of the present time."[50] In the case of Loisy, as with a number of other Modernists, this need to adapt Catholicism arose as the result of a historical study of the Bible. His understanding of the Church was based upon historical consciousness. Truth was what was historically true. The claims of historical investigation, with its resultant no-

49. Bernard Lonergan, *Method in Theology* (New York: Herder and Herder, 1972) p. 301.
50. See note 46 above.

tions of relativity and development, were intolerable from the point of view of a classicist mentality with its ''eternal verities and universally valid laws.'' Thus, the Modernists were doomed to failure because they represented a mind-set that contained components which were both unintelligible and threatening to the classicists.

From one point of view, the outcome of Modernism was disastrous. All traces of Modernism were ruthlessly eliminated from the Roman Church. Except in Germany, candidates for major orders and professors in Catholic theological faculties were required to take an oath against Modernism. The Pontifical Biblical Commission issued decrees to determine the correct Catholic position on issues of interpretation. The Pontifical Biblical Institute at Rome was established to guarantee the orthodox training of Catholic biblical scholars.[51] It is perhaps ironic that the Biblical Institute eventually produced many of the scholars who accomplished the reform of Catholic biblical studies.

It is difficult to draw any direct lines of influence between Modernism and the present reform and renewal within Roman Catholicism. Later historians with the perspective of time will have to settle that question. Because Modernism was so strongly condemned, contemporary Catholic scholars are reluctant to admit any relation between Modernism and their own positions. It is probably true that there is little direct influence. More likely, the similarities that exist between the positions of the Modernists and that of modern Catholic scholars are due to the sharing of historical method. Since Loisy emphasized the historicity of Catholic tradition, it is necessary to grasp what he understood by historical development, especially as that theory is related to religious development.

51. J. McCool, ''Pontifical Biblical Institute,'' *New Catholic Encyclopedia*, 11:554.

LOISY'S THEORY OF HISTORICAL DEVELOPMENT

Loisy had turned to German scholarship for his critical tools in the first stage of his career; he saw clearly that the solution to his questions would involve a denial of the immutability of dogma. Thus, Loisy needed a hypothesis to solve this problem, the beginnings of which he found in Cardinal Newman's *Essay on the Development of Christian Doctrine*.[52] Newman had been faced with the fact that the Vincentian Canon, *Quod ubique quod semper quod ab omnibus* ("what everywhere, always, and by everyone" has been believed), as interpreted by Bossuet and the English divines, could no longer be reconciled with the results of historical criticism. No modern church was identical to the church of the fathers. However, in one church "bold outlines and broad masses of color rise out of the records of the past. They may be dim, they may be incomplete; but they are definite."[53] This dim picture preserved in the Church of Rome was the result of historical development.

For Loisy, Newman offered a "scientific theory of Catholic Christianity," a theory that showed that "the Catholic development was in the real logic of Christianity," and furthermore that this development was "indispensable to its preservation."[54] This theory exemplifies the three points that are central to Loisy's own use of the hypothesis of development: (1) it is a scientific theory; (2) Catholicism and Christianity are mutually interchangeable terms; and (3) change is necessary for preservation.

It was in fact the critical scientific understanding of the Bible that had forced Loisy to adopt a hypothesis of development. In one of his early essays, "La Critique

52. John Henry Cardinal Newman, *An Essay on the Development of Christian Doctrine* (1845; reprint ed., Westminster, Md.: Christian Classics, 1968).
53. Ibid., p. 7.
54. "La Développement," p. 5.

biblique.'' [55] he had argued that biblical criticism should follow the same procedures that were used in the examination of profane historical documents. ''One means now by criticism the reasoned examination of the works of the human spirit.'' [56] For this reason, scholarship could not verify, nor even deal with, the inspiration of Scripture. Dogmatic concerns should not be allowed to determine the course of investigation.[57]

The mutual interchangeability of the terms Roman Catholicism, Catholicism, and Christianity was shared by Loisy with his French contemporaries.[58] For Loisy, this was not only a cultural heritage; it was also a result of his understanding of development. Protestantism did not qualify because it did not make this claim. ''He [Newman] had been forced to recognize that the Catholic tradition and the Roman tradition have walked in the same step, that there existed only one Christian development, legitimate and complete, if not absolutely perfect and definitive in all its parts, the Roman Catholic development.'' [59]

Furthermore, development and change were a necessity, for otherwise the gospel would not have been preserved. The transition from asserting the fact of development (there has been development in the history of Christianity) to the conclusion that it was therefore necessary (if it had not changed it would have died) is an argument that is used continually against Harnack in *The Gospel and the Church*. It is likewise the foundational principle for Loisy's insistence on the need for reform within Catholicism.

---

55. First published in *L'Enseignement biblique*, November-December 1892, and reprinted in *Études bibliques* (Paris: Picard, 1901) pp. 7–25.
56. *Études bibliques*, p. 8.
57. Ibid., p. 11.
58. Vidler, *The Modernist Movement*, pp. 89–90.
59. ''La Développement,'' p. 11.

The question must be raised whether Loisy's apologetic and cultural concerns have not undermined his insistence upon scientific method. Clearly it is not fair to rule out Protestantism as also a product of historical development, and conversely it is not obvious that Catholicism is the only development possible. These questions concerning the facts of development raise issues concerning legitimacy which can be settled only on theological grounds. Has not Loisy at this point violated his own canon and allowed theological (dogmatic?) criteria to stand in judgment upon historical evidence? The historical evidence which can be cited in the effort to show that Roman Catholicism is a development, in various stages and with multiple changes, from the early church, cannot be used simultaneously to prove the legitimacy of that development, nor can it justify the claim to be the only possible development.

Loisy, following Newman, distinguished several criteria for determining true development. Two of the principal criteria are unity of type and preservation of the fundamental idea.[60] Unity of type is explained on the analogy of physical growth from the embryonic state to the mature state. It is not to be understood in a mathematical sense as "an axiom of geometry in which the conclusions are deduced mathematically one from another."[61] Loisy uses this principle, on the one hand, to deny the possibility of isolating the essence of Christianity; on the other, he uses it to identify the basic historical unity of a given religion amidst the multiplicity of changes which it must undergo.[62]

Newman's second criterion, preservation of the funda-

60. It is not obvious that these principles are truly criteria; they rather appear to be descriptions post factum of how development has been recognized as true. Cf. Owen Chadwick, *From Bossuet to Newman*, (Cambridge: University Press, 1967), p. 155.
61. "Le Développement," p. 6.
62. This type of argumentation is presented at its clearest in the first part of *The Gospel and the Church*.

mental idea or impression, is reinterpreted in the hands of
Loisy; in the process he defines what he understands to be
constitutive of religion. To search for the fundamental idea
can easily mislead one into the quest for a simple "essence."
While a fundamental idea may be easy to trace in the
writing of the history of a philosophy, "it is considerably
more difficult to apply to a religion like Christianity whose
essential idea cannot be defined *a priori,* because Christianity is not only an idea but also an institution." [63] Loisy
proposes, as a fundamental assumption of his method, that
Christianity, or for that matter any religion, cannot be reduced to basic ideas. "Christianity is a living reality, not a
concept of the spirit." [64] The entire religion must be considered in its totality as a living reality, and it is that totality of religion which is subject to development.

Because religion is a living reality, it becomes for Loisy
an objective fact rather than a subjective one. This objective character of religion stems from its foundation,
"from the sentiment that man has of his absolute dependence in regard to God and from the confidence which
he placed in this very God upon whom he is absolutely dependent." [65] At the base of religion lies the distinction
between God and man; this distinction requires the objectification of the sentiment of absolute dependence, "a
certain realization of the divine." [66] This realization, or
objectification, results in traditional rites and beliefs.[67]

63. "La Développement," p. 7. Loisy understood Newman's use of
"idea" in a too exclusively intellectual way. "Idea" for Newman is
a complete process, susceptible to being apprehended in various
notions. An "idea" is an experience that leads to "realizations"
and to "principles" of life. The clarity of the "idea" is not
achieved at the beginning, but only through development. Cf. Chadwick, *From Bossuet to Newman,* pp. 149–51.
64. "La Théorie individualiste," p. 210.
65. "La Définition de la Religion," p. 197.
66. Ibid.
67. Ibid., p. 198.

While the purpose of this objectification is to bring about the protection and help of the divinity, i.e., unity with the deity, "religion . . . has always pursued the union of men with God, not simply the union of the individual with God." [68] Harnack and Sabatier have recognized, according to Loisy, only one element of religion—that of the individual, to the exclusion of the group.

Since religion deals primarily with groups of men, Loisy argues that the social element of religion is constitutive:

> It is necessary . . . to insist on this social character from which religion draws its force and which is the guarantee of its endurance. Man is not only aware of his dependence upon Him as a member of human society and with the society of which he is a part. All men who are dependent upon God are collectively (one can even say solidarily) in the same situation; this is not the individual abstracted from his every-day life concentrated in the most intimate secrets of his heart, but the entire man as he lives and behaves, as he is situated by his relations with his family and society. If all religions have presented themselves to us under a social form, this can only be in virtue of a natural necessity, a profound logic, which is as significant for the historian as for the philosopher. [69]

The religious institution is the fundamental constitutive element that objectifies the religious sentiment, the absolute dependence of men upon God. And it follows from this definition, according to Loisy, that tradition is essential to this social and institutional character of religion. "The ancestors have had the same relation with the divinity as men today," [70] and their example is necessary to preserve the right relationship with the divinity.

What is subject to development is the religious institu-

---

68. "La Théorie individualiste," pp. 203–4.
69. "La Définition de la Religion," p. 200.
70. Ibid.

tion, that social embodiment of all the rites, beliefs, and cults of the people. The social and institutional character of religion requires development to meet the changing circumstances of the people whom it serves.

Loisy's historical methodology revolves around two interrelated poles, development and institutionalization. Religion is a living fact, and, as living, is always subject to development. Since religion deals with the relation between God and men, it is objective, collective, social, and institutional. Loisy's methodology is oriented toward the religious institutions of men, toward their tradition. The individual giants of a given tradition are viewed, not in their distinctiveness, but in their contribution to the religious phenomenon. Their distinctiveness is their genius; that genius is conditioned by the context in which it is perceived and which gives it meaning.

THE KINGDOM AND THE CHURCH

It is one thing to argue for development in a given religion, but another to account for the emergence of that religion itself. In other words, how did Loisy understand the relation of Jesus to the church? In what sense is the emergence of the church a legitimate development of the demands of Jesus' ministry?

"Jésus annonçait le royaume, et c'est l'Église qui est venue." [71] This is Loisy's most famous statement, and one that is frequently used to summarize his view of the church's relation to Jesus.[72] What is ironic about this quotation is that it has come to represent the position of Har-

---

71. *L'Évangile et l'Église*, 5th ed. (Paris: Émile Nourry, 1929), p. 153.
72. Recently in Hans Conzelmann, *An Outline of the Theology of the New Testament*, trans. John Bowden (New York: Harper & Row, 1969), p. 33. Conzelmann is discussing Jesus' eschatological awareness, which he says excludes any idea of a present church, and he uses Loisy to make his point: "Loisy put [it] so perversely: Jesus expected the kingdom of God—and the church came."

nack rather than that of Loisy.[73] The statement has been taken out of its context and twisted to mean that there is no connection between the preaching of Jesus and the institution of the church, indeed that it is regrettable that the church ever came. However, for Loisy this statement is not only one of fact, but of necessity; the church had to come if the preaching of Jesus were to survive.

Because religion is a "living fact" as against a concept of the mind, Loisy begins his analysis of Jesus, not in terms of his teaching, but of his work. Loisy justifies this emphasis on the work of Jesus on the basis of the character of the sources at our disposal. Jesus can only be known "by the tradition, across the tradition and through the tradition of primitive Christians."[74] That tradition is the result of what Jesus did and accomplished; had he accomplished nothing, nothing would have been preserved. Thus, for Loisy the preaching of Jesus is viewed by the historian not as independent of Jesus' work but as derived from it, because the fragments of Jesus' teaching have been preserved by the tradition only in so far as they help clarify this work.[75]

---

73. Diether Hoffmann-Axthelm, "Loisy's *L'Évangile et l'Église*," ZThK 65 (1968) : 291.
74. *The Gospel and the Church*, p. 13.
75. Loisy has clearly anticipated the basic insight of form-criticism in his insistence upon tradition. Form-criticism, according to Rudolf Bultmann, *History of the Synoptic Tradition*, trans. John Marsh (New York: Harper & Row, 1968), p. 3, investigates the "individual units of the tradition" (Loisy's "fragments of his discourse"). *Sitz im Leben*, as the context in which a saying was preserved, corresponds with Loisy's warning that the critic must consider "the more or less notable modifications that the thought (and words) of Jesus must of necessity have endured in transmission from one generation to another" (*The Gospel and the Church*, p. 14).
  The encyclical *Pascendi* criticized this aspect of Loisy's understanding of the development of the Gospels. "The Modernists have no hesitation in affirming . . . that . . . the first three Gospels have been gradually formed from a primitive brief narration, by additions, by interpolations of theological or allegorical interpretations, or parts introduced only for the purpose of joining different passages together. This means, to put it briefly and clearly, that in the Sacred Books we

"The essence of Christianity must be in the work of Jesus or nowhere, and would vainly be sought in scattered fragments of his discourse."[76]

What is the work of Jesus? For Loisy, the answer can only be the coming of the kingdom. "The general theme of the preaching of Jesus was the reign of God, or the kingdom of Heaven."[77] This work is the one and only purpose of Jesus: "All his teaching is given to prepare for the kingdom."[78] Loisy argues that the kingdom as preached by Jesus refers to a future event very near at hand. In the Sermon on the Mount the kingdom is promised to the poor and afflicted, not as something now present, but as something in the future; he sees the parables of Jesus as the promise of the future, an immediate future, the coming of the kingdom.[79] The kingdom of heaven "is then nothing but a great hope, and it is in this hope or nowhere that the historian should set the essence of the gospel, as no other idea holds so prominent and so large a place in the teaching of Jesus."[80]

The choice of "a great hope" as a description of the kingdom is not thoughtless. To call it "a great hope" not only befits the future character of the kingdom—the fact that it cannot be fully present now—but at the same time transposes the kingdom into an impulse, something toward which the work of Jesus strives. For Loisy, the establishment of this great hope is *the work* of Jesus.

---

must admit a *vital evolution*, springing from and corresponding with the evolution of faith. The traces of this evolution, they tell us, are so visible in the books that one might almost write a history of it. Indeed, this history they actually do write, and with such an easy assurance that one might believe them to have seen with their own eyes the writers at work through the ages amplifying the Sacred Books" (as quoted in Sabatier, *Modernism*, pp. 295-96).

76. *The Gospel and the Church*, p. 13.
77. Ibid., p. 53.
78. Ibid.
79. Ibid., p. 59.
80. Ibid., p. 69.

This kingdom/hope has three characteristics which correspond to Loisy's definition of religion. (1) "It is . . . collective,"[81] since all who love God are destined to live in it. It is "of such a nature that all can enjoy it in common, and so well that their happiness cannot be compared to anything so fitly as to a great festival."[82] (2) The kingdom is objective since it "implies all the conditions of a happy life, both the physical and the moral conditions, the external and the internal conditions."[83] (3) It is a future event. "The kingdom of heaven can be spoken of as a fact that completes history."[84] This future action is cosmic and does not affect "the fate of the individual in this world, but the renewal of the world, the restoration of humanity in eternal justice and happiness."[85] Loisy acknowledges that the kingdom is not future in any absolute sense and points to the miraclès and casting out of demons to show that the power of the evil age is nearing its end, that the present virtually contains the future.[86] The futurity of the kingdom serves to make the kingdom real in the sense that the futurity provides the impulse, the driving force, which will propel the kingdom through history. Had the kingdom come, the religion of Jesus would have been without its living reality.

According to Loisy, the position of Jesus in the kingdom involves two stages: in the first he is the messenger (preacher) of the kingdom, and upon its arrival he will be its messiah. Therefore, during the period of his ministry he was the predestined messiah.[87] This character of "predestined messiah" is the key to understanding Loisy's

---

81. Ibid., p. 59.
82. Ibid.
83. Ibid.
84. Ibid.
85. Ibid.
86. Ibid., p. 60.
87. *Les Évangiles synoptiques* (Paris: Ceffonds, 1908), 1:213.

theory for the messianic consciousness of Jesus. Because the kingdom "is essentially a thing of the future, the office of Messiah is essentially eschatological." [88] While rejecting W. Wrede's contention that Jesus was only acclaimed messiah after his resurrection,[89] Loisy does recognize that most of the statements about Jesus' messiahship in the Synoptics are the product of Chritian tradition.[90] The reason why the question of the messiahship of Jesus plays so small a role in the authentic teaching of Jesus is, according to Loisy, due to the fact that the subject of Jesus' teaching is not Jesus but the kingdom. But, for Loisy, there can be no doubt that Jesus viewed himself as predestined messiah, and his evidence is threefold. First, he argues that the apostles could not have believed that Jesus was raised from the dead if they had not at first believed that he was the messiah.[91] Second, he accepts the authenticity of the condemnation by Pilate of Jesus as King of the Jews.[92] Finally, he argues that the confession of Peter contains an authentic remembrance.[93]

The collective, objective, and future qualities of the kingdom called forth even in Jesus' lifetime the organization of a definite group around Jesus—the apostles and disciples. Because of the necessity that the kingdom be

88. *The Gospel and the Church*, p. 102.
89. *Les Évangiles synoptiques*, 1:212. Wrede's important book is now available in English as *The Messianic Secret in the Gospels*, trans. J. C. G. Greig (Cambridge & London: James Clarke, 1971).
90. *Les Évangiles synoptiques*, 1:213.
91. Ibid., p. 212.
92. *The Gospel and the Church*, p. 101. In *Les Évangiles synoptiques*, 1:212, Loisy says, "If Jesus had not been condemned to death as King of the Jews, that is to say as Messiah, by his own admission, one could just as well maintain that he never existed."
93. *The Gospel and the Church*, p. 101. In *Les Évangiles synoptiques*, 2:2ff, Loisy argues that Mark 8:27ff. shows the extensive influence of the community upon this saying. Many modern scholars do not accept the authenticity of Peter's confession. For a summary of the recent debate see Raymond E. Brown, Karl P. Donfried, and John Reumann, *Peter in the New Testament* (New York: Paulist Press; Minneapolis: Augsburg, 1973), pp. 64–69.

preached, Jesus passed on to his followers a specific mission, the preaching of the gospel. Thus the kingdom, because of its qualities and its demand for preaching, called forth first the organization of the disciples and then the church, whose sole purpose was to continue this preaching. "Does it not follow that the Church is as necessary to the Gospel as the Gospel to the Church, and that the two are really one, as the Gospel and the group of believers were one during the ministry of Jesus?"[94] Loisy sees three elements emerging from the activity of Jesus: the symbol of the kingdom, the messiah (agent of the kingdom), and the apostolate or the preaching of the kingdom.[95] These elements were the living reality of Jesus' religion and work and, if they were to survive, development was necessary so that they could adapt to the changing conditions.

"There is no institution on the earth or in history whose status and value may not be questioned if the principle is established that nothing may exist except in its original form."[96] The key to this entire argument is "institution," for it is the requirements of the kingdom that allow Loisy to use the terminology of "institution." The kingdom as Jesus preached it demanded the establishment of an institution of the elect, whose purpose was to prepare for the coming of the kingdom by preaching that good news. Because it was an institution, it was necessary that it grow and develop so that the preaching of the coming of that kingdom could continue. The whole of the development of Christian history is not an aberration of the pure gospel, but a true necessity if that gospel were to survive.[97]

94. *The Gospel and the Church*, p. 151.
95. Ibid., p. 167.
96. Ibid., p. 166.
97. Ibid., p. 165.

II.

HARNACK AND LOISY

WHAT IS CHRISTIANITY?

Harnack's published Berlin lectures attracted great attention because they were one of the finest summaries of liberal Protestantism ever produced. Standing in the great line of Schleiermacher and Ritschl, these lectures are the end product of a view of Christianity which sought to demonstrate its importance and relevance to the contemporary situation. It was and is a powerful view of Christianity that still affects the present theological situation.[98] The lectures were the culmination of Harnack's historical research and meditation on Christianity.

For Harnack, the study of history was *Geisteswissenschaft,* i.e., it is first and foremost scientific and its object is the *Geist* ("Spirit") of an epoch or an individual. History deals with man overcoming nature, triumphing over himself. Without historical knowledge "routine would prevail and consciously purposeful work would be impossible."[99] For Harnack, the discipline of history is the overarching science which gives meaning to all the other

98. Cf. Rudolf Bultmann's "Introduction" to the Harper Torchbook edition of *What is Christianity?,* trans. Thomas B. Saunders (New York: Harper & Row, 1957), p. viiff.
99. "Über die Sicherheit und die Grenzen geschichtlicher Erkenntnis," *Erforschtes und Erlebtes. Reden und Aufsätze* (Giessen: Alfred Töpelmann, 1923), 4:3.

sciences. History and the historian bear a heavy responsibility. The purpose of historical study is not simply to know what has happened, as Ranke had said, but "in order to intervene in the course of history, therefore we study history and we have the right and duty to do so; for without historical knowledge we remain either passive objects of development or we become criminal misleaders." [100] What then is the object of this historical knowledge? "We want to know it as progressive objectification of the spirit and therefore as the progressive mastery over matter." [101]

This notion of "progressive objectification of the spirit" points to the two poles of Harnack's work that often stand in the greatest tension. "Progressive" denotes the evolutionary, developmental view of history that supports Harnack's historiography. The second pole is the *Geist,* which for Harnack is to be located preeminently in those rare individuals who have changed the course of history; in these rare individuals the *Geist* which the historian seeks to isolate is located.[102] Here he finds exemplified those norms and values that allow mankind to overcome history. The historian is interested in what is permanent and not what is transitory, for the transitory is only the result of development and does not represent those great planes of human consciousness. Because history must overcome history, the historian must be able to represent adequately the essence

100. Ibid., p. 7.
101. Ibid., p. 5.
102. E.g., the organization of his *History of Dogma* is built around three individuals. "We can clearly distinguish three styles of building (*Baustil*) in the history of Dogma, but only three: the style of Origen, that of Augustine, and that of the Reformers." See Harnack, *History of Dogma,* trans. Neil Buchann (New York: Dover, 1961), 1:8. Wayne Glick's important study of Harnack (*The Reality of Christianity* [New York: Harper & Row, 1967], p. 141) shows that Harnack deals with the Reformation almost exclusively in terms of Luther. The fourth German edition of *History of Dogma* was published in 1894 and 1897. Cf. Glick, p. 123, for a history of the various editions.

or reality of the past and be able to appropriate the past in a determinative way for the present and future. But since literal contact with the individuals of the past is impossible now, Harnack must presuppose *'Der Geist ist Einer'* ("The Spirit is One").[103] "How much or how little we may possess of it, it is always one and the same *Geist* ["Spirit"] which works in all of the products of history *and in us.*"[104]

The assumption that there is only one *Geist* in all history is Harnack's attempt to solve the problem of historical relativity and continuity. If history becomes so relative that the past has no dynamic relation to the present, then it would be only a museum piece, the effort to grasp it wasteful speculation. The *Geist* redeems history from this fate by allowing the historian to isolate those norms and values which affect history. But in this solution to the problem of historical relativity and continuity lies the seed of Harnack's dilemma, for, as Glick says, this *Geist* becomes a reflection of Harnack himself.[105] Harnack's predicament arose in the attempt to solve the problem that all believing historians must face: how can the gospel, a product of the first century, have an effect in contemporary affairs? For Harnack, the gospel can act today because the *Geist* of history is one.

If the historian must seek the main idea, the *Geist,* of an epoch, then Harnack certainly located the heart of his work in his conception of the gospel. The gospel is the alpha and the omega of his work. His *History of Dogma* is a history of the vicissitudes of the gospel, and the *Wesen* ("Essence") of Christianity is likewise the gospel. It is

---

103. "Was hat die Historie an fester Erkenntnis zur Deutung des Weltgeschehens zu bieten?" *Erforschtes und Erlebtes. Reden und Aufsätze,* 4:188.
104. Ibid.
105. Glick, *The Reality of Christianity,* pp. 119-21.

the principle by which the whole of dogma, the whole of Christianity, is to be judged. *Wissenschaft* was his method, but the gospel was its object.

This centrality of the gospel is seen clearly in the conception and organization of *What is Christianity?* After a general introductory lecture on the nature of historical investigation, the volume is divided into two principal sections, "The Gospel" and "The Gospel in History." This division denotes Harnack's principle that it is the duty of the historian to discern what is of permanent value, "not to cleave to words, but to find out what is essential," [106] i.e., to separate the kernel from the husk.[107] The kernel is the gospel, the husk the history in which it must of necessity become involved but for which it must not be mistaken.

For Harnack, the gospel is inseparably related to the message of Jesus Christ. He organizes Jesus' message around three interrelated poles:

> First, the kingdom of God and its coming.
> Second, God the Father and the infinite value of the human soul.
> Third, the higher righteousness and the commandment of Love.[108]

These three topics are dealt with in the first half of the section entitled "The Gospel." The first aspect of Jesus' teaching, "the kingdom of God," denotes that Jesus' message was framed within the context of Jewish apocalyptic; however, this Jewish context is of no lasting significance, for "most of the threads leading from it [the gospel] into 'contemporary history' become of no importance at all." [109] For Jesus, the kingdom of God is a moral force.

106. *What is Christianity?*, p. 13.
107. Ibid., p. 15.
108. Ibid., p. 51.
109. Ibid., p. 16.

"True, the kingdom of God is the rule of God; but it is the rule of the holy God in the hearts of individuals; *it is God himself in his power.*" [110] "It is something supernatural . . . a purely religious blessing, . . . the most important experience that a man can have." [111]

God the Father and the infinite value of the human soul, the second point in the teaching of Jesus, is for Harnack a gospel within the gospel. [112] This is the summation of the gospel because it clearly expresses the idea that the gospel calls men to become children of God and "the human soul is so ennobled that it can and does unite with him." [113] Jesus himself had pointed to the dynamics of the gospel in the prayer he taught his disciples. "It shows the Gospel to be the Fatherhood of God applied to the whole of life; to be an inner union with God's will and God's kingdom, and a joyous certainty of the possession of eternal blessings and protection from evil." [114]

Harnack's third point concerns "the higher righteousness and the commandment of Love," Jesus' ethical teaching. Jesus had broken the relationship that had existed in his day between ethics and "the external forms of religious worship." [115] Harnack again reinforces his understanding of the gospel as an interior, personal experience. Morality is determined on the basis of intention and dispo-

---

110. Ibid., p. 56.
111. Ibid., p. 62.
112. In the preface to the third edition of the fifth volume of the *History of Dogma*, p. vii, Harnack makes the same threefold division of the gospel as in *What is Christianity?* and refers to the second of these divisions as "das Evangelium im Evangelium." "The middle section connected with Matthew 11:25–30, and therefore also combined with the primitive Christian testimony regarding Jesus as Lord and Saviour, I hold, from strictly historical and objective grounds, to be the true main section, the Gospel in the Gospel, and to it I subordinate the other portions."
113. *What is Christianity?*, p. 63.
114. Ibid., p. 65.
115. Ibid., p. 71.

sition, not on the basis of law or custom (tradition).[116] Having freed ethics from ritual and self-seeking concerns, Jesus reduced all morality "to one root and to one motive— love." [117] By this means, Jesus freed morality "from all alien concern, even from its alliance with the public religion." [118]

In the second part of the section entitled "The Gospel," Harnack explains the relation of the gospel to certain modern problems:

(1) The Gospel and the world, or the question of asceticism;

(2) The Gospel and the poor, or the social question;

(3) The Gospel and Law, or the question of public order;

(4) The Gospel and work, or the question of civilization;

(5) The Gospel and the Son of God, or the Christological question.

(6) The Gospel and doctrine, or the question of creed.[119]

The gospel is not world-denying [120] and asceticism has no place in it.[121] Jesus demands a struggle against mammon, care, and selfishness, which are to be banished by a love that serves and is at the same time self-sacrificing. While Jesus did not sanction poverty and misery, but fought them and wanted others to do likewise,[122] he did not present a plan of action for the overcoming of poverty; if he had done so, the gospel would have served only the needs of its own day and "to-morrow it would have been antiquated." [123] In dealing with the gospel and the question of

116. Ibid., pp. 71–72.
117. Ibid., p. 72.
118. Ibid.
119. Ibid., p. 78.
120. Ibid., p. 84.
121. Ibid., p. 87.
122. Ibid., p. 94.
123. Ibid., p. 97.

public order, Harnack draws two distinctions. First, Jesus was not a political revolutionary [124] and brought no political ideology.[125] Second, in regard to the gospel and legal ordinance generally, Harnack argues that it is a mockery to say that the gospel supports all laws.[126] The Christian should expect all things from the Father; he should not be concerned with wordly affairs; but he should at all times be governed by love.[127] Finally, the gospel is not concerned with civilization, for that would enmesh it in mundane concerns.

Harnack's last two questions are of a different kind from the first four. Regarding Christology, his position is summarized in his one controlling principle in this matter. *"The Gospel,* as Jesus preached it, has to do with the Father, not with the Son.''[128] Finally, the question of creed is dealt with quickly. A creed stands in opposition to the gospel, and for the same reason that Christology is illegitimate: because it makes something a prerequisite for the relation between God and his children.[129]

In the final section of his lectures, Harnack comes to ''The Gospel in History.'' There can be no sense of development with respect to the gospel; it has not developed, but was fully given in Jesus Christ. What the historian investigates is the history of the church, the forms which have crystallized around the gospel. This course of study is clearly indicated in the three stereotyped questions he asks at the beginning of his treatment of Greek and Roman Catholicism.

> What did this Greek Catholicism achieve?
> What are its characteristics?

124. Ibid., p. 102.
125. Ibid., p. 108.
126. Ibid., p. 108.
127. Ibid., p. 116.
128. Ibid., p. 144.
129. Ibid., p. 146.

> What modifications did the Gospel here undergo and
> how did it hold its own?[130]

As the questions indicate, the gospel has been in a constant
battle to maintain its own. Harnack's answer to the third
question is revealing:

> What modifications has the Gospel undergone, and how
> much of it is left? Well—this is not a matter that needs
> many words—the whole outward and visible institution
> of a Church claiming divine dignity has no foundations
> whatever in the Gospel. It is a case, not of distortion,
> but of total perversion.[131]

Protestantism was a restoration of the gospel. It was the
greatest movement in history from the second century
until the present time.[132] The significance of the Reformation lay in that Christianity "was *reduced* to its essential
factors, to the Word of God and to faith." [133] But this
restoration is always in danger of being lost, for the
Protestant churches could become Catholic by "becoming
churches of ordinance, doctrine, and ceremony." [134]

In his concluding lecture, Harnack pleads for a preservation of the Reformation principles, the gospel. If only
courageously applied "modern ideas will not put any *new*
difficulties in their way." [135] Christianity must grasp the
gospel and must give proof of its spirit by facing the questions of the "social province." "Here a tremendous task
confronts us, and in the measure in which we accomplish it
we shall be able to answer with a better heart the deepest
of all questions—*the meaning of life*." [136] History must
overcome history.

---

130. Ibid., p. 218; for Roman Catholicism, see p. 246.
131. *What is Christianity?*, p. 262.
132. Ibid., p. 268.
133. Ibid., p. 269 (italics Harnack's).
134. Ibid., p. 295.
135. Ibid., p. 300.
136. Ibid.

POINTS OF DEBATE

In the introduction to *The Gospel and the Church,* Loisy locates what he judges to be the linchpin of Harnack's work:

> The whole doctrine of the book is based on this fundamental point; that the essence of the gospel consists solely in faith in God the Father, as revealed by Jesus Christ. On the validity or insufficiency of this principle depends the value of the judgements delivered on the evolution of the Church, Her dogmas, and Her worship, from the beginning, and in all the different forms of creed that are founded on the Gospel and the name of Jesus.[137]

The search for the essence of Christianity was demanded by Harnack's understanding of historical method. Loisy's understanding of method leads in the opposite direction, toward the illegitimacy of seeking such an essence. To determine the essence, Harnack must differentiate between essential and non-essential; to disprove Harnack, Loisy must invoke a method that overcomes such differentiation. He does this by means of two rules laid out in the introduction to his book. "There would be little logic in taking for the whole essence of one religion the points that differentiate it from another."[138] Because monotheism is common to Judaism, Christianity, and Mohammedanism, does this mean, asks Loisy, that monotheism is not essential to these religions? From this statement he draws a more pointed argument against Harnack, a point that is a deathblow to Harnack's position and essential to his own. "It is, therefore, in the highest degree arbitrary to decide that Christianity in its essence must be all that the gospel has not borrowed from Judaism, as if all that the gospel has re-

137. *The Gospel and the Church,* pp. 3–4.
138. Ibid., p. 9.

tained of the Jewish tradition must be necessarily of secondary value.'' [139]

A second rule established by Loisy maintains that ''we know Christ only by the tradition, across the tradition, and in the tradition of the primitive Christians.'' [140] For Loisy there never was any pure gospel of Jesus, for what Jesus preached was itself a development of Judaism which also continued to develop after him. The gospel of Jesus was both the impulse of the tradition and at the same time preserved by the tradition. Had there been no continuity between Jesus and the tradition, nothing of Jesus would have been preserved by the tradition.

These two rules proposed by Loisy represent the deciding methodological distinction between Harnack and Loisy and the pivotal point of their debate. In terms of New Testament scholarship this debate raises two fundamental problematics: Jesus and Judaism and Jesus and the church.

Jesus and Judaism. What is the relation between Jesus' teaching and that of Judaism? Harnack summarizes his position as follows: ''Jesus Christ's teaching will at once bring us by steps which, if few, will be great, to a height where its connection with Judaism is seen to be only a loose one, and most of the threads from it into 'contemporary history' become of no importance at all.'' [141] Harnack's view is not quite as simple as this statement would seem to indicate. The eschatological and apocalyptic element is present in Jesus' teaching, but is not the essence of that message. He stated this paradox very nicely in his *History of Dogma.* ''The Gospel presents itself as an Apocalyptic message on the soil of the Old Testament, and as the fulfillment of the law and the prophets, and yet it is a new

139. Ibid., p. 10.
140. Ibid., p. 13.
141. *What is Christianity?*, p. 16.

thing, the creation of a universal religion on the basis of that of the Old Testament.'' [142]

Thus, the message of Jesus was presented under the forms of apocalyptic imagery, such as the day of judgment and the coming of the kingdom. This imagery is understood by recourse to other such examples in history. ''Every time that a man earnestly, and out of the depth of his own personal experience, points others to God and to what is good and holy, whether it be deliverance or judgement that he preaches, it has always, so far as history tells us, taken the form of announcing that the end is at hand.'' [143] Because the vision of the prophet is so intense, he sees the evil of the present situation with such force that he is amazed that God has not already destroyed the world. The time left for conversion must be short in view of the enormity of the present evil state of man. By means of this psychological explanation of the forms of apocalyptic imagery, Harnack shifts the emphasis from what the prophet says to why he says it. So what is important is not the preaching of the coming of the kingdom, but Jesus' perception of the moral demand of God. This apocalyptic imagery ''threatened to obscure the simple and yet, at bottom, much more affecting maxims about the judgment which is certain to every individual soul.'' [144]

Jesus acknowledged the title messiah in his own lifetime even though it did not explain, according to Harnack, his true self-understanding. Jesus had to accept the title because ''it was an assumption that was simply necessary if the man who felt the inward call was to gain an absolute recognition within the lines of Jewish history.'' [145] It was the only option open to him to express ''that he was the

---

142. *History of Dogma,* 1:41.
143. *What is Christianity?,* p. 41.
144. *History of Dogma,* 1:101.
145. *What is Christianity?,* p. 141.

Son of God and was doing the work of God.'' [146] Jesus'
self-understanding as the Son of God was the prior and
true understanding of Jesus. ''We must assert that the
consciousness of Divine Sonship and of Messiahship could
not have existed together from the beginning; for the consciousness of Messiahship never meant anything less for our
Lord than a consciousness of *what He was about to become.*
In his soul the consciousness of what *He was* must have
come first, and only when this had attained to a height of
consciousness of Sonship could the tremendous leap be
taken to the consciousness of Messiahship.'' [147] For Harnack, the key text for Jesus' understanding of his divine
sonship is Matt. 11:25–27. He reconstructs the authentic
form of this saying as follows:

> I thank you, Father, Lord of Heaven and earth, that you
> have hidden these things from the wise and intelligent,
> and you have revealed them to babes. Indeed, Father, for
> so it was well pleasing before you. All things have been
> delivered to me by the Father, and no one has known the
> Father except the Son and to whomever the Son has re-
> vealed Him. [148]

For Harnack, in the second part of this saying Jesus
''gives clear expression to the fact that this revelation had
been vouchsafed *through himself.*'' [149] This knowledge of
God is Jesus' whole doctrine. Jesus knows the Father, he
was the first to so know him, and through him others are
coming to know the Father. [150]

This saying is the gospel within the gospel, [151] the true

---

146. Ibid.
147. *The Sayings of Jesus: The Second Source of St. Matthew and St. Luke*, trans. J. R. Wilkinson (New York: G. P. Putman's Sons, 1908), pp. 245–46.
148. Ibid., p. 295.
149. Ibid., p. 297.
150. Ibid., pp. 298–99.
151. *History of Dogma*, 5:vii.

kernel of Jesus' teaching.[152] A man acts with his age only as a coefficient,[153] and it is the duty of the historian "to determine what is of permanent value . . . to find out what is essential."[154] Judaism is Jesus' coefficient and is not what is of permanent value. Thus, to understand Jesus within Jewish categories (Messiahship) would be to totally misunderstand him.

In the introduction to *The Gospel and the Church*, Loisy remarks that Harnack had exposed himself "to the misfortune, supreme for a Protestant theologian, of having founded the essence of Christianity upon data supplied by Christian tradition."[155] For Loisy, the Matthean text was "the work of a Christian prophet, speaking in the name of Christ, in the style of the psalms and prophets of the Old Testament."[156]

As noted above, Loisy had enunciated as one of the principles of his method that one should expect "to find in Judaism and Christianity elements common to both, equally essential to both."[157] The Jesus whom Loisy reconstructs is a Jewish Jesus—a man of his nation and of that nation's religion. But Loisy is faced with the opposite problem from that of Harnack. Harnack had sought the

---

152. *What is Christianity?*, p. 130.
153. Ibid., p. 13.
154. Ibid.
155. *The Gospel and the Church*, p. 12.
156. *Les Évangiles synoptiques*, 1:907–08. In *Mémoires*, 2:121, Loisy reports that he first decided that this text, upon which Harnack was so heavily dependent, was not authentic when he read Strauss, who had suggested that this saying was dependent upon Sirach 51. Loisy does not footnote Strauss in his commentary and I can only suppose that the article to which he is referring is D. F. Strauss, "Jesu Weheruf über Jerusalem und die *sophia tou theou* Matthew 23, 34ff," *Zeitschrift für wissenschaftliche Theologie* 6 (1863): 93ff. This conjecture is not made in Strauss's *Life of Jesus* (4th ed.). In *Das Leben Jesu für das deutsche Volk bearbeitet* (Leipzig: Brockhaus, 1864; § 33) Strauss says it is not a genuine saying, but he does not trace it to Sirach 51.
157. *The Gospel and the Church*, p. 11.

distinctive and belittled the similarities. Since Loisy emphasized the similarities—and since development implies both continuity and change—what is there that is distinctive?

Jesus' argument according to Loisy, is not against Judaism but within Judaism. For example, Jesus' opposition to the Pharisees does not mean that he wished to abolish the law [158] or to stand above it. Rather, he stood against the Pharisees' tradition of the interpretation of the law. "There is precisely the originality of his teaching, which, if one takes it piece by piece, could be recovered whole from the Biblical writings or from the writings of the rabbis." [159] Jesus felt that his interpretation of the law was from God, the author of the law; he defended his interpretation by calling upon the law as evidence.[160] Nor does Jesus oppose his authority to that of Moses. "He has escaped from the shackles of the letter, and he appears so sure of himself only because he is sure of God." [161]

The foremost element of Jesus' teaching, the kingdom of God, is also inextricably bound up with Judaism. "It is even the whole of Judaism, and is intelligible only in relation to Israelite faith, all of whose traditional themes Jesus retained, without discussing them." [162] The kingdom of God would be a restoration and regeneration of the universe. "The justice of God would be manifested by the resurrection of all the true believers who had died without having received their reward." [163] According to Loisy, the notion of the kingdom at Jesus' time had three main features:

158. Loisy accepts the authenticity of Matt. 5:17. See *Les Évangiles synoptiques,* 1:564.
159. Ibid., p. 233.
160. As evidence for this view, Loisy points to the debate on divorce in Mark 10:2–12. See ibid., 2:195–201.
161. Ibid., 1:233.
162. Ibid., p. 225.
163. Loisy points to Daniel 12:2 as an example of this view of the resurrection. See ibid., p. 229.

(1) it was conceived within the national framework; (2) it would be a moral reign founded upon the religion of Israel as a universal religion; and (3) it would bring "the transformation of the world and the consummation of goodness in justice for the elite of Israel and of humanity since the beginning of the world." [164]

These three elements can also be found in the teaching of Jesus. Jesus came only to the lost sheep of Israel.[165] Although the kingdom, as conceived by Jesus, is bounded by Jewish nationalism, it is not a political kingdom, as is seen in the fact that the requirement for admission is not that one be a Jew but that one repent.[166] The preaching of the kingdom was not without political overtones since the Roman authority would be overthrown with the arrival of the kingdom.[167] While the kingdom was thus conceived within the bounds of Jewish nationalism, its joys were not political but moral and its law was God's justice.[168] Most importantly, the kingdom would be brought not by Jesus, its predestined head, but by God.[169] The kingdom was completely the work of God. "The gospel was not an enterprise of holy war with a view to effecting, through a religious motive, the national liberation, but a preparation of hearts in view of the justice which God will claim for his faithful to manifest to them his glory." [170]

The vindication of God's justice by the coming of the kingdom plays an important part in Loisy's reconstruction of the preaching of Jesus. The restoration of all things, as

164. Ibid.
165. Matt. 15:24 is, according to Loisy, a gloss upon the Marcan story of the Canaanite woman, but the redactor has correctly summed up the position of Jesus (See ibid., p. 973). Bultmann, *History of the Synoptic Tradition*, p. 155, holds a position identical to that of Loisy.
166. *Les Évangiles synoptiques*, 1:232.
167. Ibid., p. 221.
168. Ibid., p. 231.
169. Ibid.
170. Ibid., p. 232.

the act of vindication, involves the resurrection of the dead —they will be raised to show forth his justice. The resurrection is not that of man's immortal soul; it is a real restoration. "Men will be flesh and bones; they will not marry because they will be immortal,[171] but it is scarcely pure metaphor that they can be imagined as assembled at a feast."[172] Loisy defines the kingdom as preached by Jesus in the following manner: "The Kingdom of God is properly an era of goodness in justice, which was going to be inaugurated by a manifestation of power, a sudden transformation of everything, the exaltation of the Messiah."[173]

For Loisy, Jesus was a Jew whose mission and existence made sense only within the framework of the nationalist expectation of that people. There was no essence of Jesus that was not Jewish, nor was there any teaching that was not impregnated with Jewish tradition. For Harnack, Jesus in his essence stood above Judaism. Why have two such disparate pictures of Jesus emerged from men who both claimed to be following a historical, scientific method? In the case of Harnack, the answer is that such a Jesus was necessary in order to show his superiority to Judaism, with the implication that history could isolate the unique Jesus. Furthermore, if Jesus were to be meaningful, in fact decisive, for modern man, a messianic Jesus would not do.[174]

---

171. Loisy sees the debate between Jesus and the Sadducees in Mark 12:18–27 as founded upon an historical occurrence, but the redaction now present in the synoptics has been reworked to fit the church's debate with this group. See ibid., 2:339. Bultmann, *History of the Synoptic Tradition*, p. 28, maintains that this pericope "simply reflects the theological activity of the Church." But Hans Conzelmann, *Jesus*, trans. J. Raymond Lord (Philadelphia: Fortress Press, 1973), p. 69, sees the passage as authentic. "Since he says that we will be 'like angels,' he denies every deduction from this world to the next and at the same time criticizes indulging in fancies."

172. *Les Évangiles Synoptiques*, 1:238. The reference to the feast is to Matt. 8:11 and Mark 14:25.

173. Ibid., p. 237.

174. Albert Schweitzer drove this point home in a forceful manner in *The Quest of the Historical Jesus*, trans. W. Montgomery (New York: Macmillan, 1968), p. 401.

To solve the problem of continuity with the historical Jesus, a Jesus is needed who will not appear strange to modern man. Loisy's historical. and theological method did not require such a direct link between Jesus and modern man. In Loisy's understanding tradition carried on the work of Jesus, and development made this possible by allowing new interpretations of that work to be undertaken in new circumstances. It was only through, by, and across the tradition that Jesus was known.

Jesus and the Church. Harnack had located the pure essence of Christianity in Jesus himself and had distinguished the Jewish elements in his teaching as being of secondary importance. But if, as Harnack thought, the gospel has not always been preserved in its pure form, only the church can have perverted the true gospel. The illegitimate developments of Christian thought are not traced to Jesus but to the early church. So Harnack has ambivalent feelings toward the early church: it must have preserved the true gospel, for it is only through the tradition of this early church that we know Jesus; and yet it must also have prepared for the distortion that was to follow.

This ambivalence toward the early church is seen quite clearly in Harnack's treatment of the development of the primitive church. He distinguishes three factors common to the life and preaching of the early church: (1) Jesus Christ was proclaimed as the Lord; (2) religion was an actual experience; and (3) Christians led a holy life in purity and brotherly fellowship while awaiting the return of the Lord.[175]

For the primitive community, Jesus was the Lord because he was the authoritative teacher; his word and his commandments were their way of life.[176] Furthermore, he was the Lord because he had sacrificed his life for them

175. *What is Christianity?*, p. 153; *History of Dogma,* 1:78.
176. *What is Christianity?*, p. 153.

and had been raised by God, at whose right hand he was now sitting. But their understanding of Jesus' lordship could be and was couched within the framework of Jesus' own teaching. The messiahship meant sonship, and the resurrection was the confirmation of "the impression given by his person, and provided faith with a sure hold." [177]

But this proclamation that Jesus Christ became the Lord by his death and resurrection contains the seeds of a development that, according to Harnack, would eventually obscure the gospel. The death and resurrection became the whole of the gospel, and Paul actually did "reduce the whole Gospel to these events." [178] Once these two events were detached from their historical foundation, i.e., the true meaning of Jesus' preaching, the door was open to all manner of speculation, to christology. Such speculation about the mystery of Christ "necessarily withdrew from the minds of believers the consideration of the work of Christ, and the contemplation of the revelation of God, which was given in the ministry of the historical Jesus." [179] Jesus himself became the true revelation. The attempt to form a correct theory about the person of Jesus could always lead to the substitution of christology for the gospel, but, says Harnack, "it is a perverse proceeding to make Christology the fundamental substance of the Gospel." [180]

This same ambivalence toward the early church can be seen in Harnack's treatment of his second and third factors common to early Christian life. For the early believers, religion was an actual experience. Although the words and commandments of Jesus were held in the highest respect, the early Christians did not fall into the trap of allowing these words to smother the spontaneous religious

177. Ibid., p. 155.
178. Ibid., p. 154.
179. *History of Dogma*, 1:105.
180. *What is Christianity?*, p. 184.

experience by "punctilious subjection" to them.[181] That was a temptation of a later period. This religious experience of immediate relation to God was the basis of the brotherly fellowship of the early communities.[182] But the fellowship contained a danger. The early Christians were led to form societies, and from these societies came a visible church. In this manner, the individual religious experience would fall under the control of the church's laws and prohibitions. Thus in the original experience itself were sown the seeds of its own destruction.

Loisy's theory of development, like that of Harnack, involves both continuity and change. But unlike Harnack, for Loisy continuity does not imply an unchanging essence preserved in new circumstances. It is not essence which constitutes continuity for Loisy; what is inherited from the past develops in toto in order to respond to the present. In Harnack's model, the essence is the kernel, while the rest is the husk. The problem for Harnack is that the husk may be mistaken for the kernel.[183] Thus, while the early church preserved the essence, it added much more besides. There is, then, a break, a hiatus, between Jesus and the early church. Loisy's model is that of a tree, from an acorn to a full-grown tree.[184] For Loisy, there is no question of the essence becoming lost, nor of a break between Jesus and the church. Rather, the work of Jesus, as now entrusted to his followers, developed to respond to its new situation. For Harnack, the problem is change itself which threatens the unchanging essence. For Loisy, a precisely opposite problem exists: when there is no change, the tree is dead.

181. Ibid., p. 164.
182. Ibid., p. 170.
183. Ibid., pp. 14–15. Harnack also warns: "We must not be like the child who, wanting to get at the kernel of a bulb, went on picking off the leaves until there was nothing left, and then could not help seeing that it was just the leaves that made the bulb."
184. *The Gospel and the Church*, pp. 16–19.

Jesus' mission had been the preaching of the approaching kingdom, and the need for preaching this gospel had called into existence the group of disciples around Jesus. The church continued the action of Jesus by preaching and preparing the way for the kingdom. ''The gospel and the church are in identical relation to the kingdom; they prepare immediately for it.'' [185] The demand that the gospel be preached led to the institution of the church. As the area over which the gospel was preached continued to expand, the church gradually became aware that its mission was universal. In the beginning, evangelization was limited to the Jews (Matt. 10:23) ; [186] but as the kingdom failed to come, the field of evangelization increased. ''When the Gospel continued to be preached without the arrival of the glorious Christ or the kingdom arriving, Christianity was born.'' [187] The conclusion of Matthew's Gospel, which presents the risen Lord commanding the gospel be preached to all the world, is the end of the type of development that determines the scope of the gospel.[188] The church began to preach to the Gentiles, and with their entry into the church there came a new set of circumstances to which the gospel must be adapted. The church had to adapt or the gospel would have perished.[189]

The death and resurrection of Jesus brought about a new set of circumstances which had not been foreseen in the ministry of Jesus. This occurrence is for Loisy the most important development in the whole of Christianity.[190] During Jesus' ministry, the abiding concern had been the coming of the kingdom; now, it was necessary to explain the place of Jesus Christ in the kingdom. The source of

185. *Autour d'un petit Livre*, p. 159.
186. *Les Évangiles synoptiques*, 1:883–84.
187. Ibid., p. 175.
188. *Autour d'un petit Livre*, pp. 168–69.
189. *The Gospel and the Church*, pp. 129–30.
190. *Les Évangiles synoptiques*, 1:176.

continuity is the kingdom; the point of transition is the resurrection, since the resurrection is the proclamation of Jesus as the messiah of the coming kingdom. The eschatological events are now beginning, and the title of messiah now properly belongs to Jesus. While the resurrection involves a new set of circumstances to which the understanding of the kingdom must be adapted, the resurrection itself is not something unrelated to the kingdom. The coming of the kingdom involved the restoration of all things, the resurrection of the dead. It was only proper, then, that Jesus as the bringer of the kingdom should be the first to undergo this restoration. For Loisy, Christ is the product, not of the kerygma, but of the kingdom.

The resurrection is the pivotal event in the transition from Jesus to the early church. It is the risen Christ that instituted the church, not Jesus himself. The texts themselves are not clear on the precise details, but they do lead the critic to the conclusion that the mission of the church is seen as the result of the resurrection of Christ.

> The institution of the Church by the risen Christ is not therefore a tangible fact for the historian. What the historian perceives directly is the faith in this institution, the faith which inspired the writings and which interpreted itself in the discourses of Christ to the apostles. It is the continuity of faith which becomes for the historian the continuity of the gospel and the Church; because the faith in the risen Jesus continues the faith in Jesus the Messiah, and the Church, the institution of pardon for the heavenly kingdom, continues the action of Jesus, preaching repentance in view of the kingdom of God.[191]

The historian does not prove the truth of the institution of the church, but he shows the consistency of the pattern. The faith in the resurrection is the result of Jesus' preach-

191. *Autour d'un petit Livre*, p. 171.

ing of the kingdom. Faith in the resurrection called into being the church, through the perception that the resurrection demanded the proclaiming of the gospel to all nations. The historian does not prove the truth or legitimacy of this development; that decision can only be accomplished by faith.[192] The evidence of history can inform the theological argument, but it cannot decide the question of faith. "For the historian who limits himself to the consideration of observable facts, it is faith in Christ which has founded the Church; from the point of view of faith, it is Christ himself, living for faith, and accomplishing by it what the historian sees realized." [193]

Loisy has limited the powers of historical method far more than Harnack. For Harnack, the historian not only can but must make such decisions. Since it is within his ability to determine what is the essence of the teaching of Jesus, he can determine what is the truth (kernel), for the false elements (husk) must be removed to ferret out the essence. For Harnack, theology becomes history; for Loisy, theology and history are distinct modes of thought and investigation. While related to each other, they remain sovereign in their proper spheres.

THE SIGNIFICANCE OF ALFRED LOISY

Loisy's influence on contemporary scholarship is minimal. No school has followed in his wake. But his place in the history of New Testament scholarship should not be denied. Placed within their context, Loisy's historical studies are strikingly current. Loisy was a leader of the eschatological interpretation of the New Testament. Johannes Weiss had written his *Jesus' Proclamation of the*

192. Loisy does say that the theologian can argue that if the gospel as taught by Jesus is true, then the church as the outcome of that teaching is true. See ibid., p. 161.
193. Ibid., pp. 172–73.

Kingdom of God in 1892; [194] Albert Schweitzer's *Skizze des Lebens Jesu* appeared in 1901 and his *Quest for the Historical Jesus* was not published until 1906. In *The Gospel and the Church* (1902) the eschatological interpretation of the teaching of Jesus, of the kingdom of God, and of the parables is remarkably forward looking.[195] It should be noted that Loisy recognized both present and future elements in the eschatology of Jesus. Maurice Goguel pointed to this aspect of *The Gospel and the Church* as one of its most significant contributions.[196] Likewise, for its period Loisy's analysis of the Gospel texts reflects a sophisticated method. With his notion that the teaching of Jesus has been preserved only through the tradition, Loisy anticipated form-criticism. He distinguished the influence of the oral tradition from the redactional influence of the evangelists. He refused to use the Fourth Gospel as a source of information for the historical Jesus. It must be admitted that the central methodological thrust of Loisy has been vindicated by modern scholarship.[197]

Like any volume of its time, Loisy's work is in need of correction and adaptation—the progress of scholarship is unending. But *The Gospel and the Church* still represents a sound critique of Protestant liberalism[198] and marks the

194. Translated with an introduction by R. H. Hiers and D. L. Holland in the *Lives of Jesus Series* (Philadelphia: Fortress Press, 1971). In their introduction, Hiers and Holland provide a discussion of various ''eschatological theories'' up to the present-day debate.
195. Loisy himself had begun to discover the significance of eschatology for the interpretation of the New Testament by at least the early 1890s, when large sections of *The Gospel and the Church* were written.
196. A review of the fifth edition of *L'Évangile et l'Église* in *Revue d'Histoire et de Philosophie religieuses* 10 (1930):199.
197. In another area, Ernst Haenchen (*Acts of the Apostles*, trans. B. Noble and G. Shinn [Philadelphia: Westminster Press, 1971], p. 34) praises the advanced and farsighted character of Loisy's commentary on Acts (1920).
198. L. Salvatorelli, ''From Lock to Reitzenstein: The Historical Investigation of the Origins of Christianity,'' HTR 22 (1929):340.

beginning of twentieth century methodology in the investigation of the New Testament.

Loisy's most significant contribution seems to lie in his treatment of the relation of Jesus to both Judaism and the church. These two problems have been dealt with in some detail above. The problematic of the Jewishness of Jesus has remained to this day.[199] Loisy's insistence upon the Jewishness of Jesus allows for the possibility of a truly historical understanding of Jesus. Likewise, his understanding of the relation between Jesus and the church offers a possible alternative for dealing with the problematic of the Jesus of history and the Christ of faith. Rudolf Bultmann has presented an influential formulation of this problem in modern times.[200] Bultmann radically eliminated the historical Jesus as a basis for faith because the object of faith cannot be ascertained or proved by any rational act of man. The action of God is not discoverable in history by the methods of historical analysis; God can only be known by his own Word. Thus, for Bultmann the Christ of faith is knowable as an object of faith only through the kerygma, the Word of God. This problematic of the relation between the Jesus of history and the Christ of faith is for Loisy a non-problem. His theme is the gospel and the church. By concentrating his attention on the *work* of Jesus he avoids the dialectic of the Jesus of history and the Christ of faith. The work that Jesus and the church share in common is the uniting ground, and that work is, according to Loisy, expressed in the symbol of the kingdom of God. Instead of being caught in a dilemma between the

---

199. E.g., Leander E. Keck, ''Bornkamm's *Jesus of Nazareth* Revisited,'' JR 49 (1969):17.
200. For a recent discussion of Bultmann's position see Leander E. Keck, *A Future for the Historical Jesus* (Nashville: Abingdon Press, 1971), pp. 50–58.

historical Jesus and the Christ of faith, Loisy seeks to forge a middle path. Thus, the historical Jesus is presented to us as the historical being he was because he preached the kingdom of God, and the church proclaims the Christ of faith because of the demands of the kingdom in ever changing circumstances. So understood, it is correct to say that for Loisy the Jesus available to the historian and the Christ of faith are both products of the work of Jesus, the kingdom of God.

But why does Loisy, grounded in German scholarship as he is, seek this solution to the problematic? One can only suggest here, by way of a thesis yet to be tested, that Loisy's analysis in *The Gospel and the Church* is dependent upon a fundamentally Catholic vision, and that Harnack on his part represents a fundamentally Protestant vision. Paul Tillich realized the validity and importance of this question for Protestantism with his work on the Protestant Principle.[201] He characterized the Protestant Principle as prophetic, as concerned with the individual as individual, as always saying "no" to man's claims for himself, as insisting upon the radicalness of God's grace. He furthermore denotes the use of dialectics as an essential method in the Protesant Principle. Harnack, I think, represents the main elements of this Protestant Principle in his vision of the origins of Christianity. His historical imagination is dialectical; he sees the relation between Jesus and Judaism and between Jesus and the church in terms of a dialectic, of a "yes" and a "no." In this fashion, the unique individuality of Jesus is made to emerge against his cultural, religious, and historical background. Loisy's vision, like that of most Catholic theology, is analogical;

201. *The Protestant Era*, trans. James Luther Adams (Chicago: Phoenix Books, 1957), especially "Author's Introduction" and chaps. 13, 14.

therefore, he seeks order, arrangement, and relation.[202] He is concerned not with the distinctive, the "yes" and "no" of dialectics, but with that unifying vision that in all its differentiation provides the key for understanding the unity of the development of Christianity. He locates that unity, as we have seen, in the kingdom of God—not the kingdom of God understood as an univocal concept, but as a driving force and hope that has propelled Christianity through history. The dialectical and analogical visions of history are not necessarily antithetical, but they are different visions. The significance of *The Gospel and the Church* may be the question it poses to modern New Testament scholars: how do the Catholic and Protestant visions affect our understanding of the history of the origins of Christianity?

A NOTE CONCERNING THE FOOTNOTES

The text of *The Gospel and the Church* presented here is of course the translation of Christopher Home, who simply reproduced in his English edition the footnotes of the French edition on which his English translation was based. In that French edition the footnotes made constant reference to specific pages in the original German edition of Harnack, *Das Wesen des Christentums*. As a result, the Home translation here reprinted contains a number of footnote references to the German Harnack.

Wherever Loisy quoted Harnack, Home also translated into English Loisy's own French rendering of the German. For this reason there are sometimes textual discrepancies between the Harnack quotations in *The Gospel and the*

202. For a description of the analogical imagination see William F. Lynch, *Christ and Apollo* (New York: Sheed and Ward, 1960), chap. 6. The significance of the dialectical and analogical imaginations was suggested to me by David Tracy in an unpublished paper entitled "The Analogical Imagination as the Key to Catholic Theology."

Church and the corresponding Harnack expressions in the Thomas Bailey Saunders translation of Harnack, which was done directly from the German.

As an aid to the reader the following columns correlate the Loisy/Home references to the German Harnack with the corresponding pages in the Saunders English Harnack:

Loisy page and note	(Saunders' Harper Torchbook equivalent)	Loisy page and note	(Saunders' Harper Torchbook equivalent)
24[1]	31	114[3]	149
24[2]	20	117[1]	1
25[1]	22	126[1]	153
25[2]	19	127[3]	157
42[1]	24–30	128[1]	158
48[1]	30	131[1]	160
55[1]	54	135[1]	162
63[1]	55	141[1]	200
65[1]	62	141[2]	201
66[1]	56	142[1]	207
66[2]	56	142[2]	208
67[2]	64	142[3]	216
68[2]	64	144[1]	252–56
70[2]	77	145[1]	257
74[1]	79–88	178[1]	250
77[1]	88–101	183[1]	185–86
80[1]	102–16	183[2]	203
83[1]	177–23	183[3]	204
88[1]	124–46	184[1]	211
88[2]	141	185[1]	235
91[1]	127–28	186[1]	262
107[1]	144	187[1]	291–94
109[1]	145–46	227[1]	175
109[2]	142	227[2]	210
112[1]	145	228[1]	201
112[2]	146	228[2]	221
112[3]	145	228[3]	238
113[1]	146	229[1]	251
114[2]	149	229[2]	291–93

Selected Bibliography

PRIMARY SOURCES

Émile Poulat has compiled a complete bibliography of the works Alfred Loisy for his edition of Albert Houtin and Félix Sartiaux's *Alfred Loisy* (Paris: Éditions du Centre national de la Recherche scientique, 1960), pp. 303–409. The following list is a bibliography of the works of Loisy that have a direct bearing on the period from which *The Gospel and the Church* comes.

Loisy, Alfred.

Autour d'un petit Livre. Paris: Alphonse Picard et Fils, 1903.

Études bibliques. Paris: Picard, 1901.

L'Évangile et l'Église. 5th ed. Paris: Nourry, 1929.

Les Évangiles synoptiques. Volumes I and II. Paris: Ceffonds, 1908.

Jésus et la Tradition évangelique. Paris: Nourry, 1910. This work is an abbreviated version of the introduction to *Les Évangiles synoptiques*.

Mémoires pour servir à l'Histoire religieuse de notre Temps. Volumes I, II, and III. Paris: Nourry, 1930. Translated as *My Duel with the Vatican*. Trans. Richard Wilson Boynton. New York: E. P. Dutton and Company, 1924.

Le Quatrième Évangile. Paris: Nourry, 1903.

Quelques lettres sur les questions actuelles et sur des événements récents. Paris: Nourry, 1908.

The Religion of Israel. Trans. Arthur Galton, Crown Theological Library. New York: G. P. Putnam's Sons, 1910.

Simples réflexions. Paris: Nourry, 1908.

The following books come from the period after Loisy was excommunicated, but they concern themes dealt with in *The Gospel and the Church*.

Loisy, Alfred.

Les Actes des Apôtres. Paris: 1920.

The Birth of the Christian Religion and *The Origins of the New Testament.* Trans. L. P. Jacks. New York: University Books, 1962.

Histoire et mythe à propos de Jésus-Christ. Paris: 1938.

La Religion. 2nd ed. Paris: 1924.

SECONDARY SOURCES

Bonsirvan, J. "Loisy, Alfred." *Dictionaire Biblique Supplement,* 5:530–44.

Boyer, Raymond de. *Alfred Loisy.* Paris: Éditions du Centurion, 1968.

Guerin, P. "La Vie et l'Ouvre de Loisy à propos d'un Ouvrage récent." *Revue d'Histoire et de Philosophie religieuses* 41 (1961) : 334–43.

Heiler, Friedrich. *Der Vater des katholischen Modernismus: Alfred Loisy.* Munich: Erasmus, 1947.

Hoffmann-Axthelm, Diether. "Loisy's *L'Évangile et l'Église.*" *Zeitschrift für Theologie und Kirche* 65 (1968) : 291–328.

Houtin, Albert and Félix Sartiaux. *Alfred Loisy.* Ed. Émile Poulat. Paris: Édition du Centre national de la Recherche scientifique, 1960.

Marlé, René. *Au Coeur de la Crise Moderniste.* Paris: Abbier, 1960.

Petre, Maud. *Alfred Loisy, His Religious Significance.* Cambridge: University Press, 1944.

Poulat, Émile. *Histoire, Dogme, et Critique dans la Crise Moderniste.* Paris: Casterman, 1962.

Ranchetti, Michele. *The Catholic Modernists.* Trans. Isabel Quigly. London: Oxford University Press, 1969.

Ratté, John. *Three Modernists: Alfred Loisy, George Tyrrell,*

William L. Sullivan. New York: Sheed and Ward, 1967.

Reardon, B. M. G. "Newman and the Catholic Modernist Movement." *The Church Quarterly* 4 (1971) : 50–60.

————. *Roman Catholic Modernism.* A Library of Modern Religious Thought. Stanford, Calif.: Stanford University Press, 1970.

Sabatier, Paul. *Modernism.* Trans. C. A. Miles. New York: Charles Scribner's Sons, 1909.

Vidler, Alex R. *The Modernist Movement in the Roman Church.* Cambridge: University Press, 1934.

————. *A Variety of Catholic Modernists.* Cambridge: University Press, 1970.

THE GOSPEL AND THE CHURCH

INTRODUCTION

THE lectures of Herr A. Harnack on the essence of Christianity [1] have made considerable stir in the Protestant world, particularly in Germany. Embodying the profession of a personal faith in the form of a historical review, they answered without doubt to the needs of many minds, and summarized a whole group of ideas in such a way as to make a satisfactory meeting-ground for several forms of belief. But the votes of the theologians have been divided. Some have formulated reservations, others have criticized sharply a definition of Christianity which eliminates from its essence almost everything that is regarded ordinarily as Christian belief.

No doubt this work would have attracted more

[1] "Das Wesen des Christentums." Leipzig, 1900.

attention in France and even among Catholics, had it not followed the "Esquisse d'une philosophie de la réligion" of M. A. Sabatier, a book strongly resembling it in point of view and in conclusions. However, a French translation has recently been published, and already some of the Catholic reviews have drawn the attention of their readers to it, giving analyses of its contents while insisting on the need of certain amendments. The originality of such a theologico-historical synthesis strikes the intelligence, at a time when science is becoming erudite and distrustful of generalizing theories, when religious problems are discussed from a point of view that may be called purely phenomenal, when many think theology a vain thing, whilst others, on the contrary, regard it still as too divine to be concerned with all that rash investigators relate of its past. It may possibly be of some use to examine this work attentively, not so much with the object of refuting it, as of determining its exact historical position.

The aim of the work, as a matter of fact, is just to catch the point of view of history. In no sense is it an attempt to write an apologia for Catholicism or traditional dogma. Had it been so intended, it must have been regarded as very defective and incomplete, especially as far as concerns the divinity of Christ, and the authority of the Church. It is not designed to demonstrate the truth either of the gospel or of Catholic Christianity, but simply to analyze and define the bonds that unite the two in history. He who reads in good faith will not be misled.

Since the learned professor announces his work as historical, it shall be discussed solely according to the data of history. M. Sabatier sets down psychology, side by side with history, as the source of his religious philosophy. Herr Harnack appeals, above all, to facts; he sets forth less a religious philosophy, than a religion, or rather *the* religion, in the sole and unchangeable principle he deems to constitute it; this principle he extracts from the gospel, and uses as a touch-stone to test the whole Christian development, which is held of worth only in so far as this precious essence has been preserved in it. The whole doctrine of the book is based on this fundamental point; that the essence of the gospel consists solely in faith in God the Father, as revealed by Jesus Christ. On the validity or insufficiency of this principle depends the value of the judgments delivered on the Evolution of the Church, of Her dogmas, and of Her worship, from the beginning, and in all the different forms of creed that are founded on the gospel and the name of Jesus. It is not surprising therefore, that from the first a certain anxiety should be felt, to see a movement as far reaching as Christianity, based on a single idea or a solitary sentiment. Is this really the definition of a historical reality, or merely a systematic method of consideration? Can a religion that has filled such a place in history, and renewed, so to speak, the conscience of humanity, take its origin and derive its whole value from a single thought? Can this great force be made up of one element? Can such a fact be other than complex? Is the definition of Christianity, put forward by Herr Harnack, that of a historian or merely that of a theologian who takes from history as much as suits his theology? The theory set forth in the lectures on the essence of Christianity, is the same theory that dominates the author's learned history of dogma.[1] But is the theory actually deduced from history? Is not history rather interpreted by the light of the theory?

It will be remembered that Renan,[2] with some lack of reverence, compared the liberal theologian

[1] "Lehrbuch der Dogmengeschichte," i.–ii., 1894; iii., 1897.
[2] "Vie de Jésus," 13, ix.–x.

to a bird whose wings have been clipped; as long as it remains at rest, its attitude is natural, but when it attempts to fly, its movements are hampered. This comparison of the author of "Origines du Christianisme," was directed not against Catholic theologians, who, like orthodox Protestants, resemble caged birds, but against certain rationalist professors, who unite the most absolute and daring theories to a criticism so minute, that one would expect their general conclusions to be founded on experience. The remark of Renan is not an axiom beyond discussion. There is no fundamental incompatibility between the professions of theologian and historian. Possibly, there have already existed theologians who could be also historians, that is, could deal with facts as they appear from evidence intelligently investigated, without introducing their own conceptions into the texts they explored, and able to take account of the change that the ideas of past times inevitably undergo when adapted to modern thought. But it must be admitted that there have been, and always will be, a far greater number, who, starting from a general system, furnished by tradition, or elaborated by themselves under the influence of tradition, unconsciously, or perhaps sometimes consciously, bend the texts and the facts to the needs of their doctrine, though often honestly believing they avoid the danger. It must be added that the adversaries of the theologians have often brought to the discussion of these matters of religious history, prejudices acquired before the examination of the facts, prejudices that can interfere with calm and just investigation, fully as much as any theological bias.

At bottom, M. Sabatier and Herr Harnack have wished to reconcile Christian faith with the claims of science and of the scientific spirit of our time. The claims must indeed have become great, or be believed to be great, for the faith has become very small and modest. What would Luther have thought of his doctrine of salvation by faith, had it been presented to him with the amendment, "independently of creeds," or with this other— "Faith in a merciful Father, for faith in the Son is no part of the gospel of Jesus"? Religion is thus reconciled with science, because it no longer encounters it. This trust in the goodness of God either exists in a man or it does not; but it seems impossible for a sentiment to contradict any conclusion of biblical or philosophical criticism.

However, this negative reconciliation is perhaps

less solid than it seems. Every absolute assertion that defies the control of the intelligence can become, at one moment or another, an obstacle to the free and legitimate course of thought. Although this minimum of faith, extracted from the Bible, seems to authorize a complete and unlimited liberty in biblical criticism, it would nevertheless prove an obstacle to the exercise of that liberty, and an obstacle the more serious just where the exercise is most indispensable, namely, in regard to the gospel, if by chance this minimum were not to be found in the gospel, or not in the sense in which the gospel is understood. Those who would compel themselves to see it there, would be forced no longer to take the gospel as it stands. It has been said for a long time, and with reason, that the dogma of biblical inspiration, in so far as it presented the Bible as a book whose truth knew no limit, nor imperfection, nor shades of meaning, and as a book full of the absolute science of God, prevented the perception of the real and historical sense of the Scriptures; but as much might be said of the conviction, arrived at before examination of the facts, or from motives other than historical, that a certain religious system, that is believed to be true, must have been the gospel of Christ.

The gospel has an existence independent of us ;
let us try to understand it in itself, before we
interpret it in the light of our preferences and
our needs.

In seeking to determine historically the essence
of the gospel, the rules of a healthy criticism
forbid the resolution to regard as non-essential all
that to-day must be judged uncertain or unaccept-
able.   That which has been essential in the
gospel of Jesus, is all that holds the first and
most considerable place in His authentic teaching,
the ideas for which He strove and for which He
died, not only such part of them as is held to be
vital to-day.   In the same way, to define the
essence of primitive Christianity, we must seek
the dominant preoccupation of the early Christians, and all that their religion lived by.   After
applying the same analytical procedure to all
epochs successively, and comparing the results,
we can determine if Christianity has remained
faithful to the law of its origin ; if the basis of
Catholicism to-day is that which supported the
Church of the Middle Ages, or the early centuries,
and if that basis is substantially identical with
the gospel of Jesus ; or if, on the other hand,
the clear light of the gospel was soon obscured,
to be freed from the darkness in the sixteenth

century, or only in our own time. If any common
features have been preserved or developed in the
Church from its origin till to-day, these features
constitute the essence of Christianity. At least,
the historian can take account of no others; he
has no right to apply to Christianity a method
that he would not apply to any other religion
whatsoever. To decide the essence of Mahometanism, we should take from the teaching of
Mahomet and the Mussulman tradition not what
we judge to be true and fruitful, but all that
seemed most important to the prophet and his
followers in matters of faith, morality, and
worship. Otherwise, with a little good will,
the essence of the Koran could readily be discovered to be identical with the essence of the
gospel—faith in a benign and merciful God.

Further, there would be little logic in taking
for the whole essence of one religion the points
that differentiate it from another. The monotheistic faith is common to Judaism, Christianity, and
Mahometanism; but we are not therefore to conclude that the essential features of these three
religions must be sought apart from the monotheistic conception. No Jew, no Christian, no
Mussulman will admit that his faith in one God
is other than the first and principal article of his

belief. Each will criticize the particular form
that the idea receives in the creed of his neighbour,
but none will deny that monotheism is an element
of his own religion on the ground that it belongs
also to the religion of others. The essential distinction between religions lies in their differences,
but it is not solely of their differences that they
are constituted.

It is, therefore, in the highest degree arbitrary
to decide that Christianity in its essence must be
all that the gospel has not borrowed of Judaism,
as if all that the gospel has retained of the Jewish
tradition must be necessarily of secondary value.
Herr Harnack finds it quite natural to place the
essence of Christianity in the faith in God the
Father, because he supposes, somewhat hastily by
the way, that this element of the gospel is foreign
to the Old Testament. Even if the hypothesis
were well founded the conclusion drawn from it
would not be legitimate. It might present itself
to the mind of a Protestant theologian, for whom
the word " tradition " is synonymous with " Catholicism " and " error," and who rejoices to think
that the gospel was the protestantism of the law.
But the historian can see in it only an assertion,
whose proof is still to seek. Jesus has claimed
not to destroy the law, but to fulfil. We should,

therefore, expect to find in Judaism and in Christianity elements common to both, equally essential to both, the difference between the two religions lying in that "fulfilment" which is the special feature of the gospel, and should form with the common elements the whole essence of Christianity. The importance of these elements depends neither on their antiquity nor on their novelty, but on the place they fill in the teaching of Jesus, and on the value Jesus himself attached to them.

The essence of the gospel can only be determined by a critical discussion of the gospel texts, the most sure and most clearly expressed texts, and not those whose authenticity or whose meaning may be doubtful. To build a general theory of Christianity on a small number of texts of moderate authority, neglecting the mass of incontestable texts of clear significance, would be to sin against the most elementary principles of criticism. Following such a method, a more or less specious doctrinal synthesis might be offered to the public, but not the essence of Christianity according to the gospel. Herr Harnack has not avoided this danger, for his definition of the essence of Christianity is not based on the totality of authentic texts, but rests, when analyzed, on a very small number of texts, practically indeed on two passages :—" No man knoweth the Son, but the Father : neither knoweth any man the Father, save the Son," [1] and "The kingdom of God is within you," [2] both of them passages that might well have been influenced, if not produced, by the theology of the early times.   This critical prepossession might thus have exposed the author to the misfortune, supreme for a Protestant theologian, of having founded the essence of Christianity upon data supplied by Christian tradition.

No great harm would be done, from the point of view of history, if it were not that these texts are isolated by having preference given to them over the others.   It must be admitted that it is often difficult to distinguish between the personal religion of Jesus and the way in which His disciples have understood it, between the thought of the Master and the interpretations of apostolic tradition.   If Christ had Himself drawn up a statement of His doctrine, and a summary of His prophecy, a detailed treatise on His work, His mission, His hopes, the historian would submit it to a most attentive examination, and would determine the essence of the gospel, according to irrefutable testimony.   But no such treatise has

[1] Matt. xi. 27.   [2] Luke xvii. 21.

ever existed, and nothing can take its place. In the Gospels there remains but an echo, necessarily weakened and a little confused, of the words of Jesus, the general impression He produced upon hearers well disposed towards Him, with some of the more striking of His sentences, as they were understood and interpreted; and finally there remains the movement which He initiated.

Whatever we think, theologically, of tradition, whether we trust it or regard it with suspicion, we know Christ only by the tradition, across the tradition, and in the tradition of the primitive Christians. This is as much as to say that Christ is inseparable from His work, and that the attempt to define the essence of Christianity according to the pure gospel of Jesus, apart from tradition, cannot succeed, for the mere idea of the gospel without tradition is in flagrant contradiction with the facts submitted to criticism. This state of affairs, being natural in the highest degree, has nothing in it disconcerting for the historian: for the essence of Christianity must be in the work of Jesus, or nowhere, and would be vainly sought in scattered fragments of His discourse. If a faith, a hope, a feeling, an impulse of will, dominates the gospel and is perpetuated in the Church of the earliest times, there

will be the essence of Christianity, subject to
such reservations as must be made on the literal
authenticity of certain words, and on such more
or less notable modifications that the thought of
Jesus must of necessity have endured in transmission from generation to generation.[1]

"The essences of things are unchangeable,"
said the ancient philosophy, when considering the
eternal types of contingent realities. To determine such an essence in Christianity, it must be
transformed into a metaphysical entity, into a
logical quintessence, into something resembling
the scholastic notion of species, that certain theologians still fear to corrupt by admitting the idea
of evolution. Herr Harnack seems also to fear
that his essence of Christianity might be spoiled
if he introduced into it any idea of life, of movement and development. On the other hand, he
distrusts abstract essences, and has taken care not
to give any theoretical definition of religion,
which should be at the same time a definition of
Christianity, although he maintains the Hegelian
proposition that Christianity is the one absolute
religion.   He finds the essence of Christianity
in a sentiment—filial confidence in God, the

[1] Cf. E. Caird, "Christianity and the Historical Christ,"
The New World, vi. 21 (March, 1897), pp. 7, 8.

merciful Father. Therein is to lie all religion and all Christianity. The identity of this sentiment in Jesus and in all Christians, is to constitute the continuity of the religion and the unchangeableness of its essence.

But is this essence, even in these reduced proportions, actually unchangeable, and why should it be? Has the Divine mercy been understood in absolutely the same way by the apostles and by Herr Harnack? The apostles had a conception of the world, and even of God the merciful, somewhat different from the idea that is suggested in the peroration of " The Essence of Christianity." Now, sentiment is not independent of thought; if the idea change, the form of the sentiment will also change, though the sentiment retains its first direction, because of the spirit that sustains it; and if on this point (the Divine merciful Fatherhood) the attitude of Christianity is held to be unchanged, because it retains the direction and the impulse of Christ, why should not its attitude towards other points be held unchanged for the same reason? What, for instance, of the hope of an eternal kingdom, constantly preached by Christ, and never allowed to perish by the Christian Church? What of the mission of the apostles charged to propagate this hope? What of Christ Himself, Whose place as Messiah belongs to the Primitive Church, and has never ceased to occupy the thought of the Church from the beginning ?   What of all the different themes of evangelical teaching, of which not one has been regarded during the Christian centuries as accessory ?   All these elements of Christianity, in all the forms in which they have been preserved, why should they not be the essence of Christianity ?   Why not find the essence of Christianity in the fulness and totality of its life, which shows movement and variety just because it is life, but inasmuch as it is life proceeding from an obviously powerful principle, has grown in accordance with a law which affirms at every step the initial force that may be called its physical essence revealed in all its manifestations ? Why should the essence of a tree be held to be but a particle of the seed from which it has sprung, and why should it not be recognized as truly and fully in the complete tree as in the germ ?   Are the processes of assimilation by which it grows to be regarded as an alteration of the essence present potentially in the seed, and are they not rather the indispensable conditions of its being, its preservation, its progress in a life always the same and incessantly renewed ?

The historian cannot but refuse to regard as the essence of living Christianity a germ that multiplies without growing. Rather he should return to the parable of the mustard seed, comparing the new-born Christianity to a little grain. The grain was small, for the new religion was without the prestige of antiquity enjoyed by the ancient religions, still surviving, of Egypt and Chaldea; it was less, in external power, than Greco-Roman paganism : it was even less, apparently, than Judaism, of which it must have seemed a variety, with no future, since Judaism rejected it. This grain, nevertheless, enclosed the germ of the tree that we now see; charity was its sap: its life impulse was in the hope of its triumph ; its expanding force was in its apostleship, its pledge of success in sacrifice: for its general form this budding religion had its faith in the unity and absolute Sovereignty of God, and for its particular and distinctive feature that faith in the Divine mission of Jesus, which earned it its name of Christianity. All this was in the little seed, and all this was the real essence of the Christian religion, needing only space to grow to reach its present point, still living after all its growth.

To understand the essence of Christianity we

must look to those vital manifestations which contain its reality, its permanent quintessence, recognizable in them, as the principal features of primitive Christianity are recognizable throughout their development. The particular and varied forms of the development, in so far as they are varied, are not of the essence of Christianity, but they follow one another, as it were, in a framework whose general proportions, though not absolutely constant, never cease to be balanced, so that if the figure change, its type does not vary, nor the law that governs its evolution. The essence of Christianity is constituted by the general features of this figure, the elements of this life and their characteristic properties ; and this essence is unchangeable, like that of a living being, which remains the same while it lives, and to the extent to which it lives. The historian will find that the essence of Christianity has been more or less preserved in the different Christian communions : he will not believe it to be compromised by the development of institutions, of creeds, and of worship, so long as this development has been ruled by the principles verified in the first commencement. He will not expect this essence to have been absolutely and definitely realized at any point of past centuries ; he will believe that it has been realized more or less perfectly from the beginning, and that it will continue to be realized thus more and more, so long as Christianity shall endure.

Herr Harnack does not conceive Christianity as a seed, at first a plant in potentiality, then a real plant, identical from the beginning of its evolution to the final limit and from the root to the summit of the stem, but as a fruit, ripe, or rather overripe, that must be peeled, to reach the incorruptible kernel; and Herr Harnack peels his fruit with such perseverance, that the question arises if anything will remain at the end. This method of dismembering a subject does not belong to history, which is a science of observation of the living, not of dissection of the dead. Historical analysis notices and distinguishes, it does not destroy what it touches, nor think all movement digression, and all growth deformity. It is not by stripping Christianity leaf by leaf that the law of its life will be found. Such a dissection leads of necessity to a special theory, of philosophical value doubtless, but of little account from the positive standpoint of history. It is not for the theologian (unless in quite a personal exercise of his intelligence), and still less is it for the critic, to seize religion on the wing, dismember it, extract a something and declare it unique, by saying, "This is the essence of Christianity." Let us regard the Christian religion in its life, observing by what means it has lived from the beginning and is still sustained; let us note the principal features of this venerable existence, convinced that they lose nothing in reality or importance, because to-day they are presented to us under colours that are not those of a former time.

To reduce Christianity to a single point, a solitary truth that the conscience of Jesus has perceived and revealed, is to protect religion against all attacks far less than might be expected, because it is thus almost put out of touch with reality, and deprived of historical support, and of every defence against the reasoning faculty. Christ is presented as a man who had but one true thought among many false ones, and those that are now held erroneous and valueless are not those that occupied His attention the least. If the sole truth that He revealed fails to make its appeal, there is nothing else to look for from Him; and to feel this incomparable truth, to find it more true than the rest of His conceptions, the only truth in fact among them, to see in it absolute religion, it is not enough merely to contemplate it, but a kind of intellectual and moral enthusiasm is also demanded, prepared to see only this and be content.

It might be said that the God of Herr Harnack, driven from the domain of Nature, driven also from history, in so far as history is made of facts and play of thoughts, has taken refuge on the heights of human conscience, and is now only to be seen there by those who have keen perception. Is it so certain that He cannot be seen elsewhere, or that if not seen elsewhere, He will be infallibly found there? Is it not possible, if no effort is made to keep Him, that He will be driven also from this last retreat, and identified as one of "the category of the Ideal," or as "Imperfect activity aspiring to Perfection," phantoms of divinity with which the reason plays when wandering to find the explanation of itself, phantoms of no account for religion? Can the conscience keep for long a God that science ignores, and will science respect for ever a God that it does not know? Can God be goodness if He is not first—Life and Truth? Is it not as easy and as necessary to conceive Him as the Source of Life and Truth as of indulgent goodness? Shall we have need of Him to reassure the conscience, if we have no need of Him to strengthen the intelligence? Is it not with all his soul and all his might, that man should search after God to find him ?   Must not God live in Nature and in man, and must not the integral formula of true religious philosophy be "God everywhere," as the integral formula of Christianity is "Christ in the Church, and God in Christ."

But this is not the place to examine Herr Harnack's theology.   Our aim is only to determine if his "Essence of Christianity," instead of being absolute religion, absolute Christianity, entities that have little chance of taking a place in history, does not rather mark a stage in Protestant development, or form merely a basic formula of Protestantism.

SECTION I

THE SOURCES OF THE GOSPELS

INTRODUCTION

PRACTICALLY all our knowledge of the life and preaching of Jesus is contained in the Gospels. The testimony of Paul confirms rather than completes that of the evangelists, and the scanty indications found in the pagan historians are hardly worth consideration. But the Gospels are not strictly historical documents, and before using them for his definition of the essence of Christianity Herr Harnack was bound to express an opinion upon their general character and value. It was known beforehand that his opinion was comparatively temperate, but not necessarily therefore impervious to criticism.

CHAPTER I

IT is beyond question that the synoptic Gospels "supply first a clear image of the teaching of Jesus, both in its principle and its detailed application; that they then relate the end of His life, sacrificed to His work, and that they show us the impression made by Him upon His disciples, and communicated to the world by them."[1] But one would rather see more clearly the motive of these conclusions, and form a more definite idea of their object. In the present case, it is not sufficient to treat the origin of the Gospels simply as a literary problem. The question concerns the tradition itself, and the nature of the tradition must be analyzed and its progress outlined.

It will be readily conceded that the Fourth Gospel shall be set aside and the synoptic texts regarded as "the books of the gospel teaching."[2]

[1] "Wesen des Christentums," p. 20.   [2] Ibid., p. 14.

It is as well to add that "they are not partisan pamphlets," and that it was an error of former times to attribute to them certain general tendencies which would have made them actual manifestoes on behalf of Peter or Paul, or of the reconciliation between the two apostles. But it is a very summary and inexact statement concerning the composition of the Gospels, to represent that of Mark as a work at first hand; those of Matthew and Luke as having been composed later than Mark's and from another source; [1] and that of John, as founded on a special tradition, though one very difficult to recognize.[2] Is the primitive character of Mark established beyond discussion? Must not at least a third source be admitted for the Gospel of Luke? And does not the special tradition of the Fourth Gospel gradually disappear, as the sense of this mysterious book is better comprehended?

When the texts and their relations to one another are examined, without attention or regard to the life of ideas, or the development of beliefs and institutions, there is a temptation to restrain history within the limits that literary analysis imposes on documentary criticism. As the

[1] "Wesen des Christentums," p. 15.
[2] Ibid., p. 13.

second Gospel has passed almost in its entirety into the other two synoptic Gospels, it is therefore concluded that Mark is the primitive text. It is, certainly, in regard to the Gospels known to us, but no one can say that it is absolutely. Beyond the fact that its relation to Matthew and to Luke is not clearly defined on all points, there is little difficulty in seeing that it is not a book of simple growth and homogeneous editing. It is held to be both, because it cannot be collated with an edition or a document more ancient than the traditional text we possess.

The existence of a source other than Mark's Gospel is deduced from such portions of Christ's discourses as are common to Matthew and Luke, but not present in Mark, and hypothetically this source is identified with the Hebrew Gospel by Matthew and the "Logia" spoken of by Papias of Hierapolis. It begins now to be evident that Matthew and Luke must have worked from different revisions of these "Logia." The collection of discourses, therefore, underwent certain modifications before assuming the forms made permanent in our Evangelists. Why should not similar changes have happened to the Gospel according to Mark?

As Luke declares that he knows of several

Gospels, and the critics can verify only two, Mark and the " Logia," they readily suppose that a part at least of the matter that is special to the third Gospel comes from another source. There is nothing to show that it does not come from two sources or more, or from special revisions of the two principal ones. Criticism prefers the minimum number of hypotheses and rightly ; but it must at least be said that the reality appears to have been much more complex than these suppositions. As for John, the existence of a special tradition is an expedient as convenient as it is popular, to explain the divergences between the Fourth Gospel and the synoptic versions.

These results of critical labours may be thought meagre enough, unless they are looked on as indispensable preliminaries to a deeper considera- tion, which shall pass upwards from words to things, and explain the history of the gospel literature, by that of the religious movement of which this literature was the partial expression. The old school of Tübingen was right in its wish to realize the Christian books by the aid of the evolution of Christianity, only it should have been more circumspect and less artless in its conjectures, and have discussed its texts, ideas, and facts more minutely, before formulating its conclusions.

Were the criticism of Mark followed out according to the purely literary method employed hitherto, a method somewhat superficial and mechanical, it would not be difficult to discover the same phenomena of combinations, superpositions and union of different materials in the second Gospel, as are recognized in Matthew and in Luke. The discussion with the Pharisees concerning Beelzebub,[1] is as it were interpolated into the narrative of the attempt of the kinsmen of Jesus to persuade Him to return home.[2] In the chapter of the parables, three stages can be distinguished of tradition and revision : the parables themselves,[3] quite straightforward, needing no explanation ; the interpretation [4] desired by the disciples after the first parable ; the general reflections [5] on the object of teaching by parable, which come as an addition to the explanation of the allegory of the Sower. It is hardly credible that both descriptions [6] of the miracle of feeding the multitude should be due to one tradition : one must have been added by a reviser—who had come across a

[1] Mark iii. 22, 30.
[2] Mark iii. 21, 31–35.
[3] Mark iv. 2–9, 21–32.
[4] Mark iv. 10, 13–20.
[5] Mark iv. 11, 12.
[6] Mark vi. 30, 44; viii. 1–9.

second version of the miracle. The prediction of the suffering and death of the Son of man [1] appears to be intercalated between the confession of Peter [2] and the promise of the early coming of the Kingdom of God.[3] In the same way, a phrase concerning the sufferings of the Son of man [4] divides what is said of the coming of Elias in the person of John the Baptist. The parable of the wicked husbandmen [5] has been introduced between the reply made by Jesus in the temple to the chief priests, who questioned him as to the authority he claimed,[6] and the retreat of the questioners discomfited by the demand addressed by Jesus to them.[7] The prophecy of the appearance of Christ in Galilee after His resurrection,[8] comes with little fitness between the saying of Jesus as to the confusion His Passion will cause among His disciples,[9] and Peter's reply protesting his fidelity.[10] It appears, therefore, incontestable that the second Gospel has been composed by the same means as the first and third; though one of the sources of them, it is

---

[1] Mark viii. 31–38.
[2] Mark viii. 27–30.
[3] Mark ix. 1.
[4] Mark ix. 12.
[5] Mark xii. 1–12.
[6] Mark xi. 27–33.
[7] Mark xii. 12.
[8] Mark xiv. 28.
[9] Mark xiv. 27.
[10] Mark xiv. 29.

none the less itself derived from more than **one** source, and did not acquire its final form in one effort.

Would not a critical examination demonstrate further, with equal facility, that the greater part of those elements of the Fourth Gospel, that are held to show a special tradition, happen to be symbolic, and represent not the memories, but the personal conceptions of the author ?   The illusion springs from the precision of some of the information, notably the chronological indications, which do not agree with those of the first Gospels, and could not apparently have been derived from them, nor imagined by the evangelist.   Thus **it** is to be noted, first, that the ministry of Jesus includes three,[1] or more probably four [2] Easters— that is to say, a duration of three years and some months, with a stay at Jerusalem on several occasions ; while a study of the chronology of the synoptic Gospels would suggest that the preaching in Galilee lasted some months, and the preaching in Jerusalem, at the end, merely a few days.

The arguments derived from the first Gospel to confirm the chronology of the fourth are very

---

[1] John ii. 13 ; vi. 4 ; xiii. 1.   [2] John v. 1.

weak,[1] and the indications of this chronology seem subordinated to the didactic and polemical purpose of the book. If the author had wished to give a historical account of the life of Jesus, he would not have put the Galilean ministry in the background, and he would probably have described the preaching at Jerusalem differently. It is universally admitted that his aim was to show Christ upon the theatre assigned by prophetic tradition to the Messiah, and to give the impression that Christ's evengelical manifestations took place, not in an obscure corner of Palestine, but in the capital of Judaism. Viewed as history, the point of view of the Gospel of John is incompatible with that of the other Gospels, and a choice has to be made. The apparent precision of John does not alone authorize a preference, seeing that the question lies not only between two systems of chronology, but between two presentments of the Saviour, two accounts of Christ and His work. The account that is most faithful in regard to the discourses and historical appearance of Jesus, is probably also the most to be trusted in point of chronology.

It seems inconceivable that Jesus should have

---

[1] Matt. xxiii. 37 (Luke xiii. 34) is generally cited; but the passage is possibly a quotation. *Cf. infra*, p. 96.

preached at Jerusalem, declaring Himself the
Messiah, on several occasions, during several
years, without being arrested. He can but have
done so once, and paid the forfeit with His life.
The enormous gaps in the narration make the
reality of its framework a matter of suspicion.
It is clear they have not been left to be filled
from the contents of the other three gospels.
The discourses conceal the gaps in the narrative.
In the process of exhausting his doctrinal thesis,
and fulfilling the intention of his "Apologia,"
the author of the Gospel of John has found it
sufficient to bring Christ to Jerusalem for the
two first Easters,[1] to connect the miracle of the
feeding of the multitude with the third,[2] and
to bring the Saviour to the feast of Tabernacles [3]
and the feast of the Dedication,[4] while awaiting
the last.[5] If the last year includes three
journeys and three sojourns at Jerusalem, while
the previous period of more than two years
includes only two journeys and two sojourns,
the reason is that it was more suitable to reserve
to the last months and the last days the greater
part of the teaching.

[1] John ii. 13; v. 1.　　[2] John vi. 4.
[3] John vii. 2–10.　　　　[4] John x. 22.
[5] John xii. 1; xiii. 1.

It is useless to object that the evangelist would not have so far enlarged the framework of the synoptic Gospels, unless he had material to fill the space thus gained. Another consideration, equally important for the didactic purpose of the book, intervened to determine its chronological schema. Three years and a half, make half of a week of years, the Messianic number *par excellence*, and a number which plays a great part in the prophecies of Daniel[1] and in the Apocalypse.[2] The schema would conform to that needed by those passages of Scripture that suggest that the temple, which was forty-six years in building, was a type of the body of Jesus,[3] and that Jesus Himself was not yet fifty years old in the year that preceded His Passion.[4] It is known that St. Irenæus bears witness to this tradition, and maintains that he found it in the Fourth Gospel. The terrestrial life of the Saviour would be thus held to correspond to a perfect number, seven weeks of years,[5] a half week at the end being reserved for the manifestation of Christ, the Word made flesh. Jesus would have

---

[1] Dan. xii. 7–11. [2] Rev. xii. 6–14; xi. 2, 3; xiii. 5.
[3] John ii. 20, 21. The allusion is quite inadmissible to the Herodian buildings, though received by many commentators.
[4] John viii. 57. [5] Dan. ix. 25–27.

lived presumably forty-six years when He drove the money-changers from the temple; and the fiftieth year, the year of Jubilee, would coincide with His entry into Eternal Glory after His Resurrection.

This allegorical chronology then, conforming to the spirit of the book in all likelihood is not founded on a genuine traditional memory; it may well be no more actual than the Davidic genealogies of the Saviour in Matthew and in Luke, and have the same signification, to wit, that Jesus is The Christ. Similar comments might be made on the date assigned by John to the death of Jesus; the coincidence of His death with the immolation of the Paschal Lamb,[1] which, according to the synoptic Gospels, was eaten the day before,[2] is probably part of that system of symbolic adaptations that governs all this particular narrative of the Passion.

All these hypotheses, more or less probable, which could readily be multiplied, have only one result, to raise before the theologians an interminable series of difficulties, because criticism, giving most of its attention to the literary facts, too often leaves the history unexplained, not only the history of nascent Christianity, but

[1] Cf. John xviii. 28.   [2] Cf. Mark xiv. 12; Luke xxii. 7-15.

even the history of the composition of the Gospels. The points on which the synoptic Gospels differ from one another, and the differences between John and the synoptics, have been carefully accumulated, and thus limits have been set to the historical authority of the Gospels that believers cannot fail to find exceedingly narrow. The meaning of all that cannot be taken as literal history with regard to Christ escapes them, because to some extent it has escaped the critics themselves, and they have therefore failed to make it clear to believers. Faith is disquieted by conclusions and scientific conjectures that do not entirely satisfy the intelligence. They would have given rise to less trouble if they could have been understood.

But to render the development and character of the evangelical literature quite intelligible, the Gospels must not only be studied in themselves and in their relations as literary works and as simple historical documents, but must also be regarded as a partial expression of the great movement that proceeded from the preaching of Jesus. The literary tradition of the gospel has followed the evolution of primitive Christianity. The two explain one another; and if the critical analysis of the Gospels necessarily precedes the reconstitution of evangelical and apostolic history, it is none the less true that, by a sort of reciprocity, it is the primitive history of Christianity that explains the composition of the Gospels, and throws light on those particular points that are most disconcerting for minds unused to criticism. Once understood and presented as a product and a witness of an ancient faith, the Gospels, however critically analyzed, will no longer be a dangerous trial to the faith of our contemporaries.

CHAPTER II

AT the bottom of all traditions concerning the life of Christ, there is this simple statement, set forth in some of the discourses in the Acts, where are to be found specimens of the earliest Christian preaching: Jesus passed through the world, doing good, healing, because God was with Him, all those held by various maladies in subjection to the devil. Denounced by the priests, and crucified by order of Pontius Pilate, He rose on the third day from the dead, and thus became Christ and Lord.[1]   Jesus became Christ by His resurrection; that was the proof of His dignity as Messiah; and His glory is to shine forth in His approaching Second Advent. Thus His teaching and His works remain still what they actually were, and as they appeared to those who witnessed them, a first introduction to the kingdom of God and works of pity, not a formal attestation of the Heavenly

[1] Acts ii. 22–30; x. 38–40.

kingdom, nor a direct argument in favour of
Jesus as the Messiah.

The mission of Christ is not presented in the
Gospels in this primitive form. Tradition must
follow its natural tendency, and was soon to discover, in the ministry of Jesus, characteristic
features and indubitable proofs of His Messianic
dignity. The glory of the risen Lord threw new
light on the memories of His earthly career.
Thence arose a kind of idealization of His discourses and His acts, and a tendency to systematize them. If the parables, which were really
tales concerned in their application only with the
economy of the Kingdom of Heaven, are supposed
to be full of mysteries, it is because a Divine
teaching is now seen in them. If the miracles
are held to prove that Jesus is the Christ, it is
because they are now regarded as acts of Divine
Omnipotence, beyond all comparison with those
that God might permit a pious man to do for the
succour of his equals. If those possessed of
devils hail Jesus as the Son of God, their testimony acquires a special value, coming from
Satan, who thus salutes his conqueror. If heaven
opens above the head of Jesus at His baptism, it
is to hallow the Messiah.[1] If Jesus is tempted

[1] Mark. i. 9–11.

in the wilderness, it is that He may triumph from the first over him whose kingdom He comes to destroy.[1] If He gives bread to a hungering multitude, it is to signify the salvation of men by faith and in the Christian communion.[2] If He is transfigured on the mountain-top, between Moses and Elias, it is to show that the Law and the Prophets bear witness to Him as the Messiah.[3] If He predicts His Passion and resurrection, it is because He knows His future with certainty of prevision. If darkness falls over the earth, when He is on the cross, it is because the earth mourns over the expiring Christ.[4] If the veil of the temple is rent at the moment of His death,[5] it is that the new covenant, now accomplished, destroys the old and reveals its mystery. Thus everything assumes, as it were, a relation to the Messiah, and all contributes to prove that Jesus was the Christ.

Nevertheless all these arguments are not the simple expression of increasing faith. They are, for the most part, an interpretation of actual facts and occurrences, which assume a new aspect in the full glory of the Messiah, as though they now adapted themselves to the condition of the Eternal

---

[1] Matt iv. 1–11. [2] Cf. 1 Mark viii. 14–21. [3] Mark ix. 2–8.
[4] Mark xv. 33. [5] Mark xv. 38.

Christ.   Jesus did really make Himself known
to His disciples as the Messiah, and the general
tendency of His doctrine as to the Kingdom of
Heaven implied the part that was His by right in
the coming reign of God.   The miracles of healing
are incontestable, however they may be explained;
and if the Saviour did not perform them to
demonstrate His Divine mission, none the less
they prove it in a sense, since they reveal at
once the extent of His power and the goodness of
His heart.   The unhappy demoniacs did well to
salute Jesus as the Son of God, since He came,
confident in faith and charity, to bring peace to
their troubled spirits.   The baptism by John may
well have been a decisive moment in the life
of the Saviour.   The picture of the temptation
presents, in a symbolic and abbreviated form, the
psychology of Jesus and the manner in which He
looked upon His mission.   He regarded His
position as the narrative of the transfiguration
suggests, and understood the relation between His
Kingdom of Heaven and the Law in the sense that
the incident of the rent veil of the temple indicates.
He admitted for Himself, as much as for His
followers, the necessity of losing His life to find it.[1]

If the point of view is new, and differs from

[1] Matt. x. 39.

that of the immediate witnesses of the teaching
and the occurrences of the Gospels, it conforms
none the less to the rule in these matters.
It is in the nature of human affairs, that the
work, the genius, and the character of the
greatest of mankind can only be appreciated at
a certain distance, and when the actors themselves have disappeared. Christ, in so far as He
belongs to human history, has not escaped this
law. His grandeur was not perceived till after
His death, and is it not a fact that it is more and
more appreciated as the centuries pass by, that
the present is ameliorated by the influence of the
gospel, and the past illumined by all the experiences of humanity as it advances in age? It
need only be added that this inevitable and
legitimate idealization of Christ, arising spontaneously in the Christian consciousness, and not
by the aid of rigorous observation and methodical
reflection, must have affected, to a certain extent,
the form of legendary development, and presents
itself at the first glance of criticism as legendary
development, although actually it is nothing but
an expansion of faith, and an attempt, though an
insufficient one, to set Jesus on the height that is
His rightful place.

Looked at from this point of view, the question

of the gospel miracles, always so confusing for the critic, and bristling with difficulties for the apologist, is cleared up, at any rate in part, and ceases to be a dangerous and alarming theme of controversy. Herr Harnack discusses it a little pedantically,[1] and goes so far as to divide the miracles into five categories : those which are exaggerations of natural occurrences, though striking ones : those that are external and material realizations of sayings and parables, or of phenomena of intimate religious life : those that have been imagined in order to mark the accomplishment of Old Testament prophecies : the miracles of healing performed by the spiritual power of Jesus : and those whose explanation is not obvious.

It would be difficult to distribute the gospel narratives among these categories. A certain exaggeration of fact appears everywhere. It results from the presentation as a miracle of the Christ, of an incident which appeared first as a grace of God, till its miraculous character assumed a special significance in the Messianic perspective. It may be doubted if such a miraculous narrative, for instance, as that of the withered fig tree, or the feeding of the multitude, is really to be

[1] Pages 16–19.

explained as the materialization of a parable, as has been suggested; but it seems incontestable that the evangelists were always ready to see in the miracles a direct teaching of Christ, as they saw a proof of His omnipotence, and that their account has been influenced by this allegorizing tendency, as it has been in their narratives of the parables. The influence of the Old Testament is felt a little throughout, because of the preoccupation with the Messiah, and it would no doubt be more accurate to say that it colours the majority of the narratives, rather than that it has created any one of them. Finally, there is a mysterious and inexplicable residue in the most solidly guaranteed miracles. It is better not to follow a rigorous classification, which does not correspond to the reality, and assert simply the substantial truth of the tradition of the beneficent activity of Christ, while recognizing the elaboration of early memories, an elaboration more or less considerable, as the case may be, but always governed by the same principle, the faith that seeks and finds the Messiah in all the works and all the wanderings of His earthly pilgrimage.

CHAPTER III

AT this stage in its development, evangelical tradition is still kept within the limits assigned by the Book of Acts to the testimony of the apostles.[1] It includes the time between the Baptism of Jesus by John and the Resurrection of the Saviour, and it still clings to the idea of the Messiah promised to Israel, though already it tends to go beyond this idea in interpretation of the prophecies and their fulfilment. The Gospel according to Mark, which, taken broadly, represents this stage of faith, nevertheless contains traces of a more complicated doctrine, of a spirit of speculation already busy on the life and death of Christ, interpreting them to suit a more learned theology. Already there can be felt a presentiment that the framework of the Christian faith has been enlarged. From henceforward the enlargement will continue, and

[1] Cf. Acts i. 21, 22.

the historical framework will extend also to include the whole life of Jesus.

The first theory of Christ was formulated by St. Paul. This apostle, who had not known Jesus, yet became by the vicissitudes of his career the evangelist of the nations, was the first, or one of the first, to feel the need of forming an idea of Christ, a definition of Him as the Saviour, since he was compelled to explain, and could not simply narrate. Starting from his own religious experience, and from the Jewish beliefs, modified by his faith, and interpreted so as to be intelligible to the Gentiles, he affirms the eternal pre-existence of the Messiah, and formulates the theory of the Redemption. In his last epistles he comes to identify Christ, more or less, with Eternal Wisdom, attributing to Him a cosmological function, as the theory of the Redemption attributes to Him a function in regard to humanity. The author of the Epistle to the Hebrews does the same, using slightly different terms and symbols. This double theory of Christ, in His relations to the universe and to humanity, could not fail to enter into the evangelical tradition, and did in fact enter. The doctrine of the Redemption appears in Mark ;[1] that of the

[1] Mark x. 45; xiv. 24.

Eternal Christ, Wisdom of the Father, agent of all Divine Works, creeps into Matthew and Luke,[1] and finds its definite statement in the Gospel of John.

Thus, little by little, there is formed in the atmosphere of faith, beyond what can be called the historical reality of the gospel, beyond even its idealization to suit the Messiah, the dogma which aims at determining its providential meaning, its universal scope, its transcendent efficacy. It must be said, however, that the Messianic element, dominant in Mark, is still the element most in evidence in Matthew and in Luke; the theory of universal salvation, expressed in the synoptics, only enters into and appears beside the traditional matter that the doctrine of the Messiah has influenced more profoundly; and the theory of the Eternal Christ, of Divine Wisdom revealed in Jesus, appears still more discreetly. It is only in the Fourth Gospel that the doctrine of Christ as the intermediate agent of creation and the Saviour of mankind, after being clearly defined in the prologue,[2] is freely set forth in the discourses which are substituted for the traditional sentences the gospel desires to interpret, and in the symbolic narratives that

[1] Matt. xi. 27; Luke x. 22.   [2] John i. 1–18.

take the place of the Messianic miracles to signify the illuminating and eternally vivifying action of the Incarnate Word.

Nevertheless, the theological speculations of Paul and of John do not venture beyond the historical framework of the Primitive Gospel. It would even appear that Paul straitened its limits, since, while he recognized in Jesus the earthly manifestation of the eternal Christ, he invariably considers the Passion and Resurrection of the Saviour as acts of the Messiah. As for John, he limits the ministry of Jesus to the manifestation of the Word, Whose incarnation seems to be dated from the Baptism, and has no other purpose than the revelation made by the teaching, the miracles, the death and resurrection of Christ. The idea underlying John's Gospel is always a vision of faith, a faith which, in order to appreciate Jesus worthily, makes use of the loftiest elements of contemporary religious philosophy, and is expressed in the language of this mystic philosophy. Christ is the actual manifestation of the Eternal Word, and the Fourth Gospel, being a symbolic description of this truth, is a kind of incarnation, or revelation by allegorical images, of discourses and sayings of Christ, the Life and Light of mankind.

But then came the desire to know the human antecedents of Jesus, or rather the desire to represent His human origin conformably to the idea already formed of His dignity and Providential office. From the point of view of Paul, and still more from that of Mark and John, the narratives of Jesus' infancy are, so to speak, outside the history of Christ, and seem in the same way to have been foreign to the primitive tradition of the gospel. Herr Harnack writes:[1] "Two of the Gospels, it is true, include a pre-history, the history of the birth of Jesus, but we need not be concerned with this, for even were its contents more credible than they are, this pre-history would be almost without significance for the end we have in view." As a matter of fact, there is no hint there that the essence of Christianity consists in faith in God the Father, without regard to the Divine Sonship of Jesus.

It is true however, that these narratives represent a normal development of the history of Christ. The very nature of their subject, the critical examination of the two versions taken separately or compared, and an analysis of evangelical tradition, make it impossible to

[1] Page 20.

regard them as a definite expression of historical memories ; none the less they are put forward as a document of Christian faith, and in this capacity attract the attention of the historian. The idea of the Immaculate Conception by the operation of the Holy Ghost is not merely, as is readily admitted, a physical explanation of the Divine Sonship of Jesus, but also a religious explanation, like that attached to the idea of the Messiah, and a metaphysical explanation like that that belongs to the idea of the Incarnation ; it is of the nature of both, because, if the Immaculate Conception in a sense demonstrates the Fatherhood of God, the operation of the Holy Ghost has not for its immediate end the miraculous formation of a purely human being, but rather the communication of Divine life, which makes Jesus, from the earliest moment of His existence, the elect of God, the Christ anointed by the Spirit, the only Son of the Heavenly Father ; and thus is anticipated that consecration of the Messiah which the most ancient version of the synoptic Gospel referred to the Baptism. The affirmation of faith is addressed to faith, and appeals only to the judgment of faith : from the Catholic point of view, it is for the Church to determine its meaning and extent.

The narratives of the childhood of Christ are for the historian only an expression and an assertion of faith in the Messiah, that faith which is affirmed at the beginning of the Gospel of Mark, and transfigured the memories of the Apostles, which is also affirmed and developed in Paul, and then in the Fourth Gospel. This faith is, as it were, the reply made by the generations of believers in succession to the proposition of the gospel of Jesus; it increases, yet remains the same, like an echo which, reverberating from mountain to mountain, becomes more sonorous the further it travels from its point of origin.

The subject of this faith is at no stage of its development presented to the historian as an actual reality. Criticism has not to decide if Jesus is or is not the Word Incarnate, if He existed before His terrestrial manifestation, if He was consecrated Messiah from His conception, or from the day of His baptism, if the idea of the Messiah in its earliest form, and in its successive transformations, is a truth. Considered as belief, this idea is addressed to faith, that is to say, to the man, judging with all his soul the worth of the religious doctrine presented to him. The historian as such need not constitute himself either apologist or adversary. He knows it

simply as a conception or a force whose antecedents, central manifestation and indefinite
progress, he can analyze up to a point, but whose
deep meaning and secret power are not things
that can be deduced from simple analysis or
critical discussion of texts and facts.

None the less he will not deny that the
idea of Christ is essential to Christianity,—for
Christianity, at all times, from its first origin
in the gospel of Jesus, will appear to him
established on the faith in Christ. He will
recognize the substance of this faith in the best
authenticated words of Jesus, namely, the eternal
and unique predestination of the Messiah. His
unique office in the work of salvation, and His
unique relation with God, a relation not founded
merely on a knowledge of His goodness, but on a
substantial communication of the Divine Spirit—
that is to say, of God Himself—to the predestined
Messiah. The Gospels will become for the critic
the eloquent testimony to this living faith, whose
source is to be found not elsewhere than in the
soul of Jesus Himself. No page of these books
will appear negligible on the ground that it
does not directly represent the thought of the
Saviour. The Gospels are the principal documents of Christian faith, for the first period of

its history, and none of their indications can be rejected as insignificant, seeing that all, without exception and from the beginning, have been a means of expressing faith and of affirming and extending it.

SECTION II

THE KINGDOM OF HEAVEN

INTRODUCTION

THE general theme of the preaching of Jesus was the reign of God, or the kingdom of Heaven. The greater part of the parables bear either on the coming of this kingdom or on the way of making ready for it. In the Lord's Prayer, Christ makes His disciples say, "Thy Kingdom come!" All His teaching is given to prepare for the kingdom. However, as the gospel nowhere contains any express definition of its nature, there is room for discussion on the actual object of the conception, and discussion still continues. Before Jesus, the idea of the reign of God is above all concerned with the end of the world, and the system that is to take the place of the actual and imperfect order. Daniel, and the authors of

prophecies and visions, see in it the great manifestation of Divine power, which is to inaugurate
the eternal happiness of the Saints on a regenerated earth, a happiness over which God will
rule in the New Jerusalem.   Various elements
go to make up this conception: cosmology and a
transposition of cosmogony, in that the renewal
is brought about by the destruction of the present
world; national sentiment, which associates the
cosmic renovation and general judgment with the
restoration of Israel; and religious sentiment of
the Divine justice, which rewards the good and
punishes the wicked.   In the gospel, the national
element has disappeared, the nationality of Israelite
being no longer in itself a title to the kingdom ;
the eschatological element no longer fills the view,
and the religious and moral element comes into
the foreground.   But the relation between these
last two elements, which seem co-ordinated, is a
point much debated.   Several critics maintain
that the thought of Jesus was entirely dominated
by apocalyptic conceptions of the end of the
world.   Others think the moral point of view of
remission of sins and reconciliation with God is
the most important, the sole essential consideration.

CHAPTER I

THIS last opinion is that of Herr Harnack, and the eminent lecturer speaks with severity, even a little unfairly,[1] of those who support the contrary view. Recognizing that the kingdom that is to come is actually what Jesus understood by the kingdom, they yield to the desire, conscious or unconscious, to bring everything to one level, and lower that which is raised. Jesus, it is said, would share this belief in the kingdom that is to come, but for Him it would not constitute the whole of the reign of God; it would not even be the principal part, because the Saviour taught from the first, and was alone in teaching, that the kingdom of Heaven is not to be known by external signs, but exists already in the man who trusts God.

A problem of this nature is not to be dismissed by insinuations as to the tendencies of this person or that, who has sustained one or the other

[1] Page 35.

conclusion. The expositors accused of belittling Christ might easily reply that, to attribute to Him the ideas that seem to one's self to be the nearest to truth is perhaps to honour Him less than might be imagined. The gospel texts are at hand, and it is solely by their testimony that the question should be decided.

The evangelists have summed up the preaching of Jesus at the commencement of His ministry in the words: " Repent, for the kingdom of Heaven is at hand." [1] These words might also stand for an abridgment of the whole teaching of the Saviour in Galilee and at Jerusalem. They express the necessity of a moral conversion, of an internal change, of the remission of sins, but all in view of the kingdom that is at hand, that is, in view of the end of the world, for the kingdom which is near is the same that John the Baptist had announced before Jesus. The dominant idea is obviously that of the kingdom which is soon to be, and the repentance is significant in relation to the kingdom, as it is the indispensable condition of admittance therein. But the entire gospel only develops this warning. The beatitudes at the commencement of the Sermon on the Mount promise the kingdom to the poor and

[1] Matt. iv. 17.

afflicted, to the needy and the persecuted; it is promised to them as a future recompense, and is not supposed to be realized in them. When the Saviour sends His apostles out to preach, the evangelists represent Him as leaving repentance to be understood, and the message He gives them contains only the formula, "The kingdom of Heaven is at hand," [1] which, without doubt, is the essence of the gospel, the "good news" announced by Christ. When He is asked for a sign, Jesus replies that He will give no other than the sign of Jonas, [2]—that is to say, He refers His hearers to the approaching judgment of God. He assures His disciples that some of them shall be still living when the kingdom shall arrive; and when the disciples object that Elias must first come, He replies that the prophecy is fulfilled, and that Elias has come in the person of John the Baptist. [3] The parable of the workers in the vineyard [4] shows that the kingdom is assured to all who have worked for God, no matter for how short a time. In the parable of the Wedding Feast, [5] the kingdom bears the same relation to the gospel as the feast to the invitation that precedes it. Men are warned to be on their

[1] Matt. x. 7.   [2] Matt. xvi. 4; xii. 39.
[3] Matt. xvii. 12.   [4] Matt. xx. 1–15.   [5] Luke xiv. 16–24.

guard, for the kingdom will come as a thief in the night:[1] it is necessary to await the kingdom as the faithful servant awaits the return of his lord.[2] Store of merit must be provided as the wise virgins kept their oil, lest, when the kingdom shall come, the unready shall experience the fate of the five foolish ones who knocked in vain at the bridegroom's door.[3] In view of the judgment, the gifts of God must be made fruitful, as the servants, in their master's absence, employed the talents they had received from him:[4] by a good use of life and its present benefits, a part in the kingdom must be made sure, as the dishonest steward prepared a refuge for himself among his master's debtors:[5] poverty is to be endured with resignation, in the faith that the future life will atone for the miseries of the present, as is seen in the example of Lazarus:[6] consolation for the death even of the Saviour is to be found in the remembrance that, at the last supper, when Jesus presented to His disciples the symbolic cup, He bade them look forward to the meeting at the festival of the kingdom of God.[7]

[1] Matt. xxiv. 43.
[2] Matt. xxiv. 45–51.
[3] Matt. xxv. 1–13.
[4] Matt. xxv. 14–29.
[5] Luke xvi. 1–8.
[6] Luke xvi. 19–25.
[7] Mark xiv. 25.

The idea of the celestial kingdom is then nothing but a great hope, and it is in this hope or nowhere that the historian should set the essence of the gospel, as no other idea holds so prominent and so large a place in the teaching of Jesus. The qualities of this hope are as easy to determine as its object. It is in the first place collective, the good of the kingdom being destined for all who love God, and of such a nature that all can enjoy it in common, and so well that their happiness cannot be compared to anything so fitly as to a great festival. It is objective, and consists not only in the holiness of the believer, nor in the love that unites him to God, but implies all the conditions of a happy life, both the physical and the moral conditions, the external and the internal conditions, so that the coming of the kingdom can be spoken of as a fact that completes history, and is in no way confounded with the conversion of those who are called to it. It regards, and can only regard, the future, as befits its nature of hope; and this future is not the fate of the individual in this world, but the renewal of the world, the restoration of humanity in eternal justice and happiness.

If there is an anticipation of the kingdom in the teaching of the gospel and in the fruits it

produced, it is because the view of the kingdom
is of a thing close at hand ; the gospel is the
immediate and direct preparation for the kingdom, and the present looks only to this future
and virtually contains it. If the kingdom of
Heaven is compared to a feast, the gospel is
the invitation of the Father, such as is made
when the board is spread to entreat the guests
to come.[1] The principal guarantee of safety in
the kingdom will be the overthrow of Satan;
but already Satan is overwhelmed, he has found
One stronger than he, and his house is spoiled.[2]
Jesus saw in the cures He effected, especially
the cures of those possessed by devils, the
pledge of His final victory over the powers of
evil, and He could say that the kingdom of God
was come, since by the Spirit of God He cast out
the demons.[3] It may be that this assertion,
which is made in support of an argument founded
on the exorcisms practised by the Jews, and
separates rather inappropriately the two com-
parisons of the kingdom divided against itself
and the strong man, may belong to a later stratum
of evangelical tradition.[4] If it proceeds from

---

[1] Matt. xxii. 4.   [2] Matt. xii. 29.   [3] Matt. xii. 28.
[4] Cf. Mark iii. 24–27.

Jesus, it would set forth the kingdom as realized in its commencement, and not in its fulness, the power of Satan being not yet entirely overcome.

In the same way should be understood the words, " from the days of John the Baptist until now, the kingdom of Heaven suffereth violence, and the violent take it by force." [1] The kingdom of Heaven was inaugurated after John had finished his ministry, because it was then that Jesus Himself preached the gospel; but it was inaugurated in its preparation, not in its fulfilment; and those who seize it, the publicans and sinners who take possession of it, and who seem, as it were, to take it by force, do not enter into the felicity of the kingdom : they have seized it in promise, they have acquired a right to the happiness of the just.

The kingdom is for those God pardons, and God pardons all, provided they pardon themselves. Thus the kingdom is for those who are good after the example of God, and in organizing the present life on a basis of charity, the gospel realizes already the kingdom, whose full and final coming will only, as it were, assure the happiness and immortality of charitable men. But the kingdom

[1] Matt. xi. 12.

is actually this everlasting happiness. Its root is within; it lies like a precious seed in the soul of each believer; but in this state it is hidden, rudimentary, imperfect, and it awaits its perfection in the future.

CHAPTER II

In order to determine wherein consists the essence of the kingdom, of the gospel, and of Christianity, Herr Harnack starts from a principle that is far from self-evident, and is contradicted by the general attitude of Jesus towards the Mosaic religion and Israelite tradition. "Truly," he writes, "it is a difficult task, and a grave responsibility for the historian to distinguish what is traditional from what is personal, the kernel from the husk, in the preaching of Jesus as to the kingdom of God."[1] Here evidently what is traditional is the husk; what is personal, the kernel; and because the eschatological idea of the kingdom belongs to Israelite tradition, Herr Harnack finds it quite natural to consider it as merely the husk of the gospel, while the faith in a merciful God is the kernel, the original element in the teaching of the Saviour.

Such a conception of the essential and the

[1] Page 36.

accessory in matters of evangelical belief is
acceptable neither to the philosopher nor to the
historian, whose duty is only to examine what
importance Jesus Himself attaches to the different
points or aspects of His doctrine, without arro-
gating to themselves the right to decide that the
traditional element in the gospel is either suspect
or guaranteed merely by the fact that it is traditional. Now Christ has never said or given it
to be understood, that the old revelation was any
less authorized than that of which He was the
instrument. On the contrary, He had no other
pretension than to fulfil the law and the prophets;
without doubt He wished to enlarge and perfect
the former revelation, but, while enlarging and
perfecting, He meant to retain it; He is not set
before the world as the revealer of a new principle;
if He never gives His definition of the kingdom of
God it is because the kingdom of which He is the
messenger and the instrument is identified in His
thought, as in the minds of His hearers, with that
that the prophets have foretold. He holds to the
hope of the kingdom as He holds to the precept
of the love of God and faith in Him.

These three elements of His gospel are intertwined, inseparable, essential, although, or rather
because, they are traditional; they are the

essence of the gospel because they were the essence of Biblical revelation. If His way of understanding and realizing God, Love and the kingdom, is more pure, more deep, more living than that of the Old Testament, it perfects what has preceded it and does not destroy it. To seek in the gospel an element that shall be entirely new in regard to the religion of Moses and the prophets, is to seek a thing that Jesus had no desire to set there, a thing that on His own statement does not exist there.

The contradiction that has been discovered between the conception of a kingdom that is to come and that of a kingdom already present does not exist, unless we attribute to the second idea an absolute character it does not possess in the gospel. It would be far from easy to prove by clear and authentic texts that the kingdom (a supernatural gift) is purely a religious benefit,— union with the living God—and the chief experience of a man consisting in the remission of his sins.[1] Here again the great importance attached by Protestant theology to the idea of sin and justification accounts for what, from the point of view of historical criticism, is nothing but a preconceived determination to find in the gospel

[1] Page 40.

nothing but the essentials of one's own religion.
Christ nowhere confounds the kingdom with the
remission of sins, which is only the condition
of entrance into the kingdom. Nowhere does
He identify the kingdom with God, and God's
power acting in the heart of the individual.[1]
It is only by a very special exposition that this
definition of the kingdom can be found in the
parables.[2] The parable of the Sower only signifies that the kingdom is the Word of God: the
evangelical word, which is not the kingdom, is
compared to the grain the sower sows in his field,
and of which only a portion bears fruit. Part of
the seed is lost, and that is a thing that cannot
be said of the kingdom. The part that takes
root corresponds to the useful preaching, that
which attracts aspirants for the kingdom, but it
is not itself the kingdom; it bears fruit for the
kingdom, which is the end for which the seed
of the word is sown. In the same way the
parables of the Pearl and the Hidden Treasure
do not go to prove that the kingdom is God, in
the secret places of the heart, but simply that the
bliss of the everlasting kingdom is worth acquir-
ing at the sacrifice of all earthly possessions and
advantages, as the Pearl of great price and the

[1] Page 35.   [2] Page 36.

treasure hidden in the field were worth buying at the price of all the wealth of those who discovered them. The application of these parables is not doubtful, and is closely related to the eschatological conception of the kingdom. The seed which grows without the labourer heeding,[1] may suggest the idea of a moral progress accomplished within the soul; but in reality the comparison bears on the kingdom as taught and the kingdom made manifest, the first corresponding to the seed, the second to the harvest; between the two lies the time while the seed germinates and the gospel spreads. The parables of the mustard seed and of the leaven, which emphasize the contrast between an insignificant beginning and a great final result, apply also to the antithesis between the kingdom started by the evangelizing teaching and the kingdom developed to its actual manifestation. Everywhere the gospel is subordinated to the kingdom.

Some preparation is needed to find that whoever recites the Lord's Prayer prays only to preserve the strength he already possesses, and to strengthen the union between himself and God.[2] The first part of the prayer is concerned with the coming of the kingdom, and the Christian who

---

[1] Mark iv. 26–29.   [2] Page 42.

says, "Thy kingdom come," does not imagine that
the kingdom of Heaven is realized within himself.
The second part is subordinated to the first, as
the gospel is subordinated to the kingdom; for it
is in view of the near approach of the kingdom
that men pray for daily bread, to be forgiven their
trespasses, and to be delivered from temptation.
The Fatherhood of God, the heart's obedience to
His will, the certainty of having eternal possessions, and of being protected against evil, do not
exclude the eschatological conception of the kingdom, and indeed only obtain their full significance by their relations to that idea. It is evident
that the terms of the prayer would be very
different, were they not directed to guarantee the
union already existing of the individual with his
Heavenly Father.

The saying, "What shall it profit a man if he
gain the whole world and lose his own soul,"[1]
does not signify precisely "the infinite value
of the human soul,[2] an abstraction made of the
destiny of man in the future kingdom. Jesus
said that life must be lost in time to be gained in
eternity, and that he who seeks it or gains it now
loses it for the future. Now, the gain of everything else cannot compensate for the loss of life:

[1] Mark viii. 36.   [2] Page 40.

he who should gain the whole world would have
no advantage of it as soon as he were dead: and
that is the position of the man who will not sacrifice his life for the kingdom, from the wish to
keep it for the world: he will lose everything
by his death, the world he loves and has served,
and the kingdom to which he has no right. When
Jesus said, "Ye are of more value than many
sparrows," [1] it was not to exalt the value of the
soul, but to encourage His disciples to have faith;
the God that watches over the sparrows watches
even more over men. Truly the Saviour cared
for every human soul, the souls of the poor man,
the sinner, the woman, the child, but he did not
consider the value of the soul in itself in order to
sum up all religion in the actual union of each
soul with God. He made it sufficiently clear, in
the Parable of the Talents, that human existence
is of value according to the fruits it produces for
the Divine Judgment. The soul or the life has
no worth save by its destiny, through the
kingdom that God offers to it, and it ought to
deserve.

Jesus summed up all duty in the precept of
love. But this teaching does not exhaust the
moral of the Gospel and does not indicate its

[1] Luke xii. 7.

final sanction. To the man who asked what he must do to possess eternal life, that is, to have a place in the kingdom of Heaven, Jesus replied by enumerating those commandments of the Decalogue that relate to the neighbour, then enjoined him to give all he had to the poor and follow Himself.[1] Love, therefore, is not at an end in itself; charity leads to the kingdom, sacrificing the temporal to gain the eternal. It is vain to force the opinion that the kingdom is "only the treasure possessed by the soul in the eternal and merciful God,"[2] if by this treasure of actual possession charity is to be understood. Love is demanded now to assure the possession of God later, when the glory of his reign shall appear.

To support the idea of a kingdom purely personal and already present, there remains a text of the third Gospel, whose authenticity is not very certain, nor its meaning very clear. When asked by the Pharisees, when the kingdom of God should come, Jesus answered them, "The kingdom of God cometh not with observation; neither shall they say, Lo here! or Lo there! for behold the kingdom of God is within you."[3]

---

[1] Mark x. 17–22.   [2] Page 49.
[3] Luke xvii. 20, 21.

This statement is only found in Luke, and is part of the preamble that the author has drawn up for an eschatological discourse,[1] whose substance has been preserved by Matthew.[2] It is highly probable that only this discourse belongs to the source common to both Gospels, and that the saying quoted comes from Luke or his particular tradition. The general style of this introduction is that of the evangelist, who readily invents the surroundings of the discourses he repeats ; and the idea of the present kingdom does not accord well with the discourse itself, which concerns the coming of the Son of Man, unless the assertion, " The kingdom of God is within you," is to be understood as a prophecy meaning, "The kingdom of God is about to become manifest among you." The fact of revision comes out in what is said of the kingdom, " Lo here ! or Lo there ! " a phrase which really applies to the Messiah, and is, as a matter of fact, used of Him a couple of verses later. If the saying was really pronounced by Jesus and addressed to the Pharisees, as the evangelist states, it cannot mean that the kingdom of God is in them, that is, in their souls, for these

[1] Luke xvii. 23–37.
[2] Matt. xxiv. 23, 26–27, 37–39, 17–18, 40–41, 28.

Pharisees do not accept the gospel, and have no share in the kingdom. There would be much subtlety in leaving a restriction to be understood, as though Jesus had meant to say, " The kingdom of God is such that it might be realized in you, if you desired and were worthy of it." The most natural meaning would be, " the kingdom of God is in the midst of you," and it is perhaps in this way that the writer understands it, unless he has simply wished to say, that the kingdom will come when it is least expected, and before there is time to announce that it has appeared in this place or in that. Before it can be maintained with authority that Jesus understood this saying in another sense than this, other texts are needed of undoubted meaning and authenticity, expressing the internal and actual character of the kingdom. But it is evident that such texts are wanting, and as to sacrifice the rest of the gospel to the doubtful interpretation of a solitary passage would be to go contrary to the most elementary principles of criticism, under the most favourable view, and taking the authenticity of the saying for granted, Jesus must be held to have spoken of the presence of the kingdom in its commencement and its preparation by the gospel.

CHAPTER III

THE historian must resist the temptation to modernize the conception of the kingdom. If the theologian feels bound to supply an interpretation for the needs of the present day, no one will contest his right, provided he does not confuse his commentary with the primitive meaning of the gospel texts; and while this is true for the conception of the kingdom, it is also true for the appreciation of the relations of the gospel to the different aspects of human life. Nothing is easier than to determine historically the attitude of Jesus towards the world, towards earthly possessions, towards human law, towards civilization. The vision of the approaching kingdom must have inspired Him with a kind of disdain for all these things, and the texts leave no possible doubt as to His sentiments. But just as means have been found to bring back upon Himself and the present the regard that the Saviour directed towards the future, success is equally looked for if not in showing Him as positively interested in present life, social questions, political order, and human progress, at least in attenuating His indifference towards them all.

We are told,[1] that the gospel is not the doctrine of renunciation of the world, but that it merely attacks riches, anxiety for earthly matters, and egoism : the proof that Jesus was no ascetic, is that He ate and drank like all the world, that He permitted His feet to be washed and His head to be anointed ; that He permitted his followers to continue their occupations and their way of life ; that He did not organize the little group of disciples into a monastic order, with a code of laws and definite spiritual exercises ; that later the apostles taught that the labourer is worthy of his hire, and that they did not separate from their wives ; and, finally, that the gospel is opposed to the world only in that its spirit consists in humility and faith in God, the remission of sins, and the love of our neighbour.

As a matter of fact, it cannot be contested that Jesus preached self-denial, without establishing a discipline of renunciation. But the attempt to draw an absolute distinction between the spirit of detachment from the world, and the effective

[1] Pages 50-56.

renunciation of it, however legitimate in itself and useful for present-day application of gospel maxims, does not appear in a historical sense to be founded on the words of the Saviour. The expectation of the great event explains why Jesus put forward no actual disciplinary ordinance; why He submitted neither Himself nor His followers to any special mode of life that might have interfered with the preaching of the kingdom; why He considered the gospel as a message of joy, incompatible with the bodily privations and fasts imposed on themselves by the Pharisees and the disciples of John.[1] But it is for the same reason that He exacted from all those who aspired to the kingdom, not a disposition willing eventually to sacrifice possessions and family affections to the superior interest of salvation, but the immediate relinquishment of all to follow Him. A man must lose his life to save it; he must hate father, mother, wife, children, brothers, and sisters to devote himself to the work of the kingdom; he must sell his goods and give unto the poor; it is not enough to be free from avarice and temporal cares, he must abandon the riches and occupations of this world. The comparison of the disciples to the

---

[1] Mark ii. 19.

birds of the air and the flowers of the fields shows that it is not only anxiety for bodily needs, but even work that is forbidden or discouraged, and though God is to be asked for daily bread, it is not in the least intended that the prayer should show anything but confidence in God without personal anxiety; rather does he who prays thus rely entirely on God for his means of existence. The absolute nature of the hope for the impending establishment of the kingdom of Heaven corresponds to the absolute nature of the renunciation demanded for admission therein, and the absolute nature of the confidence in Him Who cares for the birds, and will assuredly come to the aid of men, His children.

It is in no way astonishing that such a discipline could not be imposed in all its rigour on every one, even during the ministry of Jesus, or that further departures from it should have occurred after Him; but this is no reason for introducing into the thought of the Master the limitations that the nature of things and the actual conditions of existence set to its detailed application. It was equally necessary for the success of the gospel that the discipline should have had in the beginning this simple, unmodified character, and that later all those modifications should have been made in it that the changing circumstances demanded, in order to adapt what had been addressed to a world believed to be near its end, to a world that had proved more enduring.

Herr Harnack[1] does not rank himself with those who see in the gospel first and foremost a social doctrine for the relief of the oppressed, either from admiration of such a teaching, or because, on the contrary, they regard it as entirely chimerical and impracticable. Nor is he among those who represent Christ as " conservative," a respecter of the priesthood, and of acquired fortunes. He thinks that Jesus, while regarding the possession of riches as a danger for the soul, did not desire general poverty as the foundation of His heavenly kingdom, and was forced to battle with misery and make it disappear. Christ neither gave nor possessed an economic programme for the conquest of poverty : He did more, by indicating a new social duty in the precept of charity. The gospel is socialistic in so far as it desires " to establish among men a community as comprehensive as human life, and as profound as human misery." Jesus appreciates the common needs of life—shelter, food, decent living; He desired that these essential possessions should be

[1] Pages 56–65.

given to all who could not procure them; He even seems to have had glimpses of a possible society wherein wealth should not exist as private property in the strict sense, but here His conception of the approaching end of the world must be borne in mind, and is it not well to consider it in regard to the rest? If Jesus did not desire general poverty as a condition of the kingdom of God, is it not because He conceived the kingdom independently of human society? It is impossible to say that He proposed to banish misery, in the sense that He was constantly preoccupied with remedying it by the regular means of a wise distribution of help, recommended to the possessors of riches. The disappearance of poverty is only foreseen, perhaps only desired, as a consequence of the establishment of the kingdom. The complete renunciation exacted from the rich man is rather in his own spiritual interest than for the relief of the poor to whom the kingdom is promised. The conception of a society where riches should be so distributed that none should lack food, clothing, and shelter, is not really present in the gospel, and it needs a certain amount of predisposition to find that when Jesus, the Son of Man, had not "where to lay His head,"[1] He

[1] Matt. viii. 20.

desired for every one the shelter He Himself did not possess.

The historical truth is that the idea of a society regularly constituted according to the principles of the gospel does not exist apart from the vision of the approaching kingdom, where there shall be neither rich nor poor, where there shall be no question of private property or collective property, and where Divine happiness is the common possession of all. There remains only for the believer the possibility, the right, the duty to draw from this ideal of the kingdom, as from that of renunciation and from the precept of charity, such applications as are suitable to any given state of human society. There is no need to quarrel with the Franciscans on the ground that Jesus, when He bade His Apostles live by the gospel, did not authorize them to beg.

In His relations with established authority, the Saviour, we are told, attacked the "political Church and the Pharisees," but took up another attitude towards "the real authority, that which bears the sword." He recognized a definite right in this authority, and never set Himself against it. Even the prohibition against taking an oath should not be extended " to include the oath taken before the authorities." Cæsar has his rights in the sphere of his purely temporal power: let his tribute be rendered to him. In itself, this power, resting as it does on force, has no moral authority. The true disciples of the gospel will keep themselves from the exercise of this power of domination: they are to know that the first among them is the servant of all. Did Jesus reject or sanction "human law"? He seems to have had no confidence in human justice, and exhorts His disciples not to claim "their rights," to let themselves be robbed and beaten without attempt to exact reparation for the wrongs done to them. From this it has been concluded that the gospel is the negation of all codes, of civil law as well as of canonical law. Herr Harnack thinks that Jesus had only individual cases in His mind, and that He was not thinking of the possibility of attack by external enemies, nor of the public authority interested in the maintenance of order and the safeguarding of the existence and welfare of citizens, nor of a nation attacked unjustly.[1]

Such a gap in the teaching of Christ could not fail to be significant. But the manner in which the learned author interprets his texts lacks exactitude. Jesus bids His disciples, without any restricting phrases, love their enemies and do good

[1] Pages 65–74.

to those who persecute them, turn the other
cheek to blows, and abandon the coat to him who
has wished to take the cloak. The persecutor,
the insulter, the robber, does not belong to the
society of the disciples, and it is not with any prevision of his possible conversion that they are
commanded to endure him : it is always by virtue
of that supreme indifference to human interests
that is, historically, the form taken by the gospel.
Why claim a right now, when eternal justice is so
close at hand ? The kingdom of heaven is for the
persecuted. What matters what one possesses,
when nothing is needed to participate in the
reign of God ? It is in the same spirit that Jesus
deals with constituted authority. He does not
contest the legitimacy of the priesthood, but He
knows that the reign of the law is about to give
place to the era of the Messiah. He is not in
revolt against Cæsar, but He knows that the
power of man is declining to its end. It is not
for Him to pronounce opinion on the value of institutions which will have no place in the kingdom of heaven. It is absolutely gratuitous to
suppose that He admitted the obligation of the
oath before authorities. When He replied to the
adjuration of the High Priest, He Himself took
no oath. His way of regarding all human and

temporal order is obviously inspired by the sentiment of His superior vocation in a totally different scheme of things, to be set in place of this temporary and defective organization, represented by unjust men, who must be endured until the destined hour shall come.

It follows that the gospel contains no formal declaration for or against the constitution of human society in the world as it is. The necessity of human law cannot be deduced from the gospel, nor can any foundation for it be found there: both exist independently of the gospel, which is not called upon to create them, or to replace them, and can only influence them by its spirit.

For the rest, it is not evident that the gospel is only addressed "to the inner soul of man that is always the same." The gospel of Jesus is addressed to the whole man, to snatch him from the conditions normal to his present life. This violent effort was indispensable for the foundation of Christianity, and analogous efforts may still be necessary to recall to men's minds that their principal interest is superior to temporal advantage. It is certain, for the historian, that the gospel has rather regarded human law and political and social economy as abstractions, and that it had no formal intention of regenerating them, unless by the radical transformation implied in the ideal of the kingdom.

Finally, observes the author,[1] if the gospel had taken any thought for science, art, or civilization, it would have bound itself to one particular form of human culture, and would have been hampered in its subsequent development, as the Roman Church is to-day through its connection with the philosophy, political organization, and general culture of the Middle Ages. Intellectual progress and civilization do not constitute the whole of man or of humanity. Moral progress is of the first importance, that progress that Jesus was conscious of preparing and safeguarding when He revealed to mankind the knowledge of the true God.

How far apart are the truth of history and the theory proposed with such ardour and conviction ! The Catholic Church is only bound to the science and political form of the Middle Ages because it does not choose to detach itself from them. If the gospel was not bound to any form of science and civilization, it was by the nature of things bound to the lack of science and of culture, which was none the less inconvenient. If it has since been the more easily adapted to different

[1] Pages 74-78.

conditions of knowledge and civilization, there has none the less remained with it, because of its origin, a kind of repugnance and distrust of civilization and science, generally returned with interest. Is Protestant orthodoxy, founded on the gospel, less troubled by the modern movement than the Catholic Church? It is incontestable that intellectual progress and civilization represent neither the supreme end of life nor the most precious possession of humanity. But does not the gospel entirely ignore their secondary value? It should be enough to say that the gospel is the factor without which science and progress do not really elevate mankind. Suppose we were asked if the gospel might not have come to an end, had it not come in contact with Greek science? Is it really certain that this alliance contributed nothing towards the preservation of its moral essence? However, from the point of view of the gospel, science and civilization were not even accessory advantages: they were nothing, and could be nothing, compared with the vision of the kingdom.

Science and civilization on their side also have justification for their existence apart from the gospel, which is not destined to promote them, and cannot take their place in so far as they are actually useful and beneficial for humanity. The independence of the gospel with regard to matters of intelligence is only a theoretical hypothesis. In historical reality, and among all those who have believed, or who do believe, evangelical faith is coloured by the relative ignorance or knowledge of its adepts.

As to the moral revolution which it is held Christ wished to bring about in the world, it cannot be too often repeated that Jesus only announced it in the kingdom about to come, and that He did not represent it as a work of slow progress. The Parables of the Workers in the Vineyard and of the Talents, that are quoted to show how the kingdom extends on the earth, have not this allegorical significance; the first means that the kingdom will be given to those who come late to faith and the practice of well-doing, as well as to those who have given all their lives to duty; the second signifies that the kingdom will only belong to those whose life has been productive of the fruits of virtue; the two complete one another, but both alike presuppose a kingdom that is to come, without assuming its existence in the present life.

In fine, it is not precisely by the knowledge of God that Christ looks to save mankind; speaking

to Jews, He supposes God to be already recognized, and does not even pretend to make Him
known in a new aspect.   The message of Jesus is
contained in the announcement of the approaching kingdom, and the exhortation to penitence as
a means of sharing therein.   All else, though it
is the common preoccupation of humanity, is as
though non-existent.

Whatever may have been the intrinsic worth and
moral efficacy of the hope of which Christ was the
interpreter, nothing was done, even at the time
when this hope was made manifest, to reconcile
it with all the realities to which it has since
accommodated itself.   The work of adaptation
still continues, and Herr Harnack, following
many others, has set himself to toil at it.   But
he is too ready to suppose that the agreement was
complete from the beginning, or at any rate that
he has only to take the gospel just as it is, to
apply it to all possible conditions of mankind.
As the gospel was appropriate to the very special
circumstances under which it saw the light, it has
first been necessary to detach it from its earliest
connections, which were not in the least with the
preoccupations of actual life (the anxiety to
ameliorate human conditions in this world, social
and political law, and the progress of culture),

but with a kind of violent and anarchic state far outside any civilization then existing. The gospel has not entered the world as an unconditioned absolute doctrine, summed up in a unique and steadfast truth, but as a living faith, concrete and complex, whose evolution proceeds without doubt from the internal force which has made it enduring, but none the less has been, in everything and from the beginning, influenced by the surroundings wherein the faith was born and has since developed. This faith took shape in the idea of the reign of God. The conception of God the Father is only one element, traditional in its origin, like all the rest, and has its history, like all the rest, in the general development of Christianity.

SECTION III

THE SON OF GOD

INTRODUCTION

GIVEN a very limited conception of the kingdom of heaven, an equally limited conception of the mission of the Saviour is sure to correspond. The Christ of Herr Harnack [1] not only differs as a matter of fact from the Christ of tradition, but also from any image that the historian can derive from a criticism of the Gospels alone. Jesus, we are told, is the Son of God in so far as He reveals the Father, but the Father alone belongs to the gospel; Jesus believed Himself the Messiah, but this Jewish conception is not otherwise bound up with that of the Divine Sonship: "it was the condition necessary for the recognition in the history of the Jewish religion of Him Who had received the inward summons; " [2] the expiatory

---

[1] Pages 79–103. [2] Page 89.

death of Jesus made Him the Lord, and whatever is thought of the narratives of the resurrection, it was in the tomb of Christ that indestructible faith was born in the victory of man over death and in an eternal life.

CHAPTER I

" JESUS has explained very clearly in one of His discourses how and why He called Himself the Son of God. It is in Matthew and not in John that the saying occurs—'None knoweth the Son save the Father, nor the Father save the Son, and he to whomsoever the Son will reveal Him.' The knowledge of God is the sphere of the Divine Sonship. It is with this knowledge of God that Jesus has learnt to regard the Holy Being Who governs the heaven and the earth, as Father, as His Father. This is why the consciousness He had of being the Son of God is no more than the practical consequence of His knowledge that God was Father and His Father. Properly understood, all that the name of Son implies is a knowledge of God. But two points further must be noted; Jesus is convinced that He knows God as none before Him has known, and He knows that His mission is to communicate to all others, by His words and deeds, this knowledge of God, and in the same way His Divine Sonship."[1]

All this edifice of argument, with its relation to Herr Harnack's conception of the heavenly kingdom which it is superfluous to point out, is founded, in the final analysis, on a solitary text, whose origin is carefully made prominent. It is a passage in the synoptics, not in John, and to be read not only in Matthew,[2] but also in Luke.[3] But this text alone ought not to serve as the basis for a historical examination of the idea to be formed, from a study of the Gospels, of the mission that Jesus attributed to Himself. It is not put forward as an explanation of the Divine Sonship, but as the expression of a permanent relation between the Father and the Son. To say that this relation constitutes, properly speaking, the Divine Sonship of Jesus, is a deduction of the theologian, not the expression of a doctrine or a sentiment that Jesus Himself formulated.

More than one passage in the Gospels can be found without difficulty, from which the conclusion is clear that the title, Son of God, was for the Jews, the disciples, and for the Saviour Himself the equivalent of the Messiah. It is enough

[1] Page 81. [2] Matt. xi. 25–30.
[3] Luke x. 21–24.

to recall the different versions of the confession of Peter in the synoptic Gospels, and the questioning of Jesus by the High Priest. In Mark,[1] Peter says to the Saviour, "Thou art the Christ." In Matthew,[2] "Thou art the Christ, the Son of the living God." In Luke,[3] "Thou art the Christ of God." In the second Gospel [4] Caiaphas says to Jesus, "Art Thou the Christ, the Son of the Blessed?" In the first Gospel,[5] "I adjure Thee by the living God to tell us if Thou art the Christ, the Son of God." In the third,[6] the priests first demand of Jesus if He is the Christ, and because He does not reply clearly, they repeat the question in the form, "Art Thou then the Son of God?" to which Jesus replies in the affirmative, as in the other two synoptic Gospels. Whatever mental or moral experience it may have been which produced this consciousness of Divine Sonship, it is certain that all who heard Jesus, friends or enemies, identified it with the consciousness of being the Messiah, or the pretension to that position. It is somewhat rash to-day to maintain that the essential significance of the title of Son of God was different for Christ Himself, and that

---

[1] Mark viii. 29.   [2] Matt. xvi. 16.
[3] Luke ix. 20.   [4] Mark xiv. 61.   [5] Matt. xxvi. 63.
[6] Luke xxii. 67–70.

its real justification was the consciousness of God as Father.

The text quoted, taken in its natural sense, has a meaning quite different from that sought to be extracted from it. It follows a prayer that Jesus addresses to God as " Father, Lord of heaven and earth;" for in the mind of Christ the idea of God the Father is necessarily bound up with that of the sovereign Ruler of the universe. The Saviour adds that "all things are delivered unto Him by His Father." Taken strictly, these words only apply to the glorified Christ, and the compiler of the first Gospel presently uses a similar expression of the Saviour risen from the dead.[1] It is only by a forced construction that they can be limited to the things that Jesus has learnt from the Father, the revelation that He has been charged to bring to mankind. It is maintained that the principal part of this revelation is the consciousness that the Son has of a good God. But the text was not intended to support such a theory. Could it be said that the Father, Who alone knoweth the Son, as the Son alone knoweth the Father, had also received a revelation from the Son of which He was to be the interpreter, and was only the Father

[1] Cf. Matt. xxviii. 18.

through His knowledge of the Son? Is there, then, a religion of the Son that the Father must teach, as the Son teaches that of the Father? Obviously the text indicates a transcendental relationship, whence springs the lofty dignity of Christ, and not a psychological reality, which in regard to God is clearly impossible. Father and Son are not here simply religious terms, but have already become metaphysical theological expressions, and dogmatic speculation has been able to take possession of them, without much modification of their sense. There is but one Father and one Son, constituted in some way by the knowledge they have of one another, absolute entities whose relationship is also absolute. The intention of the passage is not so much to explain how Jesus is the Son of God, as to give prominence to the Christ, by identifying Him, as the Son, with eternal wisdom that God alone knows in its entirety, although it is revealed to mankind, while on its side the wisdom alone possesses and represents the full knowledge of God, although it reveals God to His creatures, as far as they are capable of receiving the revelation. The gospel saying, therefore, has a totally different significance to that needed for the theory that the Sonship of Jesus was acquired on the earth by His knowledge of the Father.

On the other hand, for the historian, it proves much less, because it is difficult to see in it the literal and exact expression of a declaration made by Christ to His disciples. It occurs in a kind of psalm, where the influence of the prayer that closes the Book of Ecclesiasticus[1] is evident both in the general scope and in several details. Both passages begin with the praise of God, and there is in both a marked preference for the name of Father:[2] the declaration concerning the mutual knowledge of the Father and the Son corresponds to the praise of wisdom: the appeal of Christ to the weary and heavy laden seems inspired by the invitation that wisdom addresses to the ignorant in the last part of the prayer of *Ben-Sirach*. These correspondences are not accidental, and seeing that it is difficult to imagine that Jesus should have wished to imitate a passage of Ecclesiasticus in an oration or discourse apparently quite un-premeditated; seeing that the entire passage possesses a rhythm distinctly analogous to that of the canticles reproduced in the first chapters

[1] Eccl. li.

[2] Cf. Eccl. li. 10. Reading "the Lord my Father," and not "the Lord, Father of my Lord."

of Luke, and seeing that another passage can be found in Matthew,[1] where Christ appears to be identified with Divine wisdom, it is fairly probable that, notwithstanding its occurrence in two Gospels, the portion including the text cited by Herr Harnack is, at any rate in its actual form, a product of the Christian tradition of the earlier times.   It is always a valuable testimony, as far as concerns the conception of Christ in the early age of the Church; but a critic must use it with the greatest care, when it is a question of establishing the idea Christ in His teaching gave of Himself, His Divine Sonship, and His mission.

Thus the text upon which Herr Harnack has founded his theory of the Son of God is no more certain in its interpretation, and favours his thesis no more than does the one where he finds the definition of the kingdom of God in the heart of man. The gospel conception of the Son of God is no more a psychological idea signifying a relation of the soul with God than is the gospel conception of the kingdom. There is absolutely nothing to prove it; and even the text quoted does not say that Jesus became the Son because He was the first to know God as the Father. The compiler

[1] Cf. Matt. xxiii. 34–36 ; Luke xi. 49–51.

of the Gospel has not the least intention of
indicating that God was not known as the Father,
before the advent of Jesus: he wishes to say,
and says very clearly, that Christ (the Son) alone
knows perfectly God (the Father), and that because
He is the Son, just as the Father, God, alone
knows perfectly Christ His Son, and that because
He is the Father, because He is God. The thought
is fundamentally the same that inspires the
passage of John,[1] "No man hath seen God at
any time; the only begotten Son, which is in the
bosom of the Father, He hath declared Him."
The special knowledge of the Son has for its
subject God as He is, and is not merely concerned
with the goodness of God, as though the hearers
of Jesus needed to be taught that God was
their Father. Such a thought is as foreign to the
evangelists as it would have been to the Saviour
Himself. It is an artificial and superficial
explanation of the Divine Sonship of Jesus.

The problem of the consciousness of the
Messiah must be solved by other means, and that
without keeping the idea of the Messiah in the
background. It is truly curious to see how
embarrassed certain Protestant theologians become
over this " Jewish " conception, which they would

[1] John i. 18.

willingly eliminate from the gospel and attribute to apostolic tradition in order to shape themselves a Christ after their own heart. Some have already maintained that the Saviour did not believe Himself the Messiah, and that the faith of the disciples in the resurrection was the force that gave Him that position in their minds and for subsequent tradition. Herr Harnack does not go so far. His Christ, the Son who reveals the Divine Goodness, seems to assume the position of Messiah as a kind of costume or disguise suitable for dealing with the Jews; but the consciousness of being the Son of God preceded in Him the consciousness of being the Messiah.

It would be well to see upon what historical basis this theory rests, and if it is not a pure hypothesis. Two questions must be distinguished in it, of differing degrees of clearness, or rather of obscurity; the question as to what Jesus believed Himself to be and declared that He was, and the question of the mental processes which led Him to His conclusion. For the first point a critical discussion of the sources of the gospel should furnish sufficiently definite indications for an answer; for the second, there is only room for conjecture, on a basis of the knowledge discovered for the first.

It is not without some appearance of reason

that the idea that Jesus regarded Himself as the Messiah has been contested. Side by side with the confused idea, frequently held both now and formerly, of the kingdom of Heaven, there could only be a conception equally vague of the Messiah; and just as the way out of the contradictions involved in the idea of the kingdom seemed to lie in the denial of all that was least satisfying to the modern intelligence (namely, its eschatological character), so to escape from the difficulties presented by the conception of the Messiah, it has been thought well to suppress it, or at least subordinate it entirely to the conception formed of the Son of God.

The gospel testimony, to say the truth, seems sufficiently disconcerting. The preoccupation of the narrators to prove that Jesus was the Messiah, immediately rouses the critic to see if the point of view of the evangelists conforms to the facts. In many details an interest, either apologetic or simply didactic, has influenced the narration of discourses and occurrences; but this natural tendency would not fall under suspicion were it not that the attitude the narratives attribute to the Saviour seems at first sight inexplicable. Jesus did not, in the course of His preaching, announce Himself as the Messiah; He silenced those possessed of devils who hailed Him as the Son of God; further, the populace never imagined Him to have this mission; they made Him the subject of most extravagant hypotheses [1] without suspecting the truth. The disciples alone held Him for the Christ and finally declared their faith through the mouth of Simon; but the Master forbade them to speak of it to others, so that we must look to the end of His career, almost to His last day, to find the public avowal of His dignity. It is true that, after the Confession of Simon Peter, Jesus is said to have discoursed to His disciples several times as to the fate that awaited the Messiah; but as the general scope of His discourses is founded on the facts as they actually occurred and on the subject of early Christian preaching, and as they contain no sentence definitely reported as the saying of the Lord, such an assertion rather complicates the difficulty than throws light on it. May it not be that all that concerns Jesus as the Messiah belongs to tradition, and that the reserve of the Saviour, as narrated, was really an absolute silence, much easier to imagine than the equivocal situation described by the evangelists?

The equivocal situation does not really exist,

[1] Mark viii. 28.

if it is once understood what the name of Messiah signified to Jesus, as to His contemporaries. There seems to be no doubt that the Saviour was condemned to death for having put forward pretensions to the throne of Israel, that is, to the position of Messiah, since His claim had no political meaning. But as far as can be determined from the traditional recollections, even this point can only be established by His avowal first before the High Priest, and later before Pilate. Jesus did not say openly in Jerusalem, any more than in Galilee, that He was the Christ, the Son of God. Only at Jerusalem He made evident the direction whither His doctrine tended, and the place He claimed for Himself in the kingdom He announced. Therefore He possessed the consciousness of being the Messiah when He left Galilee, and the confession of Peter, whose historical truth there is no reason in any case to suspect, comes to clear up the situation. The conviction of the disciples was doubtless of no long standing when it was expressed by Simon; but there is nothing to forbid the thought that Jesus Himself, when He began to preach the gospel, looked on Himself not only as the messenger or prophet of the kingdom, but held Himself to be its principal agent and predestined head.

This is the key to the singularity of His attitude. As the kingdom is essentially a thing of the future, the office of Messiah is essentially eschatological. Christ is the head of the society of the elect. The ministry of Jesus was only the preliminary to the kingdom of Heaven and the fulfilment of the office of Messiah. In one sense Jesus was the Messiah, in another sense He was presently to become the Messiah. He was, in so far as He was called personally to govern the New Jerusalem; He was not yet, since the New Jerusalem had no existence and the power of the Messiah no place in which to be exercised. Jesus, then, had before Him the vision of His own coming. The question of John the Baptist,[1] "Art thou He that should come?" is thus easily understood, as is also the reply of Jesus, its indirect character and calculated reserve being due to no modesty of the Saviour, but imposed on Him by the actual conditions of the kingdom. John did not say, "Art Thou the Christ?" because the kingdom was not realized, and Jesus was not filling the place of the Messiah. He demands rather if Jesus is not about to become the Christ, and Jesus replies in a way to make him understand, that He who prepares effectively the coming

[1] Matt. xi. 3.

of the kingdom is He who must come to His fulfilment with the kingdom. When Peter says, "Thou art the Christ," he does not mean that the Saviour is already exercising His power as Messiah, but that He is the one designated for that position. It is in this way that Caiaphas understands the matter, and the discourse addressed to him by Jesus only becomes intelligible on this hypothesis. The Saviour avows that He is the Christ ; but, to support His assertion, He adds immediately, "And ye shall see the Son of Man sitting on the right hand of power and coming in the clouds of Heaven."[1] This is precisely the place of honour and the glorious coming characteristic of the Messiah. Jesus declares that He is the Son of Man who is to come.

It is easy to understand why He did not wish to avow Himself till the day of His death, and the sense in which He makes His avowal is evident. It was not for Him to declare Himself earlier, not only because He would not have been believed, or because He would have been at once exposed to the vengeance of the authorities, but because He could not, as His preaching was not the duty of the Messiah, and His coming as the

[1] Mark xiv. 62.

Christ could not be till later, at the moment decreed by Providence. It is easy to see, too, how the apostolic Church should have come to teach that Jesus became Christ and Lord by His resurrection, that is, by His entry into heavenly glory, and how it should at the same time await His *coming*, that is, His appearance as the Christ, and not His *return*, as His terrestrial ministry was not then looked upon as the fulfilment of the prophecy of the Messiah.

As to the origin of the conviction in the mind of Jesus that He was the Messiah, it cannot be deduced with certainty from the texts. The oldest tradition seems to have explained or symbolized it by a revelation made on the occasion of the Baptism in the Jordan. The tradition may have been an after-thought arising from contemplation of the later history of Jesus, although the Baptism was a definite point of departure in His ministry. In any case, the distinction that is drawn between the consciousness of Himself as the Son and as the Messiah is absolutely without foundation. The earliest tradition had no suspicion of it; nor would modern criticism have dreamed of it, had there been no theological interests at stake. Truly the filial sentiment that fills the inner life of Jesus is one thing, and the consciousness reflected from His assigned position is another. It is not the sentiment that makes Jesus the Son of God in a sense that belongs to Him alone. All men who say to God " Our Father," are sons of God by the same right, and Jesus would be only one of them, if it were merely a question of knowing the Divine Goodness and trusting in it. The critic may conjecture that in Jesus the filial sentiment preceded and prepared the way for the consciousness of being the Messiah, as His soul was elevated by prayer, confidence and love to the highest degree of union with God, till the idea of His vocation as the Messiah came quite naturally to crown the travail of His Spirit ; but in so far as the title of Son of God belongs in an exclusive sense to the Saviour, it is equivalent to that of Messiah, and takes its meaning from the rank of the Messiah ; it belongs to Jesus not because of His inner disposition and His religious experiences, but because of His Providential func- tion as the sole maker of the kingdom of Heaven It must be recognized also that the texts permit no psychological analysis of the idea of the Son of God. Jesus named Himself the Son of God to the extent to which He avowed Himself the Messiah. The historian must come therefore to the conclusion that He believed Himself the Son of God, because He believed Himself to be the Messiah. The idea of the Divine Sonship was linked to that of the kingdom: it had no definite signification, as far as Jesus was concerned, except in regard to the kingdom about to be established. Even for those who believe in the Gospel, the dignity of children of God is not un-related to the hope of the kingdom that the Father has destined for them. How much more when it is a question of the single ruler of the kingdom! He is the Son, *par excellence*, not because He has learnt to know the goodness of the Father, and thus revealed it, but because He alone is the vicar of God for the kingdom of Heaven.

CHAPTER II

To say therefore that the Father only and not the Son belongs to the gospel of Jesus,[1] is to define with little exactness the teaching of the Saviour, and the relation between the conception of Sonship and that of the kingdom. If the gospel is only the revelation of Divine Goodness, it is conceivable that the rank of the Revealer might not be formally indicated in the gospel. But as the good news (as the name gospel implies, and the teaching of Jesus proves) is, properly speaking, the announcement of the great event, the Coming of the kingdom of Heaven, the Son of God is the subject of the gospel in so far as Christ belongs to the kingdom, and it cannot be maintained that the gospel conception of the kingdom is entirely defined without the Christ.

The personality of John the Baptist remained outside the kingdom he preached, because John

[1] Page 91.

was only its prophet. The position of Jesus is quite different. If He speaks but little of Himself in His preaching, it is because the only direct object of His doctrine is the moral preparation of those who wish to accept the Divine promise, and also because He never describes the bliss to come. None the less, He assigns to Himself an essential part and a unique place in the arrival and establishment of the kingdom. What is the sign of the coming of the Reign of God ? The Son of Man appearing on the clouds. What is the place of Jesus in the kingdom ? The first; and His disciples dispute the honour of occupying the seats that shall be on His right hand and His left.[1] There is no question of a doctrine to be put forward touching Himself and His office. Jesus, who announced no dogmatic formula of the kingdom, similarly announced none of Himself. None the less, He preached the kingdom, and, with the kingdom, the Messiah. Those who believed in His message, believed also in His mission, and His grandeur was to be made manifest to them with the promised kingdom. It was quite unnecessary to put forward beforehand the theoretical definition of His dignity. No one reading

[1] Mark x. 35-40.

the gospel would doubt that Jesus demands only faith in the goodness of God without any further anxiety as to the future, or as to Himself. To affirm that "he who holds Jesus for the Son of God adds something to the gospel,"[1] is not to put forward a paradox, but simply to show an entire misconception of the nature of Christ's teaching.

It is his own religion, not that of the gospel, which Herr Harnack expounds and defends, when he announces that "God and the soul, the soul and its God, are the whole contents of the gospel."[2] The historical gospel has none of this mystic and individualistic character. The Protestant theologian must have a motive in forcing this form on it, or rather he has his faith, more powerful than any motive. The historian sees no reason for this violent interpretation, nor would he understand the tendency of an argument deduced from the despairing hypothesis that in the mind of Jesus His preaching was something merely provisional, its meaning bound to be changed after His death and resurrection, and a part of it certain one day to be negligible and held of no value. The hypothesis, as a matter of fact, would have no significance for the historian; but it is not the historian who requires it. It is

[1] Page 92.   [2] Page 90.

the theologian who may be tempted to make use of it, and Herr Harnack only escapes the necessity of such a conjecture by an argument still less acceptable. The Christ of the gospel did not divide His teaching into two parts, the one comprising all that had an absolute value, the other all that had only a relative value, fitted to the present time. Jesus spoke in order to say what He thought to be true, without the least regard to our categories of absolute and relative. But who then has distinguished in the conception of the kingdom the idea of an inner kingdom which is to have an absolute value, and the idea of a kingdom that is to come whose value is to be held only relative ? Who has found in the Filial consciousness of Christ an element of universal scope, namely, the knowledge of God the Father, and a Jewish element of which the sole advantage was to define Jesus in history, namely, the idea of the Messiah ? From a historical point of view it would be a gratuitous hypothesis to attribute to Jesus a foreknowledge of the modifications His doctrine must endure in the course of centuries after the apostolic age ; but it is far more arbitrary to limit this doctrine, in spite of the gospel, to a single point which is nowhere formally inculcated, and is not the gospel, as though this solitary point represented all that Jesus thought, desired and did.

To say that individuals shall hear the good news of the Divine Mercy and Fatherhood, and decide if they will take sides with God or with the world, is not to give a summary of the gospel, but simply to change its object, seeing that Jesus, as a matter of fact, promised the heavenly kingdom to the repentant sinner, and left it to His hearers to receive or reject this hope. He who wishes to decide historically the thoughts of the Saviour has not first to discover what can suit the mind of the man of to-day, or what can be held to be unchanged, but must take the texts and interpret them according to their natural meaning and the guarantees of authenticity they present. Further, it misleads the reader to give the impression that the idea of God the Father is entirely identical for the modern theologian and for the compilers of the gospel and that nothing in the teaching of Jesus can have been truthfully reported, except that which has not changed its meaning. Seeing that from the beginning all the mass of Christian conceptions have been constantly changing, it is neither possible nor is it true that this one idea of God the Father should have stood unshaken and should be the absolute kernel of the gospel teaching. Every development of the idea of God has exercised and will exercise an influence on the way of representing His Fatherhood.

There is nothing gained by employing traditional formulas, "the Way which leads to the Father, the Judge established by the Father,"[1] if they are emptied of their meaning. If it is desired to prove that Jesus is the Way, because He brings the knowledge of God to men and helps them to find the Father, it must be said that this is not the characteristic feature of the Saviour's mission, which may have been a mission of teaching in its outlook on the present, but was a different thing in its outlook on the future, and at bottom, in its logical and Providential unity, was that of the Introducer and Chief of the kingdom. Again, if the part played by Christ as Judge is understood in the sense that His preaching is the "critical sign" of His office because it "gives happiness and judges at the same time,"[2] then that which in the gospel is a concrete and objective hope is turned into a purely moral and abstract conception. It may be well to say that Jesus was "the personal realization of the gospel,"[3] but if by that saying

[1] Page 91.   [2] Page 92.   [3] Page 91.

it **is** understood that Jesus realized the perfect knowledge of the good God, then is His mission arbitrarily defined, and there is no exit from the same circle of systematic theology. There seems to be a desire to limit, at any cost, the office of Christ, which is universal in action as well as in thought, and is both objective and eschatological, to the measure of an individual initiative for the communication of a truth perceived in the soul, and producing all its beneficial effect to-day.

It is perfectly true that the gospel contains no theoretical doctrine, but it is impossible to say that its only dogma is the truth of God the Father.[1] Many other things are taught in the gospel as explicitly and as surely as the Fatherhood of God, and first of all is taught the reality of the kingdom that is to come, the certainty of the gospel message concerning it, and the mission of Him who announces it. Faith in the goodness of God is not conceived apart from faith in His promise, in the kingdom, and in Christ, the maker of the kingdom. The question of Christology is in no way to be confounded with the question of faith in Christ. If Jesus did not teach the Christological doctrine, it does not follow that His

[1] Page 92.

preaching and the faith it inspired had no relation to faith in Himself. As He did not call Himself the Messiah, and only announced the kingdom that was to come, Jesus asked no other faith in His mission than faith in His message, the promise of the kingdom; but it was none the less certain that, at the fulfilment of the great event, all the elect would salute the Saviour with the salutation of the Messiah. "Blessed is He that cometh in the name of the Lord."[1]

The entire gospel is bound up with a conception of the world and of history that is no longer ours, but it is the whole gospel and not only its imagined essence, which is not "inseparably"[2] bound. The proof of this assertion is to be sought in the facts, not in abstract possibility: since the gospel has little by little detached itself from its original form, it is permissible to assert that the form was temporary, and that the gospel is not inseparably connected with the conceptions of which the form bore the trace. For the rest, it cannot be said that faith in God the Father, any more than hope in the reign of justice, is "without an epoch, like man."[3] Man is not without an epoch, he is of all epochs, and changes with them. The gospel was not addressed to

[1] Cf. Matt. xxiii. 39.   [2] Page 94.   [3] Page 94.

abstract man, without an epoch, unchangeable, who never existed save in the mind of theorizers, but to real men who followed one another in time, and to them it could not fail to accommodate itself. The saying of the goodness of God, Who provides for men as He provides for sparrows, is no more susceptible to-day of a literal interpretation than the saying which promised to the generation contemporary with Jesus the spectacle of the great coming of the kingdom. Is it even so easy to-day to represent God pardoning the sinner in the way of the Father who welcomed the Prodigal Son? Have we not, for all our similar spirit of confidence, a somewhat different conception of Providence, Its mode of action and Its goodness?

It is a pitiful philosophy that attempts to fix the absolute in any scrap of human activity, intellectual or moral. The full life of the gospel is not in a solitary element of the doctrine of Jesus, but in the totality of its manifestation, which starts from the personal ministry of Christ, and its development in the history of Christianity. All that has entered into the gospel of Jesus has entered into Christian tradition. The truly evangelical part of Christianity to-day, is not that which has never changed, for, in a sense, all has changed and has never ceased to change, but that which in spite of all external changes proceeds from the impulse given by Christ, and is inspired by His Spirit, serves the same ideal and the same hope.

CHAPTER III

If the essence of the gospel and of the consciousness of Divine Sonship is set in the knowledge
of God the Father, the idea of the kingdom and
the consciousness Jesus had of Himself as the
Messiah, appear not only as accessories of purely
relative value, but as sheer illusions, a debt, as
it were, paid by the Saviour to the prejudices of
His time. Understood in this way, the personal
work of Christ appears as a fine transport of un-
reflecting enthusiasm, prevented from falling into
fanaticism by an element of pure religion, but not
losing thereby any of its chimerical character.

It is vain for Herr Harnack to begin by setting
Jesus above Socrates.[1] If the hope that centred
in the Messiah was inconsistent and false, then the
philosopher, dying in the cause of Reason, was wiser
than Christ, dying in the cause of Faith. For he
simply accepted his destiny without promising
himself in the future a compensation which he

[1] Page 1.

would have failed to realize.   It is in this way that theological rationalism, instead of explaining the gospel, comes to mutilate it, and under the pretext of safeguarding the grandeur of Jesus, lowers Him beneath, not only Socrates, but every man endowed with common sense.   The gospel and the Christ are, as it were, separated into two elements : a moral sentiment that is gladly hailed as admirable, and a dream that one dare not call ridiculous.   With a more penetrating criticism and a wider philosophy, these two elements would be found in no way heterogeneous ; it would be found that, if tradition has never separated them, it is because they are inseparable, and that the religion of the heart and the hope of the kingdom are not respectively the reality and the fantasy of Christianity, but together make up the religion of Jesus.

According to the logic of Faith, if the idea of the kingdom is real, the gospel is Divine, and God Himself is revealed in Jesus.   According to the logic of Reason, if the idea of the kingdom is inconsistent with fact, the gospel as a Divine revelation falls to the ground, Jesus is no more than a pious man, who could not separate His piety from His dreams, and died the victim of error rather than the servant of the truth that was in Him.

For Jesus suffered on the cross because He avowed Himself, and believed Himself to be, the Messiah; not because He knew the goodness of the Heavenly Father, nor because He wished to demonstrate it by His death. He died because such was the will of the Father, and because His death seemed to Him the providential condition of the definite fulfilment of the kingdom He had preached. He applied to Himself the lesson He gave to His disciples—"He that saveth his life in this world shall lose it for eternity; whosoever shall lose his life for My sake and the Gospel, the same shall save it for the kingdom of Heaven."[1] On the eve of the Passion, He presented to His disciples the bread and the wine of the Eucharist, as a symbol of the death He was about to endure, and at the same time as a pledge of the Communion which should reunite His disciples and Himself in the kingdom that was to be. He therefore died as the Messiah, filled with the idea of this kingdom, whose fulfilment He thought to ensure, the kingdom where He trusted to live again in the full glory of the Messiah. Such is the Christ of history, and the true measure of His greatness is to be sought in nothing but in what He believed and desired to be.

[1] Cf. Mark viii. 35.

Jesus, on the earth, was the great representative of faith. Now, the religious faith of humanity always has been and always will be supported by symbols more or less imperfect: its aspirations, which have infinity as their object, can only become definite in human thought in a finite form. The concrete symbol, the living image, not the pure idea, is the normal expression of faith, and the condition of its moral efficacy in man and in the world. The choice and the quality of the symbols are necessarily related to the stage of evolution of faith and of religion. The conceptions of the kingdom and of the Messiah are not merely the features that made it possible for Christianity to come forward beside Judaism, they are the necessary form in which Christianity had to be born in Judaism before spreading out into the world.

Nothing could make Jesus other than a Jew. He was only man under condition of belonging to one branch of humanity. In that in which he was born, the branch that may well be said to have carried in it the religious future of the world, this future was known in quite a precise manner, by the hope of the reign of God, by the symbol of the Messiah. He who was to be the Saviour of the world could only enter on his office by assuming the position of Messiah, and by presenting Himself as the founder of the kingdom come to accomplish the hope of Israel. The Gospel, appearing in Judæa and unable to appear elsewhere, was bound to be conditioned by Judaism. Its Jewish exterior is the human body, whose Divine Soul is the spirit of Jesus. But take away the body, and the soul will vanish in the air like the lightest breath. Without the idea of the Messiah, the gospel would have been but a metaphysical possibility, an invisible, intangible essence, even unintelligible, for want of a definition appropriate to the means of knowledge, not a living and conquering reality. The gospel will always need a body to be human. Having become the hope of Christian people, it has corrected in the interpretation certain parts of its Israelitish symbolism. None the less, it remains the shadowy representation of the great mystery, God and the providential destiny of man and of humanity, because it is a representation always striving after perfection, inadequate and insufficient.

This is the mystery that Jesus revealed, as far as it could be revealed, and under the conditions which made revelation possible. It may be said that Christ lived it as much as He made it manifest. If He had only had in view the propagation of a doctrine, the organization of an

earthly society, or even the foundation of a particular religion, Christ must have been judged not
only less wise than Socrates, but much less able
than Mahomet. He sought no such object, and
it was for no deceiving dream that he turned aside
from it. His dream was His project, the realization of perfect happiness in perfect justice, of immortality in holiness. This realization was already
complete in Him, by His union with God, His
faith in the Heavenly Father, the inner certainty
of the eternal future guaranteed to humanity in
His person and by His agency. The historian, as
such, cannot appreciate the objective value of this
persuasion: the Christian will not doubt it, and,
beyond any question, no one is Christian who does
not admit it.

It may appear to some minds, in which the
habits of abstraction and of reasoning have over-
grown the sense of vital things, that the hope of
the kingdom was too common, too imaginative, too
little in accord with actual occurrence, to be
worthy of the Saviour. Have we not already
seen learned Catholics insinuate, if not openly
profess, that the earliest Christians may have lent
their Divine Master their own apocalyptic illusion,
as though the Parousia, the advent of Christ in
glory, were not the essential element of belief

in the Messiah, and as if the appearance as Messiah were not the only historical definition of the position of Jesus? It would be impossible to show a more paltry appreciation of a fact that presents itself to the historian as the greatest manifestation of faith ever displayed on the earth.

Jesus died confident in the future of His work and in His own approaching triumph. His confidence came, not from an effort to conceal His present failure, or to overcome the terrors of death, but from the same feeling that rendered Him unable to suppose that the Divine life in Him could vanish with His last breath, or that the kingdom could fall with Him or He Himself be lost to the kingdom. No! the Messiah would live and the kingdom would come. It is because of preconceptions foreign to healthy philosophy, and to knowledge of men and of history, that men search in the gospel and in the thoughts of Christ for the abstract definition they judge the best to characterize Himself or His mission, or that they are scandalized not to find in His discourses the exact prevision of the future reserved for Christianity. Jesus has not considered or represented its future under the aspects which, according to the law of humanity, only accompany a knowledge of the past. As far as the critic can judge from the clearest and most authenticated documents of gospel history, Christ contemplated and announced the future in terms of the only kinds of belief suitable for such a purpose; He saw it and described it under the traditional symbol of Israelitish hope that He had taken possession of; it appeared to Him like a ray of light, as a single infinitely comprehensive conception, the complete and final advent of the reign of God. From a really logical point of view, no symbol can be conceived, better adapted to the conditions of His ministry and the success of His message. The idea of the kingdom of the Messiah was the sole living form, in which he could conceive, could represent to others, and make sure to Himself, the future of faithful humanity, taking root in the present.

In the gospel, then, the hope of the kingdom was a simple idea, or rather, bearing in mind the faith that it inspired, a simple reality. To the Christian historian it now appears as the concrete, rudimentary, indistinct symbol of subsequent events; namely, faith in the resurrection of Christ, in His invisible and constant presence among His own people, in His Eternal Glory; the indefinite progress of the Gospel in the world; the regeneration of human kind by

Christianity, and the anticipation of the kingdom of Heaven in the Church. From the point of view of faith, it was the certain presentiment of what is seen to-day and also of what is not seen, since the aspect presented by the reign of God, contemplated as eternal, the way in which, behind the curtain of this world, the accounts of the Divine justice and the Divine goodness are regulated, escape our experience. Let it never be said that Jesus only expected the reward of His hope, and that its fulness was never awarded to Him! For the faith, He is King and God to all eternity. As far as we can penetrate the economy of things in this world, Jesus lives in humanity to an extent and in a way never experienced by any other human being. He, the Divine Liberator, has proceeded to God by the path of sorrow and death, sure that He was not deceived, whatever were the conditions it pleased the Father to assign to the accomplishment of the work for which His earthly life was sacrificed. If His hope has only been actually realized before the eyes of faith, the philosophical historian will not hesitate to find even that an astonishingly true fulfilment, when he notes the results the hope has achieved and its inexhaustible fruitfulness.

CHAPTER IV

THE place occupied in the teaching of Saint Paul by the death and resurrection of Christ is well known: they constitute for the apostle a veritable Gospel of Salvation, because they have brought the kingdom of God, by obtaining for Jesus the glory of the Messiah, and through Jesus for them that believe, the spirit of God in the Communion with the glorified Christ. Herr Harnack writes:[1] "We may take it as certain that the Apostle Paul was not the first to seize upon the ideas of the death and of the resurrection of Christ, but that he ranked himself with the early community in attaching supreme value to both." There may be something equivocal in this statement. The early community knew full well that Christ had died on the cross, and they believed, before Paul, that he had risen from the dead; but this death and resurrection might well give rise to different conceptions that must not

[1] Page 97.

be attributed without distinction to the early believers or to Jesus Himself and to the Apostle of the Gentiles. The passage from the Epistle to the Corinthians,[1] " For I delivered unto you that which I also received, how that Christ died for our sins[2] . . . and that He rose again the third day "—by no means makes it certain that the idea of the Atonement by death existed from the beginning with the distinctness that the teaching of Paul conferred on it, or that it contributed to lay the foundations of Christology to the same extent as the idea of the resurrection.

As far as can be determined from witnesses who have all come more or less under the influence of the Pauline theology, it was the resurrection alone that made Jesus the Christ and established Him on His throne of glory; the death was only the Providential condition of the resurrection, willed by God and accepted by Jesus. Too much insistence must not be laid on the fact that the death of Christ put an end to blood sacrifices,[3] for the idea of an atoning death did not contribute alone or principally to this result. The Jews

[1] 1 Cor. xv. 3, 4.

[2] St. Paul says "according to the Scriptures," a fact showing that the historical character of the tradition he alludes to must not be exaggerated.

[3] Page 99.

only offered up sacrifices at Jerusalem, and the
disciples of the gospel would not have dreamed
of sacrificing elsewhere; their separation from the
Jews and the destruction of the Temple have
had a sequel for them that has also affected the
Israelites. It may be thought that the moral
idea underlying sacrifice ought finally to eliminate
the reality; but the logic of facts brought about
the consummation rather than the logic of ideas,
and it is not strictly true to say that the moral
idea replaced the reality. Also it is playing a
little on the double sense of the word " sacrifice "
to speak in this connection of the law which
demands that progress shall be bought for
humanity by the suffering and often by the death
of those who contribute to advancement most
effectively.[1] Between the man who dies, the victim
of his destiny, or rather of the resistance opposed
by the force of inertia to the force of progress,
and the lamb, the goat, or even the human being
immolated to a Divinity to win His favour, there
is only the analogy that explains the use of the
same word, but should not be able to deceive the
historian.

As for the idea, that as evil and sin require
punishment, there is in the suffering of the just

[1] Page 100.

a purifying expiation, it comes as an intermediary between the material notion of sacrifice and the purely spiritual conception, related to the first by the idea of expiatory satisfaction and to the second by the moral element it contains ; it is a symbolic conception which should not be forcibly translated into the expression of an absolute indestructible truth, vivid in the conscience of mankind in this particular form. This mixed conception is to be found in Isaiah ; there is no other proof that it belongs to the teaching of Jesus, and to the faith of the first community. The passage in Mark,[1] where it is said that Christ came "to give His life a ransom for many," was in all probability influenced by the theology of Paul, and as much may be said of the narratives of the Last Supper.

According to the early text of St. Luke,[2] Jesus presents the cup and the bread to His disciples, in view of His imminent death, and His future reunion with His own in the kingdom of God, but without bringing out the expiatory character and redeeming intention of His death.

---

[1] Mark x. 45.

[2] Luke xxii. 18, 19, to the words "This is my body." The rest of 19 and 20 have been taken from 1 Cor. (xi. 24, 25), and seem to be an addition to the narrative.

The narrative of Mark seems founded on a
statement very like that of Luke, and all that
is said of the "blood of the new testament"
must have been added after the teaching of
Paul; "And He took the cup, and when He
had given thanks, He gave it to them: and
they all drank of it. And He said unto them,
*This is My blood of the new testament, which is
shed for many.* Verily I say unto you, I will
drink no more of the fruit of the vine, until that
day that I drink it new in the kingdom of God." [1]
The time to say "This is my blood," was not after
the disciples had drunk, as Matthew saw, for he
associates these words with the presentation of
the cup.[2]   But the compiler of the second Gospel
did not wish to upset the arrangement of the early
narrative, and contented himself with associating
with the words said after the passing of the cup
those that, according to St. Paul,[3] were spoken
before.

The earliest believers corrected the brutal fact of
the death by the glory of the resurrection.   Paul
discovered in the death a meaning and an efficacy
able to act independently of the resurrection,
though co-ordinated with it.   But if Jesus was

[1] Mark xiv. 23–25.   [2] Matt. xxvi. 28, 29.
[3] 1 Cor xi. 25.

proclaimed Christ and Lord by the first disciples, it was not because of His death, but because of His resurrection, which displayed Him in the glory of the Messiah.

It must be granted to Herr Harnack[1] that the "message of Easter" and "the faith of Easter" are distinct things, although it is not easy to follow him in finding the distinction in the Gospels. The message of Easter (that is to say, the discovery of the empty tomb and the appearances of Jesus to His disciples, so far as these facts are taken for physical proofs of the resurrection) is not an irrefutable argument from which the historian can conclude with entire certainty that the Saviour rose in the body from the dead. The case is not one that can supply complete proof. Christ risen from the dead does not belong to the order of the present life, which is that of sensible experience, and consequently the resurrection is not a fact that can have been directly and formally established. The cure of the sick can be verified; even the return of a dead man to natural life would be susceptible of proof were it to occur; but the entry of a dead man into immortal life escapes our powers of observation. The empty tomb is only an indirect

[1] Page 101.

argument and not decisive, since the only established fact, the disappearance of the body, can be
explained in other ways than by the resurrection.
The appearances are a direct argument, but one
uncertain in its significance. Before any examination of the narratives, it is a natural thought
that sensory impressions are not an adequate
testimony to a purely supernatural reality. Jesus
after His resurrection appeared and disappeared in
the manner of a spirit; during the time of His
appearance, He was visible, palpable, and could
be regarded as a man in a normal state. Can this
mixture of qualities inspire entire confidence in
the historian who approaches the question without
previous faith? Obviously not. The historian
will reserve his conviction, because the objective
reality of the appearances is not defined for him
with sufficient precision. The critical examination of the narratives will confirm him in his
doubt, because it will be impossible for him to
reconstitute with sufficient certainty, according to
the Gospels and Saint Paul, the series of apparitions, in sequence, with the circumstances under
which they occurred. The fact of some appearances will seem to him incontestable, but he will
be unable to decide their nature and extent with
precision. Looked at independently of the belief

of the apostles, the witness of the New Testament only supplies a limited probability, hardly proportionate to the extraordinary importance of the fact attested. But is it not inevitable that every natural proof of a supernatural occurrence should be incomplete and defective ?

The faith of the apostles is not the message of Easter; it comes direct from the ever-living Christ, and hails Him as such. Compared with this faith, the imaginative representation or theoretical conception of the resurrection, and the character of the appearances, are secondary matters. However, the faith is not independent of the message. Whatever criticism may think of the difficulties and divergences that the narratives present concerning the Saviour's resurrection, it is beyond question that the faith of the apostles was stimulated by the apparitions that followed the death of Jesus, and that the apostles, even St. Paul, had no conception of an immortality distinct from bodily resurrection. The message of Easter and the faith of Easter have for them the same object and the same significance. " The history of Thomas is related solely to show that he ought to have had the faith of Easter, even without the message ; " [1] but in this narrative the

[1] *Loc. cit.*

object of the message constitutes precisely the faith; he ought to have believed that Christ was risen, in the sense of the message, without having seen the apparition. The same thing applies to the disciples at Emmaus; "they were blamed in that faith in the resurrection was wanting, although they had not yet received the message of Easter;"[1] but it is simply left to be understood, that if they had been apprehensive, the Scriptures would have taught them what the message announced, namely, that the Christ must rise from the dead on the third day after His death.

The distinction between the message and the faith can then be founded on fact, without being founded on the gospel. A fundamental element in the faith, namely, the belief in the living Christ, which is the substance of the faith, can be distinguished from its form, which resembles the object of the message. There is no space here to discuss whether or no the form is essential to the preservation of the essence. Herr Harnack desires to keep the essence and not the form, the faith without its proof, which he judges obsolete. Perhaps he is mistaken in taking for a mere proof that which in the apostolic writings is above all an expression of faith.

[1] *Loc. cit.*

Understood in this way the Easter message remains the main testimony of the faith, and the distinction between the faith and the message has only a theoretical significance of no great importance in religion. It is a mistake to oppose the faith, as an absolute thing, to the message and call the message relative: the faith has lived, and still lives, in the message, which is even its reality, in so far as it is an attempt to communicate the faith.

There is some exaggeration in dismissing Plato, the religion of the Persians, and the beliefs of Judaism after the exile, as though they had in no way aided in creating the certainty of eternal life, and as though this certainty came once and for all from faith in the resurrection of Christ.[1] The religious evolution of Judaism, in the time that immediately preceded the Christian era, contributed not a little to prepare the soil in which such a belief could take root. Jesus Himself found among the Jews a belief in the resurrection of the dead, and He spoke conformably to this belief. The idea of His personal resurrection presupposes the acceptance of the idea of a general resurrection. It cannot be questioned that faith in the resurrection of Christ gave a decisive

[1] Page 102.

impulse to later belief; but it is not for the historian to contest the relation of this faith to the belief that preceded it.

Nor can it be truly said that to-day faith in the eternally living Christ is the sole support of belief in immortality. It is one thing to say that humanity never gained this faith from philosophic speculations, and quite another to say that it derives it solely from the life and death of Christ, for ever one with God. The impression of the life and death of Jesus would be nothing on a humanity that had not in it the desire, more or less conscious, of all that Jesus brings to it, and did not already await what He promises. It is too easy to assert that the disciples, having conversed with the Saviour, knew well how intense a life He inspired, and therefore could be but temporarily shaken by His death. Even admitting this hypothesis, men who had not been familiarized with the idea of eternal life, as it was presented in the doctrine of the kingdom of Heaven, would have been ill prepared to believe that their Master had risen from the dead. Add that the moral vitality that radiated from Jesus and immortality are two quite distinct forms of life, however intertwined, and that the fishermen of Galilee would have had some difficulty in

deducing the one from the other, had they come
to the question quite unaided.

In this absolute thesis of Herr Harnack as in
his conception of the kingdom of Heaven, his
tendency is evident, to concentrate religion into a
single point where the realization of the perfect is
to be seen: this solitary point in this case would
be the eternal life acquired now by union with
the good God.   Jesus is to be regarded as the
sole herald of this unique revelation, which
remains unchangeable in this pure form, with
nothing before it to prepare the way, and itself
unchanged through the centuries that follow.   In
place of the supernatural, which he abandons
instead of explaining the idea at the back of it,
the learned theologian introduces something
equally inconsistent, a kind of revelation, human
and absolute, sudden and unchangeable, which is
held to have been produced in the consciousness
of Jesus, but is unknown to the gospel.

It is not in this way that Christianity made
its entry into the world.   If it was not (and it
was far from being) the chance product of a combination of heterogeneous beliefs, from Chaldea,
Egypt, India, Persia, and Greece : if it was born
of the incomparable word and action of Jesus, it
is none the less true that Jesus gathered up and

vivified the best of the religious wealth amassed by Israel before Him, and that He transmitted this wealth not as a simple deposit that the faithful of all time had but to guard, but as a living faith in the form of a collection of beliefs, which had to live and grow after Him, even as they had grown and lived before, by the preponderating influence of the spirit that animated them. By isolating Him in history, Herr Harnack makes his Christ no greater, but only less intelligible and less real.[1]

[1] Cf. E. Caird, *art. cit.*, p. 6.

SECTION IV

THE CHURCH

INTRODUCTION

ONCE the essence of Christianity has been restricted to faith in God the Father, almost everything that constitutes or has constituted historical Christianity becomes necessarily secondary, or adventitious, contrary, and foreign to this pure essence. The whole development of the Church, hierarchic, dogmatic, and ritual, is thus placed outside true Christianity and presented as a progressive abasement of religion. It is the Protestant and anticatholic idea pushed to its extreme limit. But if the foundation of this system of belief, the determination of the essence of Christianity, has been fixed in despite of history, it is possible that the edifice it supports is no more solid than the foundation, and that the consideration of Christian development justifies the same criticism as the consideration of the Gospel. For the historian, everything by which the gospel continues to live is Christian, and the criterion for judging of this quality cannot be an abstract essence, defined to suit the principles of a particular theology rather than to harmonize with the facts.

CHAPTER I

THE society imagined by Christ, says Herr Harnack, was something invisible and heavenly, because it concerned the inner life of man. Evangelical Christianity was as a soul without a body.[1] When He had broken with Judaism, He was forced to create forms of life and a social organization first of all : hence preoccupation with external things occupies a place beside preoccupation with the only essential : and once the purely inner sphere is left, there is no progress that has not reverses, and does not bring inconveniences.[2]

Towards the year 200 A.D. Christianity had definitely evolved towards Catholicism. A great ecclesiastical society had been established, rejecting many sects that also called themselves Christian: it was made up of different Churches scattered through the Roman Empire, which, though mutually independent, maintained constant and regular

[1] Page 113.   [2] Page 114.

relations, were organized in the same way, and professed a common doctrine, wherein rules of discipline were distinguished from rules of faith. Each Church regarded itself as the instrument of a worship which had its solemn rites, and whose principal acts could only be accomplished by priests. We are told that this means that formalism is introduced with fatal result into religions that endure, as soon as the fervour of enthusiasm that gave them birth is passed : it is in this way that " The struggle against Gnosticism compelled the Church to formulate its doctrine, its worship, and its discipline in fixed forms and with fixed laws, and to exclude whomsoever did not submit." [1] Alas for liberty ! The primitive life had vanished, " mediocrity laid the foundation of authority." [2] Nevertheless it can be seen by Acts of the martyrs, the writings of Clement of Alexandria and of Tertullian, that the Church " had not stifled the gospel." [3]

The Church, Eastern as well as Western, organized itself as a juridical institution and as a political administration. In the East, the hierarchic development only ended with the establishment of national Churches, largely dependent on the civil power. Matters went very

[1] Page 119.   [2] Page 130.   [3] Page 135.

differently in the West, where the Empire had crumbled away by the fifth century. Our critic declares, in a description wherein he seems a little carried away by his own eloquence, that "in an underhand way the Roman Church substituted itself for the Roman Empire, which in reality survived in her ; the Roman Empire did not perish, it was only transformed. . . . The Roman Church still governs the nations : its Popes reign as did Trajan or Marcus Aurelius. Peter and Paul take the place of Romulus and Remus ; archbishops and bishops replace proconsuls ; instead of legions come troops of priests and monks ; instead of the Pretorian Guard, the Jesuits. Even into minute details, peculiarities of law, even details of clothing, the influence of the ancient Empire and its institutions can be traced. It is not in the least a Church like the Gospel Communities, or like the national Churches of the East ; it is a political creation, as considerable as a universal empire because it is the successor of the Roman Imperium. The Pope, who is called 'king' and 'supreme pontiff,' is the successor of Cæsar. . . . He governs an empire. Therefore it is a useless enterprise to attack him with the weapons of doctrinal warfare only. . . . For this Church, to govern is as important as to announce the Gospel. . . .

He is held to have no piety who does not, first
of all, submit to this Papal Church, gain her
approval, and live in perpetual dependence on
her. . . . The development the Church has followed as a terrestrial State was bound to lead
logically to the absolute monarchy and infallibility
of the Pope, for infallibility in a terrestrial theo-
cracy signifies nothing more, at bottom, than absolute sovereignty in an ordinary state." [1]

This special character of Latin Catholicism has
had the effect of modifying greatly the features
common to it and to Eastern Catholicism.   Thus,
Herr Harnack observes, the principle of tradition
is proclaimed as loudly by the Roman as by the
Greek Church ; but when it becomes irksome, the
Church passes beyond it ; the Pope becomes
tradition. The same thing happens with orthodoxy ;
" the politics of the Pope can modify it ; by means
of subtle distinctions many a dogma has changed
its meaning ; new dogmas are established ; in
many respects doctrine has become arbitrary."
The tradition of ritual is no more really unchangeable than that of doctrine, and the same may be
said of religious life, the old monastical system
having been transformed to the point of becoming,
in great institutions, " the exact contrary of what it

[1] Pages 157–159.

was. This Church possesses in its organization a unique faculty for adapting itself to the course of history; it remains always the ancient Church, or at least appears to do so, and is always new." [1]

Herr Harnack does not insist on this flexibility of the Roman Church, he seems to see in it a defect rather than a merit, and without doubt he does not estimate sufficiently its importance from the standpoint of the general philosophy of Christianity and of its history. But there is a certain piquancy in meeting a liberal-minded and learned Protestant who is inclined to think the Church of Rome changes too much, and is astonished that She should change so frequently and so easily. How many others have made it a reproach to her, that She does not change enough!

[1] Pages 159, 160.

CHAPTER II

ALTHOUGH the statement has been repeatedly made
for several centuries, it is difficult to understand,
without the preparation of a special theological
education, how the Society of Christ was something
less visible and less external than the Roman
Church. This Society, comprising those who
accepted the gospel of Jesus, was not formed of
pure spirits who had no other bond than a common sentiment. They were not numerous ; but
the fewer their numbers are reckoned at, the more
distinctly they stand out against the surrounding
world. The Society was composed of certain
faithful ones who persevered to the end, and met
again after the Passion to form the nucleus of the
first Christian community. They form a circum-
scribed group, perfectly distinct, a very centralized,
even a hierarchical fraternity. Jesus is the centre
and the chief, the incontestable authority. Around
Him the disciples are not a confused mass ; the
Saviour has distinguished among them the Twelve,

and has associated them, directly and effectively, with His ministry ; even among the Twelve there is one who stands first, not only by priority of conversion or the ardour of his zeal, but by a kind of designation by the Master, accepted by the apostolic community with consequences still evident in their history.

It was a practical situation, apparently brought about by the wanderings of the Galilean ministry, but also evidently received and ratified by Jesus some time before the Passion.   There is no need to look for formal programmes, constitutional charters, pompous inaugurations.   Jesus provided for the diffusion of the gospel in the present, and thus prepared the kingdom to come.   Neither the society round him, nor the kingdom, was an invisible, impalpable reality, a sect of souls, but a society of men which carried the gospel, and was to become the kingdom.

The Church was born and endured through the development of an organization whose outline is traced in the gospel.   It was a community having as its basis a belief in the " good news " of the resurrection of Jesus ; as its law, charity ; as its end, the propagation of the great hope ; as its form of government, the distinction between the apostolic college and the ordinary disciples.   The

Twelve form a kind of directing committee, with Simon Peter at the head. As yet nothing can be seen resembling the administration of a monarchy. The saying of the Saviour, "Whosoever would be first among you shall be the servant of all,"[1] is applied literally. The community knows but one Master, one Lord, who is the Christ, and knows no dominating authority: the hierarchy that exists is that of devotion. Nevertheless, a positive power of social order belongs to the apostles, that of receiving converts into the community, excluding the unworthy, and maintaining good order.

This state of things was the result of all that Jesus did and willed: for the Saviour did not abandon the preaching of the gospel to the first comers, but confided it to those who left all to follow Him. It matters little that this first Christian group had as yet no consciousness that it formed a society distinct from Judaism: its own vital principle, obtained from its faith in Jesus, had already provided it with means of subsistence: its individuality was to grow in the struggle it had to face in order to exist and extend. The apostles were no more restricted to a purely inner sphere of action than was Jesus Himself. Their

[1] Mark x. 44.

activity tended to the formation of a religious society, and it was not only later that the inconveniences of external action became evident. The gospel of Jesus has its reverse side in the absolute character of its formula, which is at once its weakness and the condition of its entry into the world : the gospel of the apostles has its reverse side in the explosion of enthusiasm, which is an element of its force, and a disconcerting phenomenon for those who do not yet believe. Nevertheless it is always the living gospel, not spirit merely, but body also from the beginning.

Christian communities were founded among the Gentiles, and soon became the Church, entirely distinct and even separated from the Synagogue. In these communities the apostles and early missionaries established colleges of elders, or superintendents, to govern the societies as they themselves had governed the first community at Jerusalem. The organization of the body of elders, the affirmation of their rights, the pre-eminence of the bishop in the body and in the community, the pre-eminence of the bishop of Rome amongst the bishops, these changes are only defined and established in the course of time, according to the needs of the evangelical work. The Church became, at important moments, what

it had to become in order not to decline and
perish, dragging the gospel down with it. Nevertheless, it created no essential portion of its constitution. An organ which up to one moment
seemed rudimentary, and of little vigour, took on
the proportions and structure that an imminent
necessity demanded : then it existed in this
acquired form, except for accessory modifications
produced on the occasion of other developments
to preserve the equilibrium of the whole. This
equilibrium was seldom established without internal movement, having all the characters of a
serious crisis. Such, as a matter of fact, is the
law of all development, and the natural growth of
living things knows similar experiences. These
struggles do not prove a diminution of life, but
that life is threatened : when the crisis is over, and
the power of the organism is augmented, it is to
be praised for its vitality, not blamed because it
suffered or because it did not succumb. The
Church can fairly say that, in order to be at all
times what Jesus desired the society of His
friends to be, it had to become what it has
become : for it has become what it had to be to
save the gospel by saving itself.

The earliest communities could not have
lasted without the rudimentary organization their

founders gave them. The college of elders maintained order in the assemblies, and peace among
the brethren, ensured the management of alms,
and of all external relations. Just as the disciples
of Jesus had formed a society, and as the kingdom
of Heaven was conceived as a society, not as a
coalition of fervent and perfect individualists, the
Christian communities naturally formed societies,
confraternities : they needed the preservative
element of all society—authority. When there
appeared in the Churches (and they appeared
quite early) movement of ideas, tendencies more
or less marked and more or less divergent, internal and external difficulties more or less considerable, the necessity of a directing power
became still more pressing, and the only hope for
the community to hold its ground was by means
of a perfect unity. It is certain that Christianity
and the gospel would have gone under in the
gnostic crisis, without the opposition that the
ruling episcopate made to the flood of heresies,
and the episcopate strengthened its position
decidedly in this struggle. Does it not follow
that the Church is as necessary to the gospel as
the gospel to the Church, and that the two are
really one, as the gospel and the group of
believers were one during the ministry of Jesus ?

Surely there is nothing but a spirit of epigram
in the reflection on " the mediocrity " that " founded
authority." Were the Christians of Lyons in the
time of Irenæus, or those of Africa in the time of
Tertullian, so much inferior to the believers of
Corinth as we know them in the Epistles of Paul ?
Does the diminution of the early acts of grace
prove that real faith was any less strong, and is it
a matter of regret that the whole Church was not
given over to Montanism ? Even in matters of
religion, attacks of fever are not the normal
conditions of life.

In proportion as the episcopate increased, the
preponderance of the Church of Rome became
evident. Herr Harnack has himself shown this
point very well in his " History of Dogma." [1]
This Church played a considerable part in the
combat with gnosticism ; the principal leaders of
the gnostics came to Rome as to the central point
of Christendom, where it was most important to
have their doctrines approved, and there they
were condemned in succession. But it is not
only thus that the Roman community appears in
its dignity as principal Church. Each particular
Church had the sentiment of the general unity,
and even anxiety for it : it held itself within this

[1] I. 439–454.

unity while superintending the maintenance of
the standard by the others around it. But a
central body was needed to give some kind of
support to the force of the universal tendency, and
to safeguard the concerted action of the Churches,
by making its results visible and regular. This
central point and capital of ecclesiastical unity
was indicated at once by the grandest Christian
memories, and by the political situation of the
Empire. Incontestably it is owing to its rank as
the capital that Rome owed the attraction that
brought to it the two most important personages
of the Apostolic Church. Peter and Paul both
came to Rome : but whatever may have been the
prestige of Paul, that of the prince of the apostles
remained the greater in traditional recollection.
Their memory was honoured, and their tombs
guarded. Many of the elders who governed the
community towards the end of the first century
had known them, and retained full memory of
their martydom. Fifty years later, when Irenæus
came to Rome, there were certainly still faithful
to be found there who had been disciples of Peter's
and Paul's disciples, and a list of bishops was
kept, going back to Linus, the first, he who had
taken up the government of the Roman Church
after the death of Peter.

Critics have noted that the bishop of Rome, whose position is so outstanding before the end of the second century, is hardly distinguished from the body of the elders at the end of the first, and that solitary episcopal rule was constituted later in the West than in the East. The very importance of the community, which must early have been divided into several groups, aided to maintain for long the pre-eminence of the council of Presbyters, which indeed always retained at Rome a greater effective authority, under the bishop, than it seems to have had in other Churches. No doubt all the same there was from the beginning at Rome, as elsewhere, a kind of president in the body of elders, who soon became the sole bishop. The Epistle of St. Clement to the Corinthians is written in the name of the Roman Church, and the personality of the writer does not appear : nevertheless, the letter was received and kept as an Epistle of Clement, who was the responsible author and the official mouthpiece of the community. This very Epistle makes it evident that the Roman Church interested itself in the internal life of far-off Christian communities, and believed itself to have the right to intervene in their affairs with authority. Paul would not have spoken to the disunited

Corinthians with more force than Clement, although it is still from the community as the heir of the apostolic tradition, and not from the personal successor of Peter, that the word comes. This distinction is unimportant, for the sentiment of authority is identical in the case of Clement, who speaks in the name of the Church, whose mouthpiece he is, and in the case of Victor or Callixtus or Stephen, who speak in their own names, as filling the place of the apostle Peter.

It cannot, then, be contested that the central position of Rome both attracted the apostles to it and then enabled its bishop to exercise an influence that no other in another place could have had. The importance of the town contributed to the importance of the see, but it cannot be said to have created it. It is possible to believe that the force of events, acquired experience, the fact that Christianity was penetrating to Rome without them, that the Roman community was increasing, and that an apostolic intervention seemed necessary to achieve its establishment, lest a point that ought to radiate their influence should be left outside of it, that all these considerations together, led the apostles to the capital of the Empire. We may imagine also, that when they died, they little thought they were bequeathing a master to Cæsar, or even that they had given a supreme chief to the Church. The thought of the great Advent was too strong in their minds, the questions of creed and of government too little familiar, for them to see in Rome and the Roman Church anything but the providential centre of Christian evangelization. Their death consecrated what their presence had signified. Nowhere else had the evangelical tradition been more solidly implanted, nowhere else had it found a soil more favourable to its preservation. With full consciousness they made Rome the capital of the gospel. At the same time, all unknowing, they made the Roman Church the mother and queen of the Churches of the whole world; they left the inheritance of the apostles in hands capable of making its value felt.

The ease with which the bishops of Rome established their superiority over the other Christian communities was not a thing entirely unforeseen by the apostles. The head of the Empire, the accepted head of the world, ought to be also, as far as was necessary, the head of universal Christianity. It is not astonishing that this idea was never lost, and that the development of Christianity only gave it added strength as the need arose for new applications of it. A matter still less astonishing is, that the consciousness of this pre-eminence, which was a burden rather than a privilege, should have been especially vivid in the town where it had its place of action, and whence it derived its existence. The necessity of union with the Church of Rome, a union implying a certain subordination in right and in fact, on the part of the other Churches, was as profoundly felt by the Churches of the West, founded by Rome, as the idea, at Rome itself, of a kind of general responsibility for the common welfare.

It was otherwise in the East, where the Churches, not owing their existence to Rome, were less closely attached to her by tradition. It would seem that, as the idea of union with Rome was not implanted in them at their origin, it could never afterwards acquire strength enough to resist political divisions and special tendencies. The transference of the seat of Empire to Constantinople prepared the way for the schism, and it is well established that the Greek Church is, in itself, a political institution, whose principle is in no way traditional.[1] With a more complete autonomy, and with a less vivid sentiment of all that the bishop of Rome owed to the succession

[1] Cf. Duchesne, "Églises Séparées," 163-227.

of Peter, the Eastern Church during the early
centuries had yet gravitated towards Rome; it
would have continued to do so, and would have
come more and more into the orbit of the
Apostolic Church, if the normal development of
ecclesiastical government had not been fettered by
political considerations as soon as the Empire was
converted.   In proportion as the bishops of Rome
acquire a more precise idea of their function as
moderators, and translate it into a positive and
Divine right, the Easterns come to understand the
claim less and less, and finish by no longer com-
prehending it at all: they can see only Rome's
pretensions, and have no feeling of what is
demanded for the maintenance of unity beyond
the divisions of frontiers.   So completely have
they made Christianity a State religion, that once
Rome is lost to the Empire, it seems to them that
the bishop of Rome has nothing to do with their
concerns, and that the bishop of Constantinople,
the new Rome, has the same rights and powers over
the East that the bishop of the old has over the
Western countries that obey him.   At a time when
the Popes recognize no frontiers and ensure, in
the spirit for which Herr Harnack praises them,
the independence of religion before the secular
authority, the patriarchs of Constantinople are

enclosing their Church in the fragments of the Empire, and in the effort to organize their own Papacy are making that of the Emperor. By bringing Christianity back to the proportions of a national worship, they destroyed, as far as they could, that conception of Catholicism that the Roman Church had received as a sacred charge and intended to keep.

If this Church has assumed an imperial air it did not possess in the early days, if She has desired to give juridical, or rather constitutional, form to her pre-eminence and her actions, it is not only in virtue of a local and inherited tradition of dominion, which passed from the Empire to the Church, from Cæsar to the successor of Peter, but as the result of a general tendency, which, from the beginning, inclined the Church to organize herself and her government, a tendency felt in the East as much as in the West. The Church had possessions, discipline, a hierarchy; She could not dispense with legal rights. But legal rights cannot exist without an authority to guarantee them, and this authority, to be efficacious, must have its official representatives. The Popes of the fourth and fifth centuries wished to be, in the last resort, the judges of all Chistendom, as those of the two preceding centuries desired the Roman Church to be the type of all Churches for teaching, organization, and discipline. In both cases the pretension is the same, but applied to different situations. Rome claims no new power, or rather, the power is no newer than the situation it is designed to meet. The Church had to find for herself a government or cease to exist; but government in a Church, one and universal, is inconceivable without a central authority. A central ideal, with no real power, as conceived by St. Cyprian, would have been useless. Some final solution had to be found to important questions. Particular councils could not have had sufficient prestige; general councils could never have been anything but a tribunal for extraordinary occasions, and experience showed that these assemblies had many great inconveniences. The superior and permanent tribunal before which all more important cases should naturally come, by which all conflicts should be finally decided, could be only that Church, the most apostolic of all, holding the tradition of Peter and Paul, whose chiefs did not hesitate to call themselves successors of the prince of the apostles.

To the Churches maintained or established in barbarian lands, and to the nations themselves, the Pope appears not only as the supreme judge of all ecclesiastical causes and controversies. From the end of the eighth century, he acts as the depository of the Imperial tradition, transferring the title of Cæsar to Charlemagne and his successors. Towards the close of the eleventh century, all authority seems vested in him, not only over particular Churches, but also over nations. The Pope has become social instructor, tutor of monarchies, head of the Christian Confederation, while he remains and becomes more and more supreme as the chief of the ecclesiastical hierarchy, the arbiter of the faith, the guardian of discipline, the bishop of all the Churches. His two offices are not distinguished one from the other. Although the first was not conferred upon him as the direct result of a purely religious, evangelical, Catholic principle, it was found to be included in the second by force of circumstances. In the chaos in which the Empire of the West foundered, the Church maintained her structure; she alone survived, and the new kingdoms arose and advanced towards civilization in the bosom of the Church, and under her influence and direction. The Church could not accomplish the work of their conversion without becoming also their instructress in temporal order. She had to be their mistress in every branch of knowledge, and teach them the elements of ancient wisdom side by side with the gospel of salvation; she had even to make herself feared in the temporal realm, that she should not be overwhelmed in the spiritual. The individuality of the growing nations was scarcely beginning to be defined; the memory of the Roman Empire, of Roman unity, rested over them all, idealized in the sentiment of Catholic unity; a kind of great State grew into being, made up of States still unformed, a universal republic, which was a Church, and whose true and only natural leader was the Pope, having under him the temporal sovereigns whether they would or no. In this confusion, where she must dominate or perish, the Church became transformed, and grew in stature continually, grew in order to endure, because the changes which shaped themselves in her were the very conditions of her continued existence.

Had there been any actual autonomy of the individual Churches, Christianity would have been completely submerged in superstition and Germanic feudalism. Reforms became possible as soon as Rome had full power to support them, even though she had not always had the initiative to propose them. The proud temporal position of the Popes of the twelfth and thirteenth centuries was only the safeguard of their independence in the spiritual sphere; and in this sphere, the Popes were per-force what they were and what they became, in order that the Church might be still the Church, and continue to represent Christianity and the religion of Jesus. What would have happened had the Pontiffs suddenly perceived that the essence of Christianity was faith in God the Father, and that their duty consisted in representing this truth to those who might be willing to make their religion out of this alone?

From the fourteenth century onwards, the general conditions of Catholic society were modi-fied. There was no longer in any truth a Christian republic, but Christian States, sufficiently strong in themselves, and never again to be united by a common faith or a common danger in a common course of action, as they had been for the Crusades. In fact, the authority of the Pope was exercised with more and more difficulty in the political sphere; the Church, rich and powerful in every State, was sapped with increasing corruption. A great reform became essential to free it from the world, and return it to its proper path. But at this point Church and State were so in-timately bound together, that the independent organization of religious power and political power could not be accomplished without difficulties, shocks, and forcible separations. Regarding events from this distance of time, after allowing that the Papacy of the fifteenth centuries was much too preoccupied with its own interests, and not enough with the reform that was always more urgent, it is evident that if by force of circumstances, the political influence of the Church steadily decreased, the spiritual power of the Pope as steadily increased, and became that which it had to become if the Catholic Church were to be preserved in the midst of the revolutions and troubles of modern times. The Pope remains the father of the faithful and the head of the Churches. It is easy to perceive that his power will never again be exercised in the forms it assumed in the Middle ages, but this power is of constant importance for the preservation of the Church, and the preservation in the Church of the gospel.

CHAPTER III

THUS to reproach the Catholic Church for the development of her constitution is to reproach her for having chosen to live, and that, moreover, when her life was indispensable for the preservation of the gospel itself. There is nowhere in her history any gap in continuity, or the absolute creation of a new system: every step is a deduction from the preceding, so that we can proceed from the actual constitution of the Papacy to the Evangelical Society around Jesus, different as they are from one another, without meeting any violent revolution to change the government of the Christian community. At the same time every advance is explained by a necessity of fact accompanied by logical necessities, so that the historian cannot say that the total extent of the movement is outside the gospel. The fact is, it proceeds from it and continues it.

Many objections, very grave from the point of view of a certain theology, have little or no significance for the historian. It is certain, for instance, that Jesus did not systematize beforehand the constitution of the Church as that of a government established on earth and destined to endure for a long series of centuries. But a conception far more foreign still to His thoughts and to His authentic teaching is that of an invisible society formed for ever of those who have in their hearts faith in the goodness of God. We have seen that the gospel of Jesus already contained a rudiment of social organization, and that the kingdom also was announced as a society. Jesus foretold the kingdom, and it was the Church that came; she came, enlarging the form of the gospel, which it was impossible to preserve as it was, as soon as the Passion closed the ministry of Jesus. There is no institution on the earth or in history whose status and value may not be questioned if the principle is established that nothing may exist except in its original form. Such a principle is contrary to the law of life, which is movement and a continual effort of adaptation to conditions always new and perpetually changing. Christianity has not escaped this law, and cannot be reproached for submission to it. It could not do otherwise than it has done.

The preservation of its primitive state was

impossible, its restoration now is equally out of the question, because the conditions under which the gospel was produced have disappeared for ever. History shows the evolution of the elements that composed it. These elements have undergone, as they could not fail to undergo, many transformations; but they are always recognizable, and it is easy to see in the Catholic Church what stands to-day for the idea of the Heavenly kingdom, for the idea of the Messiah, the maker of the kingdom, and for the idea of the apostolate, or the preaching of the kingdom, that is to say, the three essential elements of the living gospel, which have become what they were forced to become in order to endure at all. The theory of a purely inner kingdom suppresses them and makes an abstraction of the real gospel. The tradition of the Church keeps them, interpreting them and adapting them to the varying condition of humanity.

It would be absurd to desire that Christ should have determined beforehand the interpretations and adaptations that time would exact, since they had no reason to exist before the hour which rendered them necessary. It was neither possible nor useful for Jesus to reveal to His disciples the future of the Church. The thought that the

Saviour left to them was that they must continue to wish, to prepare, to await and to realize the kingdom of God. The view of the kingdom has been enlarged and modified, the conception of its definite advent fills a smaller place, but the object of the gospel remains the object of the Church.

As a matter of fact, it is worthy of notice that the Church, for all her advanced age, for all her apparent want of anxiety as to the imminence of the final judgment, and for all the long future she anticipates still on the earth, regards herself nevertheless as a provisional institution, a transitional organization. The Church of the world, called the Church militant, is, as it were, the vestibule of the Church triumphant, which is the kingdom of Heaven realized in eternity, still held to be possible in the fulness of time. If the dimensions of the evangelical horizon have changed, the point of view remains the same. The Church has kept the fundamental idea of Christ's teaching : no terrestrial institution realizes the kingdom finally, and the gospel only prepares the way for the accomplishment. It is easy to divine why theologians, like Herr Harnack, abandon evangelical eschatology. But the question at issue is only to know if eschatology was not historically an essential element of the gospel, and if the Church, which has retained this essential element, is not the veritable continuation of Christ. What if the gospel eschatology were at bottom the expressive symbol of complex and indescribable realities; what if the eschatology of the Church be also a symbol, always striving for perfection, of the same expected benefits, the traditional theologian can still support it, and so continue to find the essence of the gospel where Jesus desired to set it. It means that Jesus and the Church have their eyes raised always in the same direction, towards the same symbol of hope, and that the Church maintains the attitude of Jesus, towards the kingdom of Heaven.

In their warfare against tradition, the most enlightened Protestant theologians, those who, like Herr Harnack, recognize a kind of relative necessity in the Catholic development, argue none the less eagerly about it, as though it were not evident that the desire to restore Christianity to its primitive form and organization is really a desire to condemn it to death, and as if change were not the natural condition of its preservation and the expression of its vitality. They are less exacting for themselves, when concerned to justify their own religious convictions, unlikely as they are to be confused with the gospel of Jesus,

What else do they do but adapt the gospel to the needs of their special consciences? The Church also, from the beginning, adapts the gospel to the needs of the men she addresses.

It is not the personal adaptation that continues the ministry of Christ, the preaching of the "good news" and the preparation of the kingdom of Heaven. Even among Protestants, the directing tradition has a considerable influence on the way the Divine word is understood, and without this tradition the effect of the written gospel on the mass of believers would probably be very slight or not always salutary. In all Christian communities there is a service of the gospel which ensures the transmission and application of the Master's word. The Catholic Church is such a service formed by the centuries and continuous from the beginning. To be identical with the religion of Jesus, it has no more need to reproduce exactly the forms of the Galilean gospel, than a man has need to preserve at fifty the proportions, features, and manner of life of the day of his birth, in order to be the same individual. The identity of a man is not ensured by making him return to his cradle.

The Church, to-day, resembles the community of the first disciples neither more nor less than a grown man resembles the child he was at first. The identity of the Church or of the man is not determined by permanent immobility of external forms, but by continuity of existence and consciousness of life through the perpetual transformations which are life's condition and manifestation. Setting aside all theological subtleties, the Catholic Church, as a society founded on the gospel, is identical with the first circle of the disciples of Jesus if she feels herself to be, and is, in the same relations with Jesus as the disciples were, if there is a general correspondence between her actual state and the primitive state, if the actual organism is only the primitive organism developed and decided, and if the elements of the Church to-day are the primitive elements, grown and fortified, adapted to the ever-increasing functions they have to fulfil.

It is the very duration of Christianity that has caused this evolution. If the end of the world had arrived in the years that followed the publication of the Apocalypse, the ecclesiastical development would not have taken place, and the Church even would hardly have existed. But the world did not perish : the Church retained a reason for existence and retains it still. Her history is that of the gospel in the world, and to find that the history is not that of the religion of Christ is only possible if the religion is placed outside history and the actual world.

If the Church were entirely a political institution, such as Herr Harnack conceives and represents her, it is certain that she would have nothing in common with the gospel, and would simply have to be regarded as the successor of the Roman Empire. We have already seen in what sense the Church really succeeded the Empire. The memories and the tradition of the Empire, conditioned, so to speak, the action of the Church, but did not change her essential character. Whatever can be said, it is a long step from Leo XIII. to Trajan, from bishops to pro-consuls, from monks to legionaries, from Jesuits to the Pretorian Guard. The Pope is not king, in so far as he is Pope, and the question is still of the Universal Church, not of the Empire. The Catholics do not regard the Pope as their sovereign, but as their spiritual guide. Although they receive their investiture from the Pope, the bishops are not simple delegates either in law or in fact; if the Pope is the successor of Peter, the bishops are the successors of the apostles, and their ministry is not of a political order nor purely administrative. It is only by way of metaphor that the faithful can be compared to an army. Secular priests and monks do not preach the policy of the Pope, even when he has one; they preach first of all the gospel, with the traditional interpretation the Church gives, and the kingdom they endeavour to extend is that of the gospel, not that of the Pope, so far as that is distinct from the kingdom of Christ. Even the Jesuits, founded to defend the Roman Church against Protestant and antipapal reform, are not political agents, but preachers of religion and religious educators, whatever may be thought of their methods and their special tendencies. The political side of the great institution, Catholicism, is naturally the one that first strikes those who are outside it, but it is wholly external, even accessory. Seen from within, the ecclesiastical organization is essentially of a religious order, and has no other reason for its existence than the preservation and propagation of religion in the world. Although the whole Catholic development, superficially observed, seems to tend solely to augment the authority of the hierarchy, or rather of the Pope, the fundamental principle of Catholicism has never ceased to be the very principle of the gospel. The faithful do not exist for the sake of the hierarchy, but the hierarchy for the sake of the faithful. The Church does not exist for the sake of the Pope, but the Pope for the sake of the Church.

Of course, the Church has put on in many respects the form of a human government, and has become and still remains a political power. None the less, she has always desired, and still desires, quite a different end. The fact that she is of political importance, and that politics must reckon with her, is the inevitable consequence of her existence, and became certain as soon as Christianity had spread sufficiently through the Roman Empire. That she should set herself up as a political power, treating with governments as an equal or as a superior, negotiating religious affairs with them as international treaties are negotiated, is a special and transitory form of her relations with human powers. In this sense the Church has not always been a political power, and may cease to be one. The actual situation now is a legacy of the past, to be dealt with only with precaution. But it is possible to foresee in the future a general comity of civilized nations, wherein the Church, as a spiritual power, in no way political in the present sense, should lose none of her prestige, none of her independence, none of her moral influence. Are not politics falling more and more from the hands of managers of men, into the hands of managers of affairs, and will they not finally remain completely there? What would the Church gain by treating directly with such men of all that regards herself, and what interest would they have to occupy themselves with such matters?

We may even go further, and conjecture that the Church, when dealing with those who recognize her authority, will find a procedure more conformable to the fundamental equality and personal dignity of all Christians. In the universal levelling of ranks which is in prospect, the members of the ecclesiastical hierarchy may be less great personages in the eyes of the world, without in any way losing the rights of their ministry, which will assume again, more visibly, their essential form of duties.

In any case, it is not true that ecclesiastical authority is, or ever was, a species of external constraint repressing all personal activity of conscience. The Church is an educator, rather than a dominating mistress : she instructs rather than directs, and he who obeys her only does so according to his conscience, and in order to obey God. In principle, Catholicism aims, as much as Protestantism, at the formation of religious personalities, souls masters of themselves, pure and free consciences. It is true, the danger for Catholicism is that of desiring too much to govern men instead of simply elevating their souls. It cannot be denied, that its tendency, reacting against Protestantism has been towards the effacement of the individual, towards the careful guardianship of men, towards a control of human activity which by no means makes for the development of initiative. But it is only a tendency. It would be going almost too far to say that there is in the Church a "legion," whose religious and political ideal is that of a society regulated in all matters of thought and action by a kind of military discipline. Yet the main defect of such an ideal is not precisely that it is contrary to the gospel, but that it is dangerous, and impossible to realize.

The gospel of Jesus was neither wholly individualistic in the Protestant sense, nor wholly ecclesiastical in the Catholic sense. It addressed itself to the mass of mankind in order to establish the free society of the elect; is it possible to form an idea of the development of personality or of the form of government in the kingdom of Heaven? It is the life and persistence of the gospel, which have made of it a permanent principle of religious and moral education, and a spiritual society where the principle is put in force. The principle has no hold without the society, nor the society without the principle. Protestantism and Herr Harnack wish to keep only the principle. It is a conception which lacks consistence and reality. Catholicism stands for both principle and society. Historical circumstances have made the social organization seem to compromise the principle more or less, even in some sort to appear to threaten it still. But it is the condition of all that lives in this world to be subject to imperfection. Whatever reservations the historian may make in details as to the way in which the action of the Church is or has been exercised, he cannot deny that Catholicism has been, and is still, the service of the gospel, continued since the days of the apostles.

The power of adaptation recognized in the Roman Church is its best title to the admiration of the impartial observer. It does not follow that the Church alters either the Gospel or tradition, but that she knows how to understand the needs of the time. It cannot be too often repeated that the gospel was not an absolute, abstract doctrine, directly applicable at all times and to all men by its essential virtue. It was a living faith, linked everywhere to the time and the circumstances that witnessed its birth. In order to preserve this faith in the world, a work of adaptation has been, and will be, perpetually necessary. Though the Catholic Church has adapted, and still adapts, the faith, though she adapt herself continually to the needs of new ages, that is no proof that she forgets the gospel or despises her own tradition, but that she wishes to display the value of both, and has confidence that they are flexible and capable of further perfection.

The "reasons of superior order,"[1] which, according to Herr Harnack, caused orthodoxy to be corrected, ancient dogmas to be interpreted, new dogmas to be produced, new practices and devotions to be authorized, are not to be sought in the caprices or calculations of an arbitrary or egoistic despotism. Whatever may have been the external circumstances surrounding any particular fact, all this development proceeds from the innermost life of the Church, and the decisions of authority only sanction, so to speak, or consecrate, the movement that arises from general thought and piety. If it does not please the Catholic Church to bury herself, immovably, in the contemplation of traditional formulas, if she scrutinizes and explains them, it is because she employs activity and intelligence in the faith. If she modifies her discipline and modes of action, it is

[1] Page 155.

because she wishes to act, seeing that she lives. As the Church she has a collective life which, notwithstanding partial failures, is the universal life of the gospel. She is not content to make only Christians, she tends to create a Christian world state. It is easy enough to understand that individualist theologians have no sense of this collective and continuous life of the gospel in the Church, and do not always see it even when they look at it. Its reality is none the less definite, and its variety does not prove that the " essence of Christianity " is, as it were, hidden and stifled there under an accumulation of foreign material, but that this essence dwells in it perpetually in action, under all the forms that display its abundant fruitfulness.

SECTION V

THE CHRISTIAN DOGMA

INTRODUCTION

PAST centuries regarded dogma as the expression and the rampart of the faith. It was believed to be immutable, although men were never weary of perfecting its formulas. Herr Harnack also teaches the immutability of dogma, but he finds but one dogma in the gospel, and the work of Christian thought since St. Paul is thus condemned totally, since its object, in the main, is other than the paternal goodness of God. The time-honoured effort to define the truth of the gospel is therefore to be held entirely vain, foreign even to the gospel it wishes to interpret. It is a fact, that the development of dogma is not in the gospel, and could not be there. But it does not follow that the dogma does not proceed from the gospel, and that the gospel has not lived and lives still in the dogma as well as in the Church. Even the teaching and the appearance of Jesus have had perforce to be interpreted ; the whole question is to know if the commentary **is** homogeneous **with the text or heterogeneous.**

CHAPTER I

EVEN if there is unwillingness to recognize in the gospel the first lineaments of Christology, they must be admitted to be present in St. Paul. The apostle, who rendered the Christian religion the eminent service of detaching it from Judaism, who presented the kingdom of God as a fact accomplished in the Redemption through Christ, who conceived the gospel as the Spirit of the Law, also laid the foundations of Christian dogma. There was, we are told, a latent danger in the conception of an " objective redemption," because of the temptation to separate it from the inner renewal of the soul. Men might be led also to count among the conditions of salvation an exact knowledge of the Saviour and of His work. Did not Paul himself attribute a celestial nature to Christ, and notwithstanding the freedom of his attitude with regard to the Law, did he not retain the Old Testament as a source of truth ? If he formulated no dogma, he set the Church on the slope of dogmatic development.[1]

However, according to Herr Harnack, this development is, properly speaking, Greek, and the direct influence of Greek thought on Christian makes itself felt about the year 130. John, it is true, had written that Jesus was the "Logos," but "he had not made this proposition the basis of all speculation concerning Christ."[2] After him came the learned men who taught that Jesus Christ was the corporeal appearance of the Logos, and this idea replaced the unintelligible notion of the Messiah. "It gave a metaphysical meaning to a historic fact; it introduced into cosmology, and into the philosophy of religion, a personality that had appeared in time and space."[3] This identification brought the Greek thinkers to Christianity. But the gnostic crisis forced the Church to trace the limits of speculation that could be called Christian. There, strictly speaking, begins dogma, and with it the menace it brings for religious liberty. "No one may feel or believe himself a Christian, that is, a child of God, unless he has first submitted his religious experience and knowledge to the control of the ecclesiastical confession. . . . He will never attain

[1] Page 115.　　[2] Page 127.　　[3] Page 128.

his spiritual majority, since he must remain in dependence on dogma, on the priest, on ritual, and on the Book." [1]

On this plane, continues our author, traditionalism, orthodoxy, and intellectualism proceed together. The gospel has become " a great cosmo-theological philosophy, wherein enter all imaginable things." Men are persuaded that " Christianity, being absolute religion, must be able to reply to all questions of metaphysics, cosmology, or history." Two features, however, separate this doctrine from Greek philosophy, namely, the dogma of creation, and especially the Christological dogma. The great factor of this dogma was a special conception of redemption which came into prominence in the third century, namely, that the salvation achieved by Christ consists in the deliverance from death, and at the same time an elevation to the Divine life, a deification of man. To obtain this benefit for humanity, the Redeemer Himself must be God, and become man. This is the reason that Athanasius fought for the consubtantiality of the Word and the Father, as though all Christianity were at stake. For the same reason, the idea of a simple moral union between the divinity and

Page 131.

the humanity of the Saviour could not be accepted. The dogmas of the consubstantial Trinity, and of the God-man, are bound up with this conception of the Redemption and fall with it. For this conception is not Christian, nor moral: it has hardly any connection with the Christ of the Gospel, to whom its formulas do not apply; it leads away from the real Christ, Whose living image it does not keep, but rather presents Him solely in the guise of "hypotheses expressed in theoretical propositions." [1]

Herr Harnack regards the Augustinian doctrine of grace rather from the point of view of piety than that of dogma. "The piety and theology of Augustine formed a special revival of the Pauline experience and doctrines of sin and of grace, of wickedness and justification, of Divine predestination, and of the defect of human liberty." "Down to our own day, in Catholicism, inner living piety and the manner of expressing it have remained essentially Augustinian." How wise is the theologian to note this contrast between the most individual piety and the Church of law and Imperialism! All Catholic reformers have been Augustinians. "It is true that the Church has joined to her dogma of grace, conceived essentially

[1] Pages 142-147.

as Augustine conceived it, a practice of confession which threatens to make the dogma completely valueless. But however wide she makes her boundaries, so as to include all who do not rebel against her, she not only supports those who think with Augustine of sin and of grace, but she desires that every one, as far as possible, should feel as strongly as he did the gravity of sin and the bliss of belonging to God." [1]

Great admirer of Luther as he is, Herr Harnack holds the Protestant Reformation to have been incomplete. In matters of dogma, there are a crowd of problems that Luther did not know, much less was able to solve ; " he was, in consequence, unable to separate *the kernel from the husk*. . . . He not only admits in the gospel the ancient dogmas of the Trinity and the two natures of Christ, . . . he constructed new dogmas ; but, generally speaking, did not know how to draw a clear distinction between dogma and the gospel. . . . The inevitable consequence was, that intellectualism was not destroyed, but formed a new scholastic dogma, considered essential to salvation, so that there remained two classes of Christians, those who understood the doctrine, and those who accepted it from those who understood and thus

[1] Pages 160–163.

continued spiritually minors." In this respect, Protestantism threatens to become an inferior type of Catholicism. Let the Evangelical Churches beware of becoming Catholicized! If they would remain truly evangelical, they must **have no** orthodoxy.[1]

[1] Pages 182–185.

CHAPTER II

CHRISTIAN thought at the commencement was
Jewish, and could not be other than Jewish,
although evangelical Christianity contained the
germ of a universal religion.   The first change,
the most decisive, most important, most rapid
also, perhaps, it ever experienced, was that which
made out of a Jewish movement, founded on
the idea of the reign of the Messiah, a religion
acceptable to the Greco-Roman world and to humanity.   However rapid it was, the change was
effected in successive stages : St. Paul, the Fourth
Gospel, St. Justin, St. Irenæus, Origen, mark the
steps of this progression in the evolution of ideas,
and the adaptation of the faith to the conditions
of intellectual culture in the first centuries of
our era.   The transformation was effected in spite
of the traditional and conservative tendency
inherent in every religion, and manifest from
the beginning in Christianity.   The obligation of
the Mosaic Law was abrogated in spite of the

Judaizers : the theory of the Logos triumphed in spite of the adversaries of the Johannic writings, to whom St. Epiphanes gave the name of Aloges ; the theology of Origen was accepted, with some amendment, by those who contested it. Each step of the doctrine, taken in spite of resistance, is achieved by some sort of accommodation with those that preceded it. The thesis of St. Paul on the law of servitude and the gospel of liberty, the Johannic conception of Christ, entered into the tradition of the teaching Church under condition of adaptation to primitive Christianity. In order to assimilate the greater part of Origen's theology, the Church cut up his system into fragments, and even condemned certain philosophic hypotheses which were not to her liking.

In a sense, it may be said that the Hellenization of Christian doctrine dates from the Apologist Fathers, because they were the first to present Christianity as a philosophy, and because they elaborated the theory of the Logos, which was not enunciated in the Fourth Gospel as a speculation, but as a series of assertions of faith and mystical pictures. This opinion would be inexact if it were held to involve, as Herr Harnack seems to think, the conclusion that the idea of the Logos, or, more exactly, the idea of the Incarnate Word, does not dominate entirely the Fourth Gospel. There is not a single verse of the Gospel of John written independently of this influence. But the conception of the Logos enters, so to speak, into a living faith, enlarges the formula of the faith, and changes its own nature : it ceases to be a purely theoretical conception upon which are founded speculations of the same order, and becomes Christian by serving to define the Christ: it is a vital theology, mystical, not abstract, in no way scholastic, whilst the doctrine of the Fathers develops the cosmological point of view merely indicated in the prologue of John.

The Pauline theory of salvation was indispensable in its time, if Christianity were not to remain a Jewish sect without a future. The theory of the Incarnate Logos was also necessary when the gospel was presented, not only to the proselytes of Judaism in the Empire, but to the whole pagan world, and to every one who had received a Hellenic education. The learned theology of Origen was the synthesis of doctrine, that could make Christianity acceptable to the most cultivated minds. It was the bridge between the new religion and the science of antiquity. The Greek world would never have admitted the necessity of circumcision, nor have become converted to the Messiah of Israel, but it could and did become a convert to the God Who became man, to the Incarnate Word. All the development of Trinitarian and Christological dogma, which, according to Herr Harnack and other critical theologians, has weighed so heavily on all Christian orthodoxies, binding them to an effete doctrine and to the science of Plato and Aristotle, long since passed by modern knowledge, was, in the beginning, a vital manifestation, a great effort of faith and intelligence, which enabled the Church to link her own tradition to the science of the age, to fortify one by the other, and transform both into a learned theology which believed it contained the knowledge of the world and the knowledge of God. Philosophy could become Christian without being obliged to deny itself, and yet Christianity had not ceased to be a religion, the religion of Christ.

This work of Christian thought must not be judged as a scientific achievement. It did not pretend to be, and had it desired to be, it must be confessed its method would have led to failure. It was not erudite research that determined its character and fixed its results, but the instinct of faith in souls otherwise saturated with the Greek spirit. Further, the Hellenization of Christianity was not anticipated by professional philosophers,

like the gnostic doctors, nor desired by skilful
politicians, who would have carefully fostered
every chance of success for the work of conversion, and would have taken pains to remove
from Christianity every sign of its Jewish origin,
that in a Greek guise it might penetrate the
pagan world more easily. The cause of the movement lay deeper, and, so to speak, was more
profoundly necessitated. The development of
Christian dogma was brought about by the state
of mind and culture of the earliest converts,
who were Gentiles, or under Gentile influence.
So far as they were won over to Jewish beliefs,
they were prepared to understand and appreciate
primitive Christianity, and to this extent they
became attached to it. So far as they were
imbued with Greek culture, they felt the need
of interpreting their new faith to themselves.
They did so, the more promptly and the more
willingly, because some explanation was essential
to any one who wished to speak of Christianity
to pagans ignorant of Judaism. In this way,
progressively, but beginning at a very early date,
the Greek interpretation of the Christian doctrine
of the Messiah came into being through the
spontaneous effort of the faith to define itself,
through the natural exigencies of propagandism,

and thus the Christ, Son of God and Son of man, predestined Saviour, became the Word made flesh, the Revealer of God to humanity.

All the development of Christological doctrine up to the end of the third century comes from this double impulse, which at the same time accelerates its progress. It is moderated and controlled by the principle of tradition which compels it to remain always in close relation with its point of departure, the monotheistic conception, and the real humanity and historical personality of Jesus. Israelitish monotheism was a doctrine much more religious and moral than philosophic ; to it is adapted the metaphysics of Plato and Philo, without which, faith in the one God would have hardly had any meaning for the Greeks, much more "intellectual" than religious. In the same way, the Divinity of Christ, the Incarnation of the Word was the only conceivable way of translating to Greek intelligence the idea of the Messiah. God does not cease to be One, and Jesus remains Christ ; but God is triple without multiplication of Himself, Jesus is God without ceasing to be man, and the Word becomes man without losing its single identity. Each step of dogma marks the introduction of Greek philosophy into Christianity, and a compromise between this philosophy and Christian tradition.

For philosophy was not introduced into the Faith as such, nor entirely, but only in so far as an explanation or a learned formula was borrowed, or rather stolen, from it to give value to tradition. The apologists may speak of philosophy in connection with Christianity, and Origen regard theology as a true science, a gnosis superior to the common faith, but the official representatives of the Church affect to know nothing but tradition, and do not acknowledge, having no consciousness of them, the loans that Christianity has made before them, and is making still through them, from Hellenic wisdom. Orthodoxy is nourished by Plato, Philo, and Origen, and condemns them all more or less, for it does not always draw from them directly. The principle of tradition, a religious, moral, and social principle, a principle of government rather than of science, generally wins the day over the principle of free speculation, which is that of philosophy, and always wins at decisive moments. It is, therefore, permissible to say that Christian theology undertook a work of selection from Greek philosophy. But if it is true, in a sense, that it absorbed philosophy, seeing that it took the place of it, after assimilating a good part of its elements, it is certain that primitive Christian tradition was never exchanged for philosophy, nor Greek science substituted for the gospel, nor Plato taken for master in place of Christ and the apostles. From a historical point of view, it may be maintained that the Trinity and the Incarnation are Greek dogmas, since they are unknown to Judaism and Judaic Christianity, and that Greek philosophy, which helped to make them, also aids in their comprehension. None the less, they are not scientific dogmas transported from Pagan philosophy into Christian theology; they are religious dogmas, which owe to philosophy only certain theoretical elements and their formulas, not the spirit which penetrates elements and formulas, nor the special combination of conceptions which constitute them. The evolution of the idea of the Divine life in the Trinity does not proceed from Israelitish monotheism without the influence of Hellenic speculations, but the maintenance of unity, the definition of the three terms of the Divine life are dictated by Jewish tradition and Christian experience. In the conception of the Incarnation, the idea of the Word comes from Philo as much as from the Bible, but it does not cease to be partly Biblical, and, above all, it is fixed, made concrete, turned, as it were, from cosmology towards revelation, directed towards Christ in such a way as to derive an original significance in its relation to Him and to the Christian faith.

It is not astonishing that the result of so special a labour seems to lack logic and rational consistency. However, it is found that this defect, which would be fatal to a philosophic system, is, in theology, an element of endurance and solidity. May it not be said that all heresies are born of deductions followed out in a special sense, starting from one principle of tradition or of science isolated from all the rest, erected into absolute truth, from which, as a result of reasoning, conclusions are drawn incompatible with the general harmony of religion and traditional teaching ? Orthodoxy seems to follow a kind of politic line, balanced and obstinately conciliatory, between the extreme conclusions that can be drawn from the data it preserves. When it can no longer perceive the logical agreement of the assertions it seems to set one against the other, it proclaims the mystery, and does not purchase unity of theory by the sacrifice of an important element of its tradition. So it acted in the case of the Trinity, when the principle of the consubstantiality of the three

Divine Persons finally triumphed, and it was no longer possible to oscillate between Modalism, which admitted but one Person manifested in three works, creation, redemption, sanctification, and Subordinationism, which attributed the three works to three unequal Persons. So also it acted in the case of the Incarnation, when the dual nature was definitely affirmed in the one Person, and when it was necessary to take a stand simultaneously against Nestorianism and Monophysism. Christian tradition refused, more or less consciously, to limit the real nature of religious things by the rational nature of our conceptions ; its aim was rather to render to the eternal truth the only homage that is of value, by holding it always higher than our intelligence, affirmations which seem contradictory being, perhaps, compatible at the limit of infinity. There is but one eternal God, and Jesus is God— that is the theological dogma. The salvation of man is entirely in the hand of God, and man is free to save himself, or not—that is the dogma of grace. The Church has authority over men, and the Christian is only responsible to God—that is ecclesiastical dogma. Abstract logic would demand that throughout one or other of these strangely linked propositions should be sacrificed. But attentive observation shows that such a course would compromise the living equilibrium of religion.

The dogmas of the Trinity and the Incarnation are associated with an idea of Redemption influenced by Hellenism; but neither is the idea purely Hellenic, nor is its relation with the dogmas so close that they absolutely depend on it. If Herr Harnack's judgment is that the gospel does not, by Redemption, intend to signify exemption from death, it is because he began by considering eternal life to be the actual possession of God through faith in His mercy. But we have seen that this hypothesis is founded on an interpretation of gospel teaching, which is of very doubtful value. Eternal life, in the teaching of Jesus, is not the possession of God by man through faith, but the possession of the kingdom in the life to come, the life that is unending. Thus the immortality guaranteed to those who will see the great advent, and those who will rise from the dead to partake in it, is an element in the gospel, and the necessary and explicitly formulated condition of participation in the kingdom of God. The gift of immortality is not yet conceived as a ransoming, a restoration of humanity; it constitutes the recompense promised to the righteous. The reconciliation of sinners in the parables of mercy is not represented as a redemption. God pardons the repentant sinner who thus acquires a title to eternal life.

But St. Paul already sets forth Christian righteousness and blessed immortality as an effect of the mediation and sacrifice of the " heavenly man " Christ, Who restored to humanity the gift it lost by the fault of our first parent, the " earthly man." [1] The author of the Fourth Gospel makes little of the idea of propitiation ; but he associates the idea of life in God with that of life in the kingdom, and thus conceives the eternal life both as to come and as already present. This life is a deification of man ; for if the deification of Jesus consisted in the full communication of the Divine Spirit, which was the Incarnation of the Word, that of man is realized by the partial communication which is made of the same Spirit to believers, united to God in Christ, as Christ Himself is united to His Father.

The dogmatic theory of the Fathers of the Church is, therefore, already present in the New Testament. The reasoning of Athanasius, and the other doctors, only gave it the rigour of a system. John had said that man participates in the Divine life and triumphs over death by

[1] 1 Cor. xv. 35–57

the gift of the Divine Spirit, which Christ, Incarnate God, obtains for him. The defenders of
consubstantiality said that Christ could not thus
deify man, unless He Himself were God. The
reasoning of the ecclesiastical theologians is
founded on the assertion of the evangelist, and
all the Greek development is linked to one
element of the teaching of Jesus, wherein the
Messiah was already the messenger and the
agent of immortality. On the other hand,
the dogma of the Trinity does not rest only on
the idea of the deification of man by Christ, but
on the assertion of faith which first presented
Jesus as Christ and Lord, hallowed by the Spirit
of God, and later, as identified with the Divine
Word, and on the assertion which, before all
doctrinal systematization, conceived the Spirit
which acted in the Church as a Divine Personality, dependent and distinct from the Father
and the Son. The Apostles' Creed and the
formula of baptism are of a date anterior
to the third century, and it cannot be denied
that they contain the essential elements of the
dogma of the Trinity. The systematic definition
of the dogma is in relation to the systematic
definition of Redemption, but the ideas which supported these definitions existed before them in

Christian belief, and their evolution has its starting point in the gospel of Jesus and apostolic tradition.

The development of the dogma of grace, and that of the dogma of the Church, has been effected under the same conditions as that of the theological dogma. The West has never had much liking for the speculations wherein the genius of the ancient East has always delighted to wander, and frequently to go astray. Her religion, instead of being a matter of transcendental metaphysics, or of cosmological epic, was a wellspring of inner piety and an instrument of social order. At Rome, and in the Latin countries, religion is readily conceived as a discipline and a social duty. For the Germanic races, it is a principle of inner life, the poem of the soul, where nothing is really visible but " God and the soul, the soul and its God." The spirit of government, inherent in Rome, contributed to the ecclesiastical development, and prepared for modern times the development of the dogma of the Church. The spirit of piety was not lacking in any fraction of ancient Christianity; nevertheless, it gave rise to no special development peculiar to the Latin Church, except through St. Augustine and the influence of Augustinism, an influence that must not be altogether confused with the credit the

Augustinian system of grace has enjoyed among theologians. As Herr Harnack has said, the history of Western Christianity, since the fifth century, is made up of the relations that have existed between two factors; the spirit of piety, which tends to make religion a personal matter, and the spirit of government, which tends to make it an official thing, regulated throughout by the sovereign authority of the Roman Pontiff. Religious individualism is the extreme limit of the first tendency, ecclesiastical absolutism of the second. From their equilibrium, the life of Christianity results, a life that will vanish promptly enough on the day when one of these tendencies fails to counterbalance the other, for Protestantism only exists as religion by means of fragments of hierarchy and traditional organization, and Catholicism derives its vitality at least as much from the intimate ardour of piety as from the solidity of the hierarchical bond, or the rigour of administrative centralization.

St. Augustine contemplated the Christian idea from the point of view of individual salvation, an abstraction made from the cosmological gnosis. He does not regard salvation alone as a final end, but first of all in the guise of that spiritual regeneration, which constitutes its reality for the present life. The history of Christianity becomes a psychological drama: Adam and Eve were righteous and holy; they had within them the grace of God, and the power to do good, but nevertheless, in such a way, that in the trial of the forbidden fruit, they had the faculty of obedience without the overwhelming compulsion to fulfil their duty; they failed, the attraction of the flesh gaining the day over the spiritual force of grace, and so destroying the harmony God had established in His chosen creation; henceforth, the lust of the flesh, that is, sin, in a permanent and abiding form, reigns in man; all the sons of Adam are born sinners, because they are born of the lust of the flesh, and bear within them the deadly principle which brought them to birth; but as the evil, so is the remedy; the grace deserved through Jesus, which is essentially the gift of faith and love of God, is an attraction of another order, all-powerful and Divine, by which man acquires the liberty of righteousness, by becoming capable of resisting effectively the deadly attraction of lust; as long as he lives on the earth, the lust of the flesh is not plucked up by the root, it is simply combated and overthrown by the superior attraction of the grace of God.

The doctrine of grace is no more Roman in origin than the doctrine of the Incarnate Word. The African Church was Roman neither in race nor in spirit, notwithstanding its close and permanent relations with the community of Rome. The sense of the personal dignity of the Christian and of Christian holiness was preserved there very vividly ; although they had not followed Tertullian into the chimerical realm of Montanism, they had, so to speak, the worship of the Spirit and of the sacraments that confer it : for a long time they refused to accept the baptism of repentant heretics, and a formidable schism, that of the Donatists, arose from the same cause as the error of Cyprian and the rebaptizers ; in the same way that baptism given by a heretic could not be valid, because the heretic, not having the Holy Spirit, could not communicate it, so the ordinations made by the "Traditors," those who, during the persecutions of Diocletian, had been so weak as to hand over the sacred treasure of the Scriptures to the Roman authorities, were necessarily void, because a "Traditor" bishop is deprived of his grace, and cannot confer what he no longer possesses. It is in such an atmosphere that the dogma of efficacious grace was sure to be born. Alexandria might be interested in the Divine Essence, Antioch in the theandric constitution of Christ, Rome in rules of ecclesiastical government, but Carthage and the Church of Africa were concerned with the holiness of the Church in its chiefs and in its members. This way of understanding religion was defined by Augustine in a theory, which had the advantage over the principle that guided Cyprian and the Donatists, that it did not disturb the constitution of the Church, since it accepted from common tradition both the theological dogma and the form of ecclesiastical institution.

By presenting to each believer a scheme of moral redemption founded on the profound senti-ment of human weakness, and the mysterious efficacy of grace, through faith, hope, and love, the dogma of grace was found to be absolutely fitted to the spirit of the new nations the Church had soon to convert, who are now the Christian nations, Catholic and Protestant, of Western Europe. These nations have taken religion as a spiritual medicine, the condition and fruit of an inner struggle, the second birth of the indi-vidual and his progress towards moral perfection, liberty above all the freedom of social order, the principle of righteous action and of righteous life, and the deification of man, no longer only in the radiance of God, but by the life of God in himself and by the activity of love.

This dogma, psychological and human, somewhat modified by the interpretations of a later tradition, is bound up with the teaching of Jesus neither more nor less than the theological dogma. It proceeds directly from St. Paul. The apostle considered salvation not only as a cosmological function, but first of all as an interest of humanity in general and of the individual in particular; from his meditations on the relations of the Law and the Gospel, on Sin and Redemption, was derived his theory of salvation, through faith in Jesus and the grace of God alone, without the works of the Law. Man, since Adam, is inclined to sin—in his natural state, a sinner: far from serving him, the Law, by multiplying precepts, multiplies transgressions; it is only an instruction, a guide; through the Law has no one ever been saved.

Faith is the true remedy for sin; but faith is founded only on Jesus Christ, Who delivers men from the Law, from sin, and from death, having left this triple burden buried in the sepulchre whence He ascended, free and glorious; the "heavenly man" made flesh has redeemed all sinners, the descendants of the "earthly man:"

He has condemned sin in the flesh, He has crucified it; unjustly smitten in virtue of the Law, He has broken the Law in pieces: dying of His own free will, He has destroyed the empire of death; thus He remains a principle of justice and eternal life for those who believe in Him.[1] St. Augustine disentangled these ideas from their connection with the question of the Law, which was an essential matter for Paul, but had no significance for the Church; drew from them a logical system; made precise the conception of original sin and that of personal sin, of grace and of nature, and interpreted as a theologian the institutions and subtle polemic of the apostle.

As the reformers made much of the Pauline and Augustinian theory of justification, and as liberal theologians readily find therein their conception of salvation or of eternal life acquired through faith in God the Father, it is seldom insisted that this dogma of grace is no more expressly taught in the gospel than the Christological dogma. But the teaching of the Saviour would be searched in vain for a doctrine of sin and of justification. The Kingdom of Heaven is promised to him that repents, in such a way that the gain of eternal life seems subordinated to two

[1] Cf. Rom. **v**.

conditions; one implicit, namely, faith in the Divine mercy and in the coming kingdom, and one explicit, namely, repentance; otherwise the conditions of salvation, which is, as a matter of fact, offered only to Jews, are not discussed. It is easy to see all that St. Paul adds to the gospel, where are to be found only ordinary ideas of sin, pardon, and eternal life, without any theory.

Just as truly as the Christological dogma, the dogma of grace is an interpretation of the salvation of the Messiah and of the theology of the heavenly kingdom, and this interpretation also was made necessary by the circumstances in which the gospel was perpetuated, and by the problems presented by the conversion of pagans, problems which had to be resolved by drawing inspiration much more from the Spirit of Jesus than from His formal declarations.

It is since the Reformation especially, that the conception even of the Church has become a matter of dogmatic development. Previously the Church grew without much speculation on the nature of her progress. Protestantism first threw doubt on her authority, thus throwing doubt on the Church herself. Now, the main point at issue between Catholic theologians and those of the reformed communions may be stated in these simple terms : Is the gospel of Jesus in principle individualist or collectivist ? The question which seemed of prime importance to past centuries, namely, if the object of faith is to be determined by Scripture alone or by tradition with Scripture, retires into the background; for, in spite of appearances, it is no longer a question of knowing if Scripture contains the plenitude of the revelation or no, but whether it is for the individual Christian himself to build up his own faith and all his religion with the aid of Scripture, or whether Christian faith and religion ought not to be and are not rather a perpetual and universal work, to which each contributes and from which each derives benefit.

In opposition to Protestantism which leads the Christian religion logically to absolute individualism, that is, to indefinite subdivision, Catholic Christianity has kept a clearer consciousness of itself, and has declared itself a Divine institution as an external and visible society, with a single chief who possesses to the full, powers of teaching, of jurisdiction, of sanctification, that is to say, all the powers that are in the Church, powers which earlier centuries placed in the general episcopate under the hegemony of the Pope, without specifying whether the Pope alone possessed them wholly. The definitions of the Vatican are to some extent sprung from reality; but if the centralizing tendency that led to it seems to have reached its limit, theological reflection has not yet spoken its final word on the subject. It is possible that the future will make observations on the true nature and object of ecclesiastical authority, which cannot fail to react on the manner and conditions of its exercise.

Any one who has followed the progress of Christian thought from the beginning must perceive that neither the Christological dogma nor the dogma of grace nor that of the Church is to be taken for a summit of doctrine, beyond which no prospect opens for the believer or can ever open except the dazzling distance of infinite mystery; it is not to be expected that these dogmas will remain firmer than the rock, inaccessible even to accidental change, and yet intelligible for all generations, and equally applicable, without any new translation or explanation, to all states, and to every advance of science, life, and human society. The conceptions that the Church presents as revealed dogmas are not truths fallen from heaven, and preserved by religious tradition in the precise form in which they first appeared. The historian sees in them the interpretation of religious facts, acquired by a laborious effort of theological thought. Though the dogmas may be Divine in origin and substance, they are human in structure and composition. It is inconceivable that their future should not correspond to their past. Reason never ceases to put questions to faith, and traditional formulas are submitted to a constant work of interpretation wherein "the letter that killeth" is effectively controlled by "the spirit that giveth life."[1]

[1] 2 Cor. iii. 6.

CHAPTER III

IT is only by starting from a scholastic conception, abstract and unreal, of revelation and of dogma that a conclusion is reached condemnatory of all the fruit of Christian reflection upon the object of Christianity. It is clear that if the unchangeable essence of the gospel had been only faith in God the Father, all Christian development of doctrine, as well as of ecclesiastical organization and ritual, would have been a vast aberration. But besides the fact that the gospel is not to be summed up in such a belief, it would be absurd to suppose that the statement of this faith could remain unchangeable, or become so if it were judged expedient for mankind to content themselves with it. If the attention of the first believers had not been directed towards the Son of God, it would have turned to the Father Himself, and become occupied with His nature and relations with the world, thus leading speculation back to cosmology. Interest would have been roused in this goodness, which had its essential significance in relation to mankind, its historical manifestations would have been tentatively defined, or, at any rate, its secret action in each believing soul, a process leading thought again to Christology and the economy of Divine Grace. Sooner or later attention would have been brought to bear on the normal conditions of evangelization, and the problem of ecclesiology would have arisen. Doctrinal Christian development was inevitable, therefore, and in principle, legitimate; on the whole, it has served the cause of the gospel, which could not exist as a pure essence, but being constantly transformed into living doctrines has itself lived in these doctrines, whose development is therefore justified in fact.[1]

It is easy to say that the Catholic Church does not even recognize the existence of this development, and condemns the very idea of it. Perhaps it would be nearer the truth to say that she has never had consciousness of it, and that she has no official theory concerning the philosophy of her own history. That which is taught by Vincent de Lérins, modern theologians (except Cardinal Newman) and the Council of the Vatican, touching the development of dogma, applies in reality to the definitely intellectual and theological phase

[1] Cf. E. Caird, *art. cit.* p. 10.

of its development, not to the first budding and formation of beliefs, or at least includes in an abstract definition, much work for which this definition is no adequate expression. It is just the idea of development which is now needed, not to be created all at once, but established from a better knowledge of the past. The acquisition of this new dogma will have no different effect to that of the old ones. These latter were not contained in primitive tradition, like a conclusion in the premises of a syllogism, but as a germ in a seed, a real and living element, which must become transformed as it grows, and be determined by discussion before its crystallization into a solemn formula. They existed as more or less conscious facts or beliefs, before they were the subject of learned speculations or of official judgments. The Christological dogma was, before everything, the expression of what Jesus represented from the beginning to Christian consciousness; the dogma of grace was the expression of the Divine work accomplished in the souls that were regenerated through the gospel; the ecclesiological dogma was the expression of the permanent position of the Episcopate and the Pope in the Church. If ever a dogmatic conclusion is formulated on the subject of Christian development it will almost certainly be an expression of the law of progress which has governed the history of Christianity from the beginning. Till now, Catholic theologians have been especially preoccupied with the absolute character that the dogma derives from its source, the Divine revelation, and critics have hardly noticed the relative character that its history makes manifest. The efforts of a healthy theology should be directed to a solution of the difficulty, presented by the unquestionable authority faith demands for dogma, and the variability, the relativity, the critic cannot fail to perceive in the history of dogmas and dogmatic formulas.

We have seen how the whole development of Christian doctrine is not outside the faith, but within the faith, which dominates it entirely. The traditional principle and the religious sense have always overcome the need of scientific adaptation, and have saved the originality of Christianity. The ancient dogmas have their root in the preaching and ministry of Christ, and in the experiences of the Church, and their development in the history of Christianity and in theological thought: nothing else was possible. Further, it is no less natural that the creeds and dogmatic definitions should be related to the state of general human knowledge in the time and under the circumstances when they were constituted. It follows that a considerable change in the state of knowledge might render necessary a new interpretation of old formulas, which, conceived in another intellectual atmosphere, no longer say what is necessary, or no longer say it suitably. In such a case, a distinction must be drawn between the material sense of the formula, the external image it presents, related to ideas received from antiquity, and its proper religious and Christian significance, its fundamental idea, which can be reconciled with new views of the constitution of the world and the nature of things in general. The Church still repeats every day in the creed of the apostles, "He descended into Hell, He has ascended to Heaven." These propositions have for many centuries been taken literally. Generations of Christians have followed one another believing Hell, the abode of the damned, to be beneath their feet, and Heaven, the abode of the elect, above their heads. Neither learned theology nor even popular preaching maintains this localization to-day : and no one any longer will hold that he can determine the place of the soul of Christ in the interval between His death and His resurrection, nor that of His glorified humanity since His ascension. The real dogmatic meaning of these sentences remains unaltered, because by them is always taught a transitory relation of the soul of Christ with the just under the ancient law, and the glorification of His risen humanity. May we not say, looking at the transformation that the apparent sense of the formulas has undergone, that the theology of the future will again construct a more spiritual idea of their content? It is quite true that the Church corrects its dogmatic formulas by means of distinctions, sometimes rather subtle. But, in so acting, she continues in the way she has walked from the beginning, she adapts the gospel to the constantly changing condition of human life and intelligence.

It is not indispensable to the authority of belief that it should be rigorously unchangeable in its intellectual form and its verbal expression. Such immutability is not compatible with the nature of human intelligence. Our most certain knowledge in the domains of nature and of science is always in movement, always relative, always perfectible. It is not with the elements of human thought that an everlasting edifice can be built. Truth alone is unchangeable, but not its image in our minds. Faith addresses itself to the unchangeable truth, through a formula, necessarily inadequate, capable of improvement, consequently of change. When Jesus said, in all solemnity, "Verily I say unto you, There be some of them that stand here, which shall in no wise taste of death, till they see the Son of man coming in His kingdom," [1] He put forward a dogmatic proposition much less absolute in reality than in appearance ; He demanded faith in the approaching kingdom, but the idea of the kingdom and of its proximity were two very simple symbols of very complex matters, and even those who were the first to believe must have attached their minds more to the spirit than to the letter of this statement, to find it always true. The dogmatic formulas stand in the same position as the words of the Saviour, and it is no demonstration that they are objectless, to discover at any given moment that the reality has passed them by.

The singularly defective logic which seems to preside over the formation and growth of dogmas, is in no way difficult to understand, and may even be called normal, by the historian who considers the proofs of faith as expressions of its vitality rather than the real reasons of its origin.

Nothing is more precarious, from the point of view of the ordinary rules of human reasoning

[1] Matt. xvi. 28.

and textual criticism, than certain arguments by which the gospel is founded on the Old Testament, and Catholic Christianity on the whole Bible. The work of traditional exegesis, from whence dogma may be said to proceed by a slow and continuous elaboration, seems in permanent contradiction with the principles of a purely rational and historical interpretation. It is always taken for granted that the old Biblical texts and the witness of tradition must contain the truth of the present time, and the truth is found there because it is put there. Catholic theologians had a right appreciation of this state of affairs when they laid down the rule that the infallibility of the Church applies to dogmatic definitions, not to the preambles that stated the reasons of them, even when the preambles were expressed in the official declarations of Councils and Popes. A distinction of this kind would be useful for the New Testament, wherein the resurrection of the dead is proved by the text, "I am the God of Abraham, and the God of Isaac, and the God of Jacob," [1] the independence of the Christian from the Mosaic law by the history of Hagar and Sarah,[2] and quotations from the ancient Scripture applied generally in a sense that did not originally

---

[1] Mark xii. 26.   [2] Gal. iv. 21–31.

belong to them. As for tradition, it suffices to recall how the Fathers and theologians prove the Trinity of Divine Persons by the words of Genesis, "Let us make man in our image, after our likeness," [1] and by the three angels that visited Abraham; [2] how the two swords that Peter is said to have carried at Gethsemane [3] demonstrated, according to Boniface VIII. and the mediæval doctors, the double power, spiritual and temporal, of the Popes. It is well known, also, how texts, in themselves perfectly clear, like the lamentations of Job and the psalmists over the annihilation of man by death, the assertions of the Saviour and the apostles upon the approaching end of the world, the saying of Christ as reported by John, " The Father is greater than I," [4] are not held to mean that which they obviously signify.

May it not be said that, in the order of things moral and religious, human logic has no care for itself, that the effort towards improvement runs ahead of the reasoning that justifies it, and that it bears within itself a truth superior to all the arguments that seek to establish it ? Thus the best apology for all that lives lies in the life itself. All the scaffolding of theological and

[1] Gen. i. 26. [2] Gen. xviii. 2.
[3] Luke xxii. 38 ; John xviii. 10. [4] John xiv. 28.

apologetic argument is only an attempt, and a necessary one, to figure the relation of the past to the present as well as the continuity of religion and religious progress from the beginning. The artifices of interpretation serve ceaselessly to enlarge and spiritualize the meaning of the symbols, to promote the development and intelligence of religion by the ever renewed perception of analogies, higher and more worthy of their mysterious object. External imperfections, which are above all, imperfections relative to us to the critical knowledge of the sources of history and to the modern education of intelligence, do not render this great work vain nor prejudice the importance of its results. If the gospel had been a philosophical thesis, the thesis would have been very badly constructed and developed, but as the gospel was a living religion, the theological work of Christian centuries testifies that this religion has really lived, as an infinitely powerful movement, of which those who supported it and whom it supported had only a partial consciousness, the whole of whose depth, those who to-day attempt to analyze it are incapable of sounding. How vain it is to proclaim the end of dogma because the doctrinal flower of this great life appears withered, and to imagine that the fruitfulness of

Christian thought is definitely exhausted, and that the old tree can never again renew its adornment for a new epoch, a new springtime!

From the moment the gospel is believed, it is impossible not to think of the belief, not to work at the thought, and so produce a theology of faith. It is equally impossible to keep the faith without transmitting it, for it demands to be communicated, being universal hope and charity; and it cannot be communicated without a certain teaching, a dogma regularly put forward for belief. There is a mastership of the faith. Reasoning in the abstract, it is possible to say that faith springs up in the soul at the contact of the gospel as expressed in its text. But in fact, faith is born of Christian instruction, and the gospel is explained to those who are taught to believe. The distinction of masters and pupils is therefore inevitable. It is impossible that no science of religion should exist, or that it should be indifferent to the preservation of faith in cultivated society. Equally is it impossible that this science should be accessible to all, that all should be doctors of religion. From the beginning all the faithful could not be apostles. Under the conditions which are prescribed for the gospel in this world, masters are needed to propagate it, and doctrines to express it. A durable society, a Church, can alone maintain equilibrium between tradition, which preserves the heritage of acquired truth, and the incessant toil of human reason to adapt ancient truth to the new needs of thought and knowledge. It is inconceivable that each individual should recommence the interrogation of the past on his own account, and reconstruct, for his own use, an entire religion. Here, as elsewhere, each is aided by all, and all by each one.

It is no longer a matter for astonishment that the Church presents herself as an infallible mistress to those believers who venture forth without her. Her attitude is as easy to understand as that of the Protestant theologians who, seeing the powerlessness of the individual to formulate a creed for others besides himself, and knowing no other religious principle than individualism, take refuge in one solitary idea, which they wish to believe is alone evangelical and accessible of itself to all souls. But their hypothesis has the inconvenience of being unfounded and impracticable, whilst the Catholic hypothesis is a real institution that continues the real gospel. It was not without reason that Luther retained a dogma, and that organized Protestantism tends to orthodoxy in spite of itself.

Is this the same thing as to say that Christian dogma thus becomes a ready-made belief, before which it is wise to bow, without too close investigation, lest contradiction be called for? Even as the constant flexibility of ecclesiastical teaching brings it about that no conflict of dogma with knowledge can be considered as irreducible, so the very character of this teaching causes the authority of the Church and its formulas to be not incompatible with individuality of faith, and does not necessarily bring with it that perpetual subserviency which seems, to Protestant theologians, the normal condition of the Catholic believer. The Church does not exact belief in its formulas as the adequate expression of absolute truth, but presents them as the least imperfect expression that is morally possible; she demands that men respect them for their quality, seek the faith in them, and use them to transmit it. The ecclesiastical formula is the auxiliary of faith, the guiding line of religious thought: it cannot be the integral object of that thought, seeing that object is God Himself, Christ and His work; each man lays hold of the object as he can, with the aid of the formula. As all souls and all intelligences differ one from the other, the gradations of belief are also of infinite variety, under the sole direction of the Church, and in the unity of her creed. The incessant evolution of doctrine is made by the work of individuals, as their activity reacts on the general activity, and these individuals are they who think for the Church while thinking with her.

This is not the place to examine whether the tendency of modern Catholicism has not been too tutelary, or if the movement of religious and even scientific thought has not been more or less impeded by it. The object of this chapter is simply to show that the Catholic conception of dogma and of faith excludes neither the personal character of belief nor the vitality of dogma.

SECTION VI

THE CATHOLIC WORSHIP

INTRODUCTION

HISTORY knows no instance of a religion without a ritual, and consequently the existence of a Christian ritual should surprise no one. But it is easy to conceive that, if the essence of Christianity is such as Herr Harnack has defined it, so pure a Christianity must exclude all external forms of worship. A singular religion, designed, one would think, for angelic hosts, where every individual constitutes a separate species, rather than for men destined to live together on the earth!

CHAPTER I

As the rupture with Judaism obliged the primitive community to take the form of a distinct society, so also it led to the establishment of forms of worship. "No religious movement can exist without a body."[1] We are yet told that Christian ritual was the result of the struggle of the Church against gnosticism. The Church assumed forms similar to those it reproved in its adversaries.[2] By the end of the second century she is an organ of worship, the separation of the priests from the laity is an accomplished fact, and intermediaries are admitted between God and man. Just as Greek philosophy influenced Christian faith from the year 130 onwards, so a new era of Hellenization began towards the years 220 to 230 : "then Greek mysteries and Greek civilization, in all the fulness of their development, acted upon the Church, but not Greek mythology nor Polytheism. In the century following, pure

[1] Page 113.   [2] Page 130.

Hellenism, with all its creations and acquisitions, is established in the Catholic Church. Here also there were reservations, but they often consisted only in a change of label, the thing being taken just as it was, and in the worship of the saints a Christianity of a lower order was born." [1]

Judged by its external appearance, the Greek Church (and in matters of ritual the same may be said of the Roman Church) has collected, we are told, the impressions, superstitions, knowledge, and practices of unknown ages; with its solemn rites, its relics, its images, its priests, its monks, and its mysteries, it is connected with the Hellenic worship of the Neo-Platonist epoch, and not with the Church of the first centuries. "It appears not as a Christian creation with a Greek thread, but as a Greek creation with a Christian thread. The Christians of the first century would have fought it as they fought the worship of the Magna Mater or of Zeus Soter. . . . It is the natural product of the alloy made with Hellenism, split up by oriental influence and Christian preaching." [2] The worship in spirit and in truth is become a worship of signs, formulas, and idols. "Jesus Christ gave Himself to be crucified in order to destroy religion of this kind." [3]   The Greek

---

[1] Page 126.   [2] Pages 137, 138.   [3] Page 148.

mystery is associated in the Latin Church with the idea of contract, of salvation depending on definite conditions; the Sacraments are means of union with God, conceived as obligatory acts; the discipline of penitence resembles a code of civil procedure: even as the dispenser of salvation, the Roman Church is a juridical institution as "polytheistic," in any case, as the Greek Church.[1]

Herr Harnack holds, with Luther, that grace is not given in fragments; that the only grace is God Himself; that all the doctrine of sacraments is an "outrage on the majesty of God and a servitude of souls." But he holds that the reformer was wrong to be led away into distressing discussions on the means of grace, on the communion, and the question of infant baptism, whereby he ran the risk of exchanging his lofty conception of Divine grace for the Catholic idea; in this respect he has left his Church a fatal heritage.[2]

[1] Pages 155, 156.   [2] Pages 175, 183, 184.

CHAPTER II

It may be said that Jesus, in the course of His ministry, neither prescribed nor practised any external rite of worship which would have characterized the gospel as religion. Jesus no more decided the form of Christian worship beforehand than He laid down the constitution and dogmas of the Church. The reason is that, in the gospel, Christianity is not yet a religion with a separate existence. It has taken up no independent position in regard to legal Judaism; the Mosaic rites, practised by the Saviour and His disciples, take the place of any other form, and satisfy the need that all religion feels to express itself in acts of worship. The gospel, as such, was only a religious movement within the bosom of Judaism, an attempt to realize perfectly its principles and hopes. It would therefore be inconceivable that Jesus should have formulated a ritual before His final hour. He could only have begun to think of it at that supreme moment when the immediate accomplishment of the reign of the Messiah appeared impossible in Israel, and another accomplishment, mysterious in its prospect, to be obtained by the death of the Messiah, remained the last chance for the kingdom of God on the earth. The supper of the Eucharist, then, stands out as the symbol of the kingdom, that the sacrifice of Jesus is to bring; and more distinctly still, this communion, on the day of its first celebration, signifies the abrogation of the ancient worship and the approaching advent of the kingdom, rather than the institution of a new ritual, as the thought of Jesus was bent, as always, on the idea of realizing the kingdom of Heaven rather than the direct idea of founding a new religion and a Church.

However, it was the Church that came to the world, and by force of circumstances took shape more and more outside the pale of Judaism. In this way Christianity became a religion, distinct, independent, and complete; as a religion it needed a ritual, and obtained it, of such a nature as its origin permitted or compelled. At first the worship was imitated from that of the Jews, so far as concerned the external forms of prayer, and also certain important rites, such as baptism, anointing with oil, and laying on of hands. The central act of worship, the celebration of the

Eucharist, was really the creation of Jesus. It became, in the Church of the Gentiles, the great mystery, and without it Christianity would not have been received as a perfect religion.

A ritual was already organized in the apostolic communities, and the promptitude with which it was established shows clearly how it responded to an intimate inevitable necessity of the new body. It would have been an absolute impossibility to gain proselytes to a religion with no external forms and sanctifying acts ; Christianity had to find a ritual, or cease to exist. For this reason, it was from the first the most living worship that can be imagined. Attempt merely to conceive those baptisms, with laying on of hands, and sensible manifestations of the Divine Spirit ; that breaking of bread, and the meal where the very presence of the Master, Who had just left the earth, was felt ; the songs, celebrating the acts of grace, that burst forth from the heart, the signs, sometimes strange ones, of the overflowing enthusiasm. Is it not true that, just as there is there no cold and abstract belief, so there is no purely symbolic rite, the material expression of such a belief ? Everything is living, the faith and the rite, the baptism and the breaking of bread ; the baptism is the Holy Ghost the

Eucharist is the Christ. There is no speculation about the token, no hint of physical efficacy of the sacrament in baptism, nor of transubstantiation in the Eucharist; but what is said and believed goes almost beyond these theological assertions. The worship of that primitive age might be defined as a kind of spiritual realism, knowing no pure symbols, and essentially sacramental by virtue of the place that rites hold in it as the vehicle of the Spirit, and the means of Divine life. St. Paul and the author of the Fourth Gospel are witnesses to it.

The same necessity that presided at the birth of Christian ritual caused its increase. The ritual of the apostolic Church could respond to the essential needs of Christian society in all times; in its special form it corresponded to the special conditions of nascent Christianity. As the Church did not attain, at one stroke, the normal development she still continues to pursue, her ritual has developed, and is developing, under the permanent influence that gave it birth.

Exactly the same experience had overtaken Israelitish worship. It is as an effect of theological perspective, from the point of view of faith, that this worship is represented in the Sacred Books as a homogeneous whole, proceeding

from a Divine revelation, regulating the least
details of liturgy and sacerdotal costume. In
reality, Moses, as far as the historian can gather,
only did relatively for the Israelitish ritual what
the apostolic Church did for the Christian; he
authorized, or instituted, the fundamental practice,
the worship of the ark, where Jehovah, the God
of Israel, was present without an image. All the
rest of the forms of worship may have been
borrowed, before Moses, or after him, from other
religions, with certain changes affecting the meaning, rather than the form, of the rites. While
running the risk of corruption through the ad-
mixture of foreign elements, the Mosaic ritual
realized successively the transformations that its
preservation and progress demanded. The Jews
of the captivity were descendants of the Hebrew
companions of Moses, of Joshua, of David, and of
the inhabitants of Canaan, who had little by little
become assimilated to the children of Israel.
When human groups are thus mingled, not only
physical and racial, but also intellectual and moral
qualities, customs and traditions are blended
together. More than one Canaanitish rite has
been canonized in Deuteronomy or Leviticus.
It would have been as difficult to discern the
features derived from Canaan in the Jewish

type of the fifth century B.C., as to distinguish the non-Israelitish contribution to the Pentateuch. The worship, as a whole, however diverse the services of its elements, was one by the spirit that penetrated it, the spirit of Moses and the Prophets, eliminating or neutralizing the spirit of pagan tradition.

All that happened in the history of Israelite religion, happened also in that of Christianity, but under different, that is to say, more regular, and less perilous, conditions. Suppose that the pagan origin of a certain number of Christian rites can be demonstrated, these rites ceased to be pagan, when accepted and interpreted by the Church. Suppose that the great development of the worship of saints, of relics, of the Virgin, is due, in some degree, to a pagan influence, it is not to be condemned on the sole fact of its origin. If apostolic preaching had converted only Jews, there would not, properly speaking, have been any Christian ritual, any more than there would have been a Christian Church or Christian dogmas. But Christianity, by remaining Jewish, could not have become a universal religion, it would not have become Christianity; and to become universal it was not enough that it should lay aside its Jewish form. It cannot be maintained that it had no need to assume a Greek, a Roman, or a German form, but should have conquered the world by might of its principles alone. Principles are the soul of religion, but principles, without religious institutions and doctrines, are, in sober truth, a soul without a body, something which has neither reality nor consistence in the realm of present life. Now, the institutions, the external and traditional forms, which are indispensable to the existence or to the preservation of a religion, are necessarily adapted, in one way or another, to the surroundings wherein they are established; they even result, to some extent, from their surroundings, as the adaptation is made by virtue of a reciprocal action, since if religion marks with its influence the men who accept it, the men in their turn, as nations or as individuals, stamp their impression on the religion they receive.

The number and variety, even to some extent the quality of the symbols, are things indifferent or unimportant in themselves; custom gives them their credit, and their value depends upon the significance attached to them. Of what value in itself is the rite of circumcision? Less than nothing, since in the abstract it may be considered absurd and ridiculous. Nevertheless, in the time of Antiochus Epiphanes, when it was a symbol of fidelity to God, it became something worthy, noble, and holy. It would be puerile to blame the Jews for practising the rite, or the prophets for not condemning it. At no epoch of history before the great upheaval brought about by Christianity, and the conversion of the pagans to Jesus outside the Law, could the idea of dispensing with it have occurred to any pious Jew, and he would have been mad to wish to suppress it as a practice. It was the consideration of the Gentiles that forced the apostolic Church not to exact it.

But the Gentiles, who thus succeeded in obtaining exemption from a Jewish custom, might well obtain, on the other hand, power to retain their own customs, on condition of imparting to them a Christian significance. They could in no way bring themselves to Judaism; and they could only settle down as Christians by imparting to Christianity something of themselves, forms of thought and forms of worship. The Church has adopted no rite that resembles circumcision; she has proscribed all the bloody and magical rites of ancient religions, and thereby has guaranteed, as far as is necessary or possible, the spiritual character of the Christian religion. But just as any way of representing God, the economy of

salvation, redemption, the action of the glorified
Christ, cannot fail to have some analogy or historic
relation to philosophical or religious conceptions
of Greco-Roman antiquity, so also the Catholic
worship cannot fail to retain something from
the ancient religions it has supplanted. It could
not do otherwise, once it took their place:
Christianity could not become the religion of
Greeks, Romans, or Germans, unless it became
one with them, unless it received many things
from them, unless they themselves, as it were,
entered into it, and made it in truth their own
religion. In matters of worship, the religious
feeling of the masses has always preceded the
doctrinal definitions of the Church as to the
object of their worship. The fact is full of significance ; it attests the law which demands a form
of worship suitable to all the conditions of existence and to the character of the people that
believe. The real communion with Christ in the
Eucharist was exacted by the Christian conscience
as imperiously as the Divinity of Jesus ; nevertheless the Divinity of Christ is not a dogma
conceived in the spirit of Jewish theology, neither
is the Eucharist a Jewish rite ; dogma and rite
are specifically Christian, and proceed from the
apostolic tradition, without altering the fact that

the influence of Greek wisdom can be perceived
in the traditional way of understanding the first,
and in the manner of understanding the second,
an element doubtless at bottom common to several
religions, if not to all, but which recalls rather the
pagan mysteries than the unadorned conception of
sacrifice of post-exilian Judaism. If it were not
to become Greek, Roman, or German in its form
of worship, Christianity must have avoided the
Greeks, Romans and Germans; the adaptation
of Christianity was inevitable. The important
question is whether the adaptation has served the
spread and preservation of the gospel, or whether
the gospel itself has been lost in it. Have the
institution of the ecclesiastical ministry, the sacrament, the worship of Christ and the Virgin, of
saints and angels, compromised the gospel, and
are they foreign to its spirit ?

Since Christianity has become a religion, and,
becoming a religion, has become a form of worship,
it has needed ministers. No assemblies of many
persons could take place regularly and frequently
without chiefs, presidents, superintendents, and
minor officers to ensure order. The college of
elders, more or less imitated from the synagogues,
was, in each community, what the apostolic
college had been at first in the community of

Jerusalem. The presidency was naturally an attribute of the elders, and it was also natural that one of them should occupy the leading place in the celebration of the Communion. The hypothesis of a rotation of officials, a presidency exercised by each elder in turn, set forth by some critics, is not authorized by any evidence, and is unlikely. Besides the leaders, the elders, presbyters (priests) or bishops, there were inferior ministers, the deacons. When the extraordinary ministry of the apostles and the missionary preachers came to an end in due course, with the enthusiasm that stimulated the prophets, towards the close of the first century, the duties of instruction and direction of the community passed entirely to the resident chiefs, or rather administrators, who doubtless exercised these functions in part from the beginning. They alone decided the question of the admission of neophytes, and, except in exceptional cases, alone conferred baptism ; in proportion as a discipline of penance required organization for baptized Christians, they determined its conditions. The hierarchy of order, in three degrees, became constituted when the first of the elders was really separated from the presbyteral group, and reserved the title of bishop for himself.

The needs of the liturgical service determined later on the creation of minor officers, who are to be regarded as a division of the diaconate: the Church of the East had subdeacons and leaders, with exorcists, fulfilling their individual ministry and not constituting an order of the clergy; the Church of the West had its subdeacons, acolytes, readers, exorcists, who had all regular duties in the preliminary ceremonies of baptism, and door-keepers. In any case, the orders below the subdiaconate, later even the subdiaconate, and finally the diaconate itself, ended by becoming in the Latin Church no more than preparatory steps to the priesthood, which remains the only really active ministry below the episcopate. The liturgical functions of the other orders have ceased, in fact, to be specialized; the highest are exercised on occasion by priests and the lower by laics, and thus a special example is constituted of what may be called suppressed development, like a stunted branch on a tree that grows vigorously in another direction, or like the rudiment of an organ no longer existing actually in the living body.

The organization of this service has been related to the development of the system of sacraments and must not be judged independently of it. The

Church herself counts ordination, that is, the ceremony by which her ministers are invested with their powers, among the sacraments. As to their origin, it stands with the sacraments as with the Church and the dogmas, they proceed from Jesus and the gospel as living realities and not as expressly defined institutions. It is only from the twelfth century onwards that Western tradition has determined their number. The primitive Church knew but two principal: baptism, with which confirmation was associated, and the Eucharist; the number of secondary sacraments was indefinite. Such indefiniteness would be inexplicable if Christ, in the course of His mortal life, had drawn the attention of His disciples to seven separate rites, destined to be the basis of Christian worship for all time. The sacraments are born of a thought, an intention, of Jesus, interpreted by the apostles and their successors, in the light and under the pressure of facts and circumstances.

It may be by a sort of anticipation that the Fourth Gospel shows Christian baptism practised during the Saviour's ministry. It is a fact that Christ gave no formal precept on the subject before His death. Baptism was a Jewish rite, raised to special honour by John the Baptist, and Jesus

Himself received it at the hands of John. Just as the Saviour's baptism served as the introduction to the gospel, so baptism introduced each believer into the evangelical society, substituted for the kingdom of Heaven. It was not purely a symbol of remission of sins and spiritual regeneration, but the effective sign of the reception of the Spirit by the faithful, and of their incorporation with the Church. The idea and the practice of baptism have undergone no important change in Catholic tradition. The custom of baptizing infants constitutes a disciplinary development, which makes no change in the significance of the Sacrament, though perhaps it has a little diminished it, and has contributed to redoubling the significance of penance.[1] Baptism, followed by confirmation and communion, was the rite of Christian initiation and of remission of sins; but the Eucharist remained the real sacrament of the initiated. The idea of the Christian as a reconciled sinner was not held at first, and the Church was slow in becoming accustomed to it. It was supposed that ordinary failings were atoned for by a kind of continuous effect of baptism, by prayer, by communion, and by all good works, especially by works of charity. Very grave and scandalous

[1] Cf. Newman, "Essay on Development" (1846), p. 154.

sins set the sinners outside the Church and the regular economy of salvation. Soon, however, such sinners were admitted to a perpetual penance, accepted gladly, in the interest of their salvation, although as yet the Church did not take it on herself to pardon, and left the repentant sinner to the Divine mercy. But the multiplication of sins was sure to produce the indulgence, and an institution of pardon. It was at first in regard to sins of the flesh that discipline was slackened. Calixtus, the Bishop of Rome, decided that these sins could be remitted after a penitence more or less prolonged. Concessions were soon made in cases of apostasy, notably after the persecution of Decius. The principle of temporary and absolving penance, with reconciliation by the authority of the Church, either at the moment of death, or after a definite lapse of time, was established: it exists as a second baptism, a plank of salvation after shipwreck. But if penance thus became a Christian institution, and the reconciliation of sinners a function of the Church, as yet there was no thought of employing the name of sacrament to designate such a duty: it was a shameful sacrament. The sinner must submit to it, if he desired reconciliation, but whoever endured public penance, and there was no other form, was disqualified as a Christian ; clerks were only admitted to it by losing their status, and a reconciled penitent could be no member of the clergy. The discredit attaching to penance gradually disappeared, through the multiplication of cases wherein it was judged necessary, through the fact that many Christians submitted, in a spirit of mortification of the body, to a life very analogous to that enjoined as penance, and finally through the fact that this rule of public penance was transformed and gave way to that of private penance. The fourth Council of the Lateran (1215) definitely consecrates and regulates private penance, and all mortal sins must be submitted to the proper pastor or priest, once a year, before the Easter Communion, which is declared obligatory. The priest will enjoin a penance proportioned to the faults, and will give absolution. From the twelfth century penance follows absolution instead of preceding it, a fact which tends to augment the character of grace in absolution, and even gives it the form of a sacramental grace. The development of discipline has had an effect upon the institution as a whole, upon the subject and object of penance, the declaration of sins, the character, duration and place of satisfactory penance, and even upon the formula of absolution, which was at first deprecatory, the bishop or priest asking of God the pardon of him whom they sought to reconcile, but has become imperative, the minister of the Church saying, " I absolve thee," because he gives a sentence and confers a sacrament.

We know that development did not stop there, and that penance, instituted to deal with mortal sins committed after baptism, became, in fact, especially after the Council of Trent and in the Church of the latter centuries, a common practice of Christian perfection, whose use is only neglected by the real sinners. The sacrament of penance has assumed the character of a moral discipline, whose efficacy can only be equitably judged by those who make use of it, and they find it an aid and not an obstacle to piety.

The development of the Eucharist has been mainly theological and liturgical. At bottom the belief and the rite have no more changed than have the belief in baptism and its rite. The Supper of the early Christians was a memorial of the Passion and an anticipation of the festival of the Messiah, whereat Jesus was present. There is no very marked difference between the Pauline conception of the Eucharist and the idea that simple Christians have of it to-day, those who are strangers to the speculations of theology, who believe that they enter into real communion with God in Christ by taking the consecrated bread. The entire Christian worship developed round the supper of the Eucharist. The simple blessing and distribution of bread and wine, detached from the Love feast, surrounded by readings and prayers and hymns, became the offering of the Mass. Since the death of Jesus was conceived as a sacrifice, the act commemorating this death naturally partook of the same character. The liturgical form helped to impart the same thing, by the real offering of the bread and wine, and the participation of all the faithful in the sanctified food, as in the sacrifices of the ancients. Thence came the idea of a commemorative sacrifice, which simply perpetuated that of the Cross, took nothing from its significance or its merit, and satisfied all the aims included in the common prayer of the Church, interests spiritual and temporal, the salvation of the living and the dead. The Christian sentiment which has preserved, in a sense, the Divinity of Jesus against certain speculations of learned metaphysics, has protected the Eucharist against speculations of abstract symbolism, and as the evolution of penance ended by bringing about the confession of the devout, the evolution of the rite of the Eucharist ended in private masses for the priests, and communions of piety for the faithful.

Jesus seems to have commanded or permitted His disciples to anoint the sick with oil, and pray over them with a view to relieve or even to cure them. Possibly, He even set them the example of this procedure:[1] that is, in the gospel, the whole sacrament of extreme unction. The history of this custom in the first Christian centuries is obscure enough. The use of applications of oil has probably never ceased since primitive times, but the use of sacred oil was very variable. The anointing of the sick in danger of death, by the priest, was distinguished by its special significance and more solemn character. From a historical point of view, it was this use of the oil that gave it a place among the sacraments when the catalogue was drawn up, limited to the number seven.

Christ recognized monogamy as a Divine institution, and declared it indissoluble: that in the gospel is the whole sacrament of marriage. Among Christians marriage was very soon the object of a special benediction; nevertheless, this prayer of the Church was never regarded as an indispensable consecration of the conjugal bond. Marriage entered the list of sacraments by reason

[1] Cf. Mark vi. 13.

of those words in the Epistle to the Ephesians,[1] wherein it is presented as the symbol of the union between Christ and the Church, and because of the use of the word " sacramentum " in the Latin Vulgate, although the word in this place has the meaning of allegorical mystery, and does not stamp marriage in itself as a sacred rite.

The sacramental system is thus found to include and consecrate the hierarchical organization of the Church and the principal moments of Christian life. Without any previously constructed scheme, an institution became realized which surrounds human existence with a Divine atmosphere, and is, without doubt, by the intimate harmony of all its parts and the intensity of its influence, the most remarkable creation that has ever proceeded spontaneously from a living religion. The period at which the Church fixed the number of the sacraments, is only a special point in the development, and marks neither the beginning nor the end. The starting-point of the system is, as has been indicated, the baptism of Jesus and the Last Supper. The end is still to come, as sacramental development, continuing to follow the same general lines, can only end with the Church herself.

[1] Ephesians v. 32.

The importance, therefore, of the work of scholastic theologians must not be exaggerated, though they fixed the number of sacraments before the Council of Trent, and united in the same rubric actions as different as baptism and matrimonial contract, absolution of sins and extreme unction, finding in each, according to the Aristotelian formula, a substance and a form. All these things existed, more living in themselves than in the studied description made of them, and have not ceased to surpass the description, which bears the same relation to them as an incomplete anatomical statement to a real organism. Regarded historically, the development shows a persevering effort on the part of Christianity to penetrate with its spirit the whole existence of man. Is not this effort the very essence of a perfect religion, and is it astonishing that a religion that has taken to itself absolutely, not only its founder, but the first generations of its adherents, demanding the sacrifice of their life, should have left outside its sphere of action no part of man nor of human life?

This religion considers man wholly as its property. This power of possession is signified in a way by all the sacraments, as was necessary. Christianity has not escaped the need of symbol, the normal form of worship, as well as of religious knowledge. It announces its right, the right of God revealed in Jesus Christ, at the same time it acts on man by sensible signs, rites, and formulas, appropriate to the particular ends it has in view. The signs that are employed have not been chosen hap-hazard, but have been suggested or imposed by past tradition, by customs of life or by circumstances. Christianity has found in them an indispensable refuge made to its needs, since the evolution of rites has been conditioned by the constant evolution of religion and piety. Christianity needed sacramental signs, and needed sufficient of them; they have been such as the conditions of the Christian institution indicated; they were sure to be modified, at least accidentally, and they have developed under the influence of the external and internal conditions in which Christianity has lived.

There is little need to show how the worship of Jesus was born in, or rather with, Christianity. In their daily intercourse with their Master, the disciples had no other worship for Him than a religious reverence. Even after the confession of Peter, there was no alteration of the simplicity that governed the relations between Christ and the apostles. The glory of the Messiah was still to come, and no homage would be rendered till the glory was made manifest. But the respective situations of the Saviour and His followers were entirely changed as a result of the Passion and the Resurrection. Jesus had then entered, for His part, into the splendour of His reign; He was living and immortal, seated at the right hand of the Father, participating in His power: He was no longer only the Master who taught with authority the revelation of God, He was the Lord whom God had set as the governor over His Kingdom. " Ye men of Israel, hear these words; Jesus of Nazareth, a man approved of God unto you by mighty works and wonders and signs which God did by Him in the midst of you, even as ye yourselves know. . . . God hath made Him both Lord and Christ, this Jesus whom ye crucified." [1] " All authority hath been given unto me in heaven and on earth. Go ye therefore, and make disciples of all the nations. . . . I am with you alway, even unto the end of the world." [2] It was thus that Christian consciousness represented the founder of Christianity, following all that Jesus had Himself proclaimed of His coming glory. It was therefore very natural that men should pray to God through Jesus, with Jesus,

[1] Acts ii. 22–36.   [2] Matt. xxviii. 18–20.

in Jesus, and soon come to pray to Jesus Himself, if indeed they did not do so from the beginning, since He was always with His own, ready to hear and with power to grant their prayers.

It is impossible even to conceive how Christianity could have failed to be the worship of Christ, and it is a probable supposition that this worship preceded in some way, sustained, and inspired the work of Christian thought on the person of the Redeemer. The intercourse of the Christian was in heaven with his Lord; if he distinguished God from Christ, none the less he saw God in Christ, so close and indissoluble was the union of the two; praying to Christ he prayed to God, although the solemn prayers of the community were addressed to God through Christ. Jesus was, as it were, the countenance of God turned towards humanity. Christian piety continued to place the Saviour at an ever higher degree of glory, seeking God in Him and finding Him, adoring Him in heaven, and endeavouring to follow His example on earth, drawing strength from His double character—the Divine and the human. Therein has always lain the life of Christianity, and the principle of its moral fruitfulness. Those are bold indeed who believe this conduct to be an alteration of its essence. It is unnecessary to

add that the same piety under different forms
continues to exist in the numberless devotions
that have become linked to the worship of Jesus,
and have continued down to our own day, principally the worship of the Eucharist and of the
Sacred Heart, the latter more recent in appearance
than in reality.

The worship of martyrs is hardly less ancient
than martyrdom itself. From the earliest times
care was taken to preserve the remains of dead
brethren, especially of those who died for the
faith, because of the belief in the approaching
resurrection of the body at the second coming of
the Lord. This conception of resurrection had a
more powerful influence on minds then than it
has to-day over the most sincere believers. The
care of dead bodies finds thus a most natural
explanation, and this care was accompanied by a
sense of piety, having for its object these remains
hallowed by the spirit and by an immortal hope.
The kingdom they had awaited, and still expected
so eagerly, was now visibly constituted beyond
mortal vision by all the blessed who rejoined
Christ in His glory, and were none the less united
in Him, even as He was, to the Church on the
earth, the organ of evangelical preaching and of
the preparation of the kingdom of Heaven.

The worship of the Saints is, therefore, the natural complement of the worship of Jesus, and the worship of Jesus is the Christian worship. Christianity without this worship is only a philosophy—if it is preferred, call it a mystic philosophy—which would gladly take the name of religion, but has no right to it, having kept no definite religious form. It is not Israelitish monotheism, seeing that this religion finds its form in the privilege which makes the sole God the God of Israel alone. Christianity is a religion, and a universal one, because it incarnates the sole God in the Son of man, and adores in God Man the God of all humanity.

Save for the special importance of its development, the worship of Mary presents itself under the same conditions as the worship of the saints. Primitive evangelical tradition was entirely filled with the memory of Jesus; the mother of Christ is barely mentioned in one situation where her intervention had no favourable significance.[1] Later thought centred on Mary in the consideration of the origin of Jesus. The virginal conception, which tended merely to heighten the personality of the Saviour, and cause appreciation of His Divine Sonship, came to imply a special honour for the

[1] Mark iii. 31.

Virgin Mother. It may be said that the worship
of Mary has profited by every advance of the
Christological dogma. Belief in the virginity
maintained after the birth of Christ, and in the
material virginity maintained even in the birth,
completed the idea of the virginal conception;
it served to glorify Jesus, and incidentally more
and more to glorify the mother of Jesus. It seems
that here, too, common piety preceded learned
theology, and that the Council of Ephesus, in
proclaiming Mary the mother of God, far less gave
a new direction to worship than a dogmatic consecration to a very vivid sentiment of Christian
consciousness.

It has been remarked that Mary occupied in
theology later than the Council of Nicæa, the
place that Arius assigned to the Word of God.
The substitution, though unconscious, was not
therefore accidental; it arose from a kind of
unseen necessity, as though Catholic piety could
not dispense with this intermediary power that
the heresiarch desired to personify in Christ and
orthodoxy actually personified in His Mother.
Again, it was popular or monastic devotion that
initiated the later progress of the worship of Mary
and of what may be called Mariology. It is
known that the festival of the Conception

preceded, and in a way provoked, the doctrine of the Immaculate Conception.

Thus there was formed in Catholicism a human ideal that has continued to grow incessantly. The historical justification of the assertions of faith, of which this ideal is composed, has never been sought otherwise than by the collection of testimony wherein these very assertions are formulated, testimony which is an expression of Catholic Christianity. It is perhaps less easy than is believed to show that this ideal is contrary to the gospel, and has in no way proceeded from it.

CHAPTER III

If, however, the moral necessity of this development can be proved, does it not also follow that it has been " natural," as Herr Harnack calls it, and outside that worship of the spirit that the Saviour came to establish? Truly the development has been natural, inasmuch as it has been a historical fact, arising to satisfy the innate needs of human nature. In this sense it may just as well be said that confidence in God is natural to man, and that the gospel of Divine goodness is as little supernatural as the Christian ritual. If all movement whose sequence can be perceived is to be called natural, and if the nature of God's action in the soul, and the confident impulse of the soul towards God, are to be classed as outside nature, then Christian worship is natural in its external characteristics and co-ordinated to a supernatural effect, in so far as it acts on the soul by a sensible means to aid in producing that which is properly supernatural in man, namely, life in God.[1] The evangelical word, the indispensable means of faith, is just as natural as a text, as the sacraments are as a sign, but it is none the less the vehicle of a supernatural good.

The conception that Protestant theologians readily form of the worship in spirit is no more rational than evangelical. It is impossible to unite men in a worship that is purely an affair of the soul, and it would be vain to impose such worship on human beings, who are bound by their physical conditions, and can only think through being able to hear and to speak. Their religious life cannot be independent of every sensible element, which aids them to become conscious of it, to define and affirm it. Jesus was the first to give His disciples a formula of prayer; He observed the practices of Jewish worship; He never recommended to His followers a worship without external forms, and never intended to establish such a worship. The saying of Christ in the Gospel of John, as to the worship "in spirit and in truth,"[2] does not oppose a purely inner worship to an external one; but the worship that may be called inspired, spiritualized,

[1] Cf. Newman, "Essays critical and historical," ii. 230 194–196.
[2] John iv. 23, 24.

the Christian worship known to the evangelist, and animated by the spirit given to the faithful, is substituted for a worship localized at Jerusalem or on Mount Gerizim.

The same evangelist who gives the formula of worship in spirit, gives also the formula of the Incarnation; the two correspond to one another; God is a Spirit, as is also His Word; the true worship is spiritual, since it is founded on the communication of the Divine Spirit. But just as God the Spirit is made manifest in the Incarnate Word, so the life of the Spirit is communicated and maintained by Spiritual sacraments, the water of baptism, the bread and wine of the Eucharist. The system of John is a perfect whole; neither the discourse to Nicodemus nor the instruction concerning the bread of life contradict the statement made to the woman of Samaria, and the whole agrees with the conception of the Incarnation, the Divine manifesting itself in the human, the spiritual acting in the sensible, the eternal reality figured in the terrestrial symbol and communicated by it. Catholic worship does nothing but apply the theory of John, and this theory was the description of the evangelical fact.

From the point of view of pure reason, the efficacy of the sacraments is not so very difficult a thing to conceive. It is with the sacraments as with ordinary language, the virtue of ideas passes into the words, acts through the words, is communicated really, physically, by the words, and only produces its effect on the mind by the aid of the words. Therefore it is fair to speak of the virtue of words, for they contribute to the existence and fortune of ideas. In so far as an idea has found no formula capable of striking the mind by a clearness, at least in appearance, by its simplicity and its vigour, it has no power of action. It is true that the action of the formula depends on the historical circumstances of its production, but this fact by no means lessens the analogy between words, the natural expression and indispensable means of communication of ideas, and the sacraments, the expression of inner religion and means of communication with God. The significance of the sacramental symbols has also been determined by the historical circumstances connected with their establishment and use. Thence comes their efficacy; they are signs appropriate to their end, as words can be appropriate to the expression of thought; they are Divine signs because they are religious; they are Christian, because they proceed from Christ. On all these grounds they are efficacious, and their

power comes not from him on whom they are
conferred, but is exercised in him and upon him;
it is bound up with the tie that links them to
Jesus, which makes them, as it were, actions of
Christ living in the Church, and it is conditioned
at once by the special application of the symbol
to him who receives it and by the disposition it
finds in him.

These considerations help to make clear the
doctrine of the Catholic Church regarding the
sacraments, and the essential harmony of this
doctrine with the gospel. This is not the place
to set forth the theory of the efficacy of the
sacrament in itself, as a definite institution of
Christ, in its substance and its form, that cannot
be modified without destroying its effect. The
formulas of sacramental theology, like the greater
number of dogmatic definitions, were conceived
in opposition to assertions rejected by the Church
as erroneous, namely, that sacraments have no
real efficacy, that they do not come from Christ,
that the choice of them is arbitrary and without
relation to the effect. Positive doctrine, as a
counterblast to condemned opinion, is always
capable of explanation and of progress. It
matters little that sacraments are held to be
composed of form and of substance; there would

be nothing unsuitable in abandoning these notions of ancient philosophy, artificially applied to the sacraments, and considering them in themselves, taking them for what they are, namely, religious acts, endowed with supernatural efficacy. This efficacy does not belong to them merely as religious acts, but in so far as they are the acts of religious Christians, related to Christ through the Church, men in whom Christ lives and acts, as He lives and acts in the Church and the Church's teaching.

The life of a religion consists not in its ideas, its formulas and its rites as such, but in the secret principle which first gave an attractive power, a supernatural efficacy, to the ideas and formulas and rites. The sacraments have no meaning for the Christian except through Jesus or His Spirit acting in the material symbol; they figure and realize the constant action of Christ in the Church. Jesus established them so far as they are a permanent institution proceeding from Him, powerful through Him. The incontestable and important changes undergone in the management and arrangement of several of them do not deprive them either of their character or their value as sacraments of Christ. The Church has always believed that she possesses in herself the Spirit of Jesus to direct her in all things. The action of the Spirit is linked to the forms of her government, her teaching and her worship. The sacramental institution is not an inert instrument, but a principle, a mode of action transmitted from Christ to the Church, susceptible of varied application, changeless only in itself, its general direction and essential form. The Church regulates its progress and action, regarding herself as the authorized interpreter of the intentions of its founder, and of the suitable way to execute it. The sacramental system is the historically established form taken by the Christian institution, the Church, inasmuch as it is a sanctifying organization through which the immortal Christ continues to act.

It is, perhaps, true that God is the only Grace, as He is the supreme good of man and his final end. But human life cannot be resolved into a simple act of union with God, to contain the whole of religion. It is written that the "Grace of God" is "manifold," [1] and truly it must adapt itself to very varied conditions of existence, bringing God to them, whose inexhaustible nature can no longer be summed up for man in a single aspect. The activity of the Father is not exhausted by the single movement of pardon. Why should

[1] 1 Pet. iv. 10.

not His permanent assistance be recalled and guaranteed by material symbols? These symbols take nothing from the Divine majesty, if it is well understood that their efficacy is in no way magical, and if, instead of interposing between God and man, they only remind human beings of the constantly beneficent presence of their Creator. Nor does the administration of the sacraments come between man and his Supreme Master, to take the place of God. The social character of Christianity exacts a regulation of external worship and a division of duty in the acts which constitute it; but none the less is there a direct relation between God and all those who, under different titles, participate in the symbolic actions of Christian ritual. God is no farther from the simple believer than from the bishop or the priest. Clerics and laity come together to God, pray together, are sanctified together. There is between them only a "diversity of gifts and of ministrations," as St. Paul says, but "the same Spirit"[1] is in all. The gospel is not the enemy of order, and it is difficult to see how the regular economy of Divine service can impede the operation of the grace of God.

Every religion is sacramental; every religion is

[1] 1 Cor. xii. 4, 5.

also more or less *deifying*, offering man a means of raising himself to Divinity, conceived first by analogy in the image of man. Perhaps it would not be very difficult to prove that the worship of man is, in all known religions, associated in some way with that of God. But in pagan worship this association is made definitely, to the detriment of Divinity, whose essential feature, that of remaining infinitely above humanity, is not recognized. Christianity avoided this confusion, while satisfying, by the worship of Jesus and the sacraments co-ordinated therewith, that need of deification which seems inseparable from human nature. It renders to Christ the worship the Jews rendered to the hidden God, Whom no human being could look on and live. It has been able to do so without falling into Polytheism or man-worship, because it distinguishes, in the object of its adoration, the Eternal God and the human nature in which this God was manifested on earth. Christ is none the less seated on the right hand of the Father, and humanity is raised in Him up to Divinity. It may be said that humanity adores itself in Jesus, but it must be added that, so doing, it forgets neither its own condition nor that of God.

Herr Harnack does not expressly condemn the

worship accorded to Christ, but he regards it all
the same as a kind of idolatry, born of ancient
polytheism. For him, the worship of Jesus is no
more legitimate than the dogma of His Divinity.
Did the apostles adore Christ even when they had
acquired belief in His resurrection ? Was Jesus
for the first Christian generation any other than a
Divine mediator, with Whom, and through Whom,
men could pray to and worship the Father, instead
of One to be worshipped ? But these circumstances only serve to make more evident the need
of a worship deifying humanity, since from a
rigorous monotheism, whose formula has been
strengthened rather than weakened, was derived
the worship of a human being, whose human
character has been never denied, though His
Divinity has been proclaimed; while, after this,
Christian piety has made for itself a whole hierarchy of intercessors from heavenly spirits and
spiritual ancestors, as though to aid Christ in His
position of intercessor, and at the head of them
has set the Virgin Mary.

Neither the worship of Christ nor the worship
of the saints could be part of the gospel of Jesus,
nor does either belong to it: they arose spontaneously, and have increased one after the other,
and then together, in Christianity as it became

established. All the same, the worship, both of
Jesus and of the saints, proceeds from what may
be called, in all truthfulness, the primitive revelation, the revelation that has never been specified
in a formal doctrine, that mankind bears in the
depths of its religious consciousness written in
indistinct characters. The sole article that constitutes this unexplained revelation, that Jesus
manifested in Himself and in His life as much as
in His teaching, and was the first to show in a
clear and intelligible manner because He realized
it in Himself, is that God reveals Himself to man
in man, and that humanity enters with God into
a Divine association. Man had always believed
it, and only understood it vaguely; Jesus made
it intelligible, and from that moment, as it were,
the direction of prayer was changed, and the
mythological cloud dissipated, while at the same
time the barrier of law and verbal revelation was
overthrown. The most Divine thing in the world
is not the crash of the thunder, nor the light of
the sun, nor the unfolding of life; it is beauty of
soul, purity of heart, perfection of love in sacrifice,
because this is the sovereign gift of God to man,
the grandest work and supreme manifestation of
God in the universe. In this way Jesus revealed
to men the secret of God and religion, because

God was in Him revealing Himself; in this way men felt that in Jesus they possessed God revealed to them. The impression was deeper among the Gentiles, who knew not God, than among the Jews, who knew Him better, but were accustomed to adore Him in His redoubtable majesty. It is certain that the eternal principle of the passage of the Divine through the human then received a new application, very clear and very fruitful, that this application was the Christian religion and the worship of Jesus, and that it could be nothing else.

This application of the principle itself refused to be limited to the worship of Christ. All those who bore witness to the revelation of God in Jesus, who had not feared to die rather than disavow their certainty, who had demonstrated its power by the practice of Christian virtues, and had died in the peace of the Lord, all these equally received on their foreheads a ray of Divinity. It was not the full light, the unmeasured communication of the Spirit and of the glory of God, but it was a part of this gift, to be saluted with reverence.

In fact, it is as an extension of the worship of Jesus that, from the Catholic point of view, the worship of the Virgin and the saints is justified.

The saints live, not only in the memory of the Church, but in her present work, by the lasting influence of their personal activity, and of the ideal signified by their name. Worship of them, like that of the Virgin and of Christ Himself, has become what it might and ought to have become under the circumstances and in the times where it has developed. The Christian spirit gave life, and still gives it, to practices apparently trivial, and easily becoming superstitious ; but the point at issue is whether those who follow them do not find Christ therein, and whether they would be capable of finding Him more easily elsewhere. From the actual point of view, the Virgin and saints are religious types inferior to Christ, but united to Him, leading to Him, acting through Him and for Him. From the point of view of theological symbolism and popular conception, Christ alone is the mediator, all powerful by reason of His Divinity ; the Virgin is a sub-ordinate intercessor all-powerful through Christ ; and the power of the saints is equally subordinated to that of Jesus.

It may be said that the government of this world, even of moral things, should not be divided into provinces according to specialities which recall a little too vividly the lesser gods of paganism. Yet all that ever was has an eternal life and action in God, wherein all things abide. He who suppresses intercession is on the way to suppress prayer. Is it not true in the strictest sense for the Catholic, that he goes to God through Jesus, to Jesus through the saints? Is it not true that Christianity endures by the force of all its past, from Jesus to the Christians of our own day, worthy of the name? Is it not true that all the fruits of the gospel in Christianity are still the gospel? Is it not true that to have recourse to the saints is to have recourse to Jesus —to Jesus, then to God; and that to turn to God with a simple faith is to rise above one's self, to enter into religion and make it a personal reality? Is it not true that by all those means the Protestant finds so vulgar and so ridiculous—by wearing a scapulary, by telling beads, by gaining indulgences on the merits of saints for this life or for souls in Purgatory—the Catholic places himself effectively in the communion of the saints, which is the communion of Jesus, which is the communion of God?

Assuredly it would be wise to moderate this worship in some of its manifestations, and above all to make clear its real significance. The general considerations which allow, from the Christian

point of view, prayers of intercession, as a means
of attaching the soul to God by the intermediary
of those in whom God was especially made manifest, demand also that these prayers should be
different in spirit from pagan superstitions, and
should not be sustained by wild imaginations.
After all, it will be said, if St. Antony of Padua
has not really the power to cause the recovery of
things that are lost, the winning of the great prize
in the lottery, the gaining of diplomas by devout
but lazy students, it is possible that a naïve
credulity may provide the hope of supernatural
intervention that is solicited in these cases, so
that the religious and moral value of such prayers
is not superior to that of the requests commonly
addressed to pagan deities : far better recommend
students to deserve success by their work, advise
all to look to their affairs and count at once on
Providence and on themselves for the success of
their enterprises.

Nevertheless the apparent puerilities of devotion
are less removed from religion than they seem.
The face of the world is twofold. Man is placed
between nature, where all seems inevitable, and
consciousness, where all appears free. The universe
for him is a gigantic mechanism, which encom-
passes him on all sides, and will overwhelm

him without mercy if the opportunity arise; and, at the same time, it is the revelation that a Being, good and omnipotent, gives of Himself. The contradiction evident in the conduct of man demanding to be freed from inevitability, exists also in the world, where necessity and liberty meet in opposition. No prayer is insignificant or ridiculous for the man of faith, so long as it does not misrepresent God in His goodness and respects His sovereignty. No prayer is justified as an act of pure reason and of perfect piety, save by the uprightness of its intentions, its application to duty, and submission to the Divine will. Taken solely in its natural and primitive significance, the Lord's Prayer in some respects would be as open to critical objection as a prayer to St. Antony of Padua to recover an object that has been lost. Would not the demand, "Give us this day our daily bread," considered in its strict historical meaning,[1] be subversive of social economy? Practically, as a general rule, the adult healthy man can and should earn his bread with his own powers. To-day, the Christian requests that this activity be blessed by Heaven, but the original sense of the words he uses was very different. In the same way the meaning of

[1] Cf. supra.

the request, " Thy Kingdom come," is very different for the modern Christian from the sense the first converts attached to it. Thus the prayer derives its value from the feeling that prompts it and determines its moral efficacy, not from the occasion that provokes it, not even from the good to which it seems directed. This efficacy of prayer is independent of its formal fulfilment, and is no more a matter of question for the Christian than the personal existence of God.

It must not be imagined that sentence of condemnation has been passed on the worship of saints, of relics, of the Virgin, and of the Saviour Himself because such worship appears to the historian as a concession to the tendencies of popular religion.[1] It is essential that every religion that lives should be a concession of this kind, though Christianity may be asked to raise the character of the concession by the spirit that informs its worship and its practices. The tendencies in question are a fundamental law of religion, and a condition of religious development. All is well so long as the forms of worship are not esteemed beyond and at the expense of the spirit that should animate them. The Church is unable to suppress the religious instinct, and as

[1] Cf. Newman, " Development."

little disposed to leave it to itself: she sets out to regulate it, and devotions are to her a means of maintaining religion. The piety of any Catholic nation does not, perhaps, represent the ideal of Catholicism, but it is all that Catholicism can obtain from that nation. What can be asked of the Church beyond a constant effort to obtain more than has as yet been given? This effort exists. Herr Harnack recognizes [1] that devotions paid to the Sacred Heart, the Holy Virgin, and others, have become in the Catholic Church a source of blessing and a means of reaching the good God. This is because the Christian spirit has penetrated to the depth of the devotion, and set the gospel there. These devotions, far from being a hindrance to religion, are a support to it, just as the sacraments do not take Christ from the believer, but give Him.

Protestant critics, when they express surprise that the Christian spirit is still found in Catholicism in spite of the Church, faith in spite of dogma, true piety in spite of the multiplication of external rites, take for obstacles the real guarantees and normal conditions of the good that the gospel, now become a religion, has given to the world, good that their own speculations on

[1] "Dogmengeschichte," iii. 670, n. **3.**

the pure essence of Christianity are unable to procure. Does not Protestantism itself exist as a religion through that amount of ecclesiastical organization, official doctrine, and confessional worship that it has retained ?

It is true that as a result of the evolution, political, intellectual, economic, of the modern world, as a result of all that may be called the modern spirit, a great religious crisis, affecting Churches, orthodoxies, and forms of worship has arisen to a greater or less extent everywhere. The best means of meeting it does not appear to be the suppression of all ecclesiastical organization, all orthodoxy, and all traditional worship—a process that would thrust Christianity out of life and humanity,—but to take advantage of what is, in view of what should be, to repudiate nothing of the heritage left to our age by former Christian centuries, to recognize how necessary and useful is the immense development accomplished in the Church, to gather the fruits of it and continue it, since the adaptation of the gospel to the changing conditions of humanity is as pressing a need to-day as it ever was and ever will be. It is no part of the present book to say what difficulties— more apparent, perhaps, than real—this work may encounter in the Catholic Church, nor what incomparable resources exist for it, nor in what way the agreement of dogma and science, reason and faith, the Church and society, can be conceived to-day. This little volume is full enough if it has shown how Christianity has lived in the Church and by the Church, and how futile is the desire to save it by a search after its quintessence.